Raising Curious,
Creative, Confident Kids

Raising Curious, Creative, Confident Kids

The Pestalozzi Experiment in
Child-Based Education

Rebeca Wild

Shambhala
BOSTON & LONDON
2000

Shambhala Publications, Inc.
Horticultural Hall
300 Massachusetts Avenue
Boston, Massachusetts 02115
www.shambhala.com

9 8 7 6 5 4 3 2 1

First Shambhala Edition

Printed in the United States of America

♾ This edition is printed on acid-free paper that meets the
American National Standards Institute z39.48 Standard.

Distributed in the United States by Random House, Inc.,
and in Canada by Random House of Canada Ltd

Library of Congress Cataloging-in-Publication Data
Wild, Rebeca, 1939–
[Erziehung zum Sein. English]
Raising curious, creative, confident kids: the Pestalozzi experiment in
child-based education/Rebeca Wild.—1st Shambhala ed.
p. cm.
Includes bibliographical references.
ISBN 1-57062-455-0
1. Alternative schools—Ecuador—Case studies. 2. Montessori method
of education—Ecuador—Case studies. 3. Educational innovations—
Ecuador—Case studies. 4. Pestalozzi, Johann Heinrich, 1746–1827. I. Title.
LC46.8.E2 W55 2000
371.04—dc21 00-032201

Contents

Raising Curious,
Creative, Confident Kids

CHAPTER ONE

Before the Beginning

It is 1982, two weeks after the start of summer vacation in the Ecuadorean Andes. The dry season has suddenly set in just before the end of the school year. Rainless white clouds rush across a dark blue sky, driven by strong winds that relentlessly bend the slender eucalyptus trees from one side to the other. If you close your eyes, you can imagine yourself to be at the seashore—so loud is the roar of the wind through the long rows of trees that border the grounds of the Pestalozzi School.[1]

Behind us lie five very busy years of work. The construction of an alternative school, the blazing of new trails, and the day-to-day routine of operation have taxed our strength as never before. The "active system" demands a high degree of preparation, an inexhaustible capacity for the new, and the continual invention, production, collection, organization, and maintenance of materials. The days seem too short, and there are not enough hands to realize the myriad ideas that often come into our minds in a rush while work-

---

1. Swiss educator Johann Heinrich Pestalozzi (1746–1827) was a pioneer in articulating and implementing principles of developmental education and in his commitment to social justice—educating children from disadvantaged backgrounds in their native language, for example.

ing with the children. During these last few years, I have felt the desire so many times to put some of our experiences into writing and share some of the wealth of observations we have made about "free" children. But this project kept being shelved, put aside for more urgent tasks: talks with parents; meetings with teachers; courses with teachers, parents, and students from different disciplines; discussions with Indian groups from remote parts of the country or with the Ministry of Education and Culture—an endless list of activities directly or indirectly related to the school that all absorbed our afternoons, evenings, and weekends.

Yet my urge to share our experiences in Ecuador with our friends in Europe has become stronger and stronger in the last few months. More and more young people from many different nations have visited us recently. They raised many questions and showed that a certain dismay and confusion over the meaning and purpose of existing educational methods prevailed even in the developed countries. This impression was further confirmed by various European periodicals that happened to come to our attention in these months.

This desire to communicate our experiences to our European friends in more detail than had previously been the case coincided with a growing personal need: by remembering, reflecting on, and setting down certain experiences, I wanted to achieve a better balance between our all-too-active life and a more contemplative one, to bring some order into my thoughts and feelings and perhaps gain some new insights here and there.

Not long ago we welcomed a young friend from Hamburg who visited us during a trip through South America from which he hoped to gain new perspectives and make a decision about what to study. His first impressions here led him to the conclusion that this type of work could never be achieved through the initiative of a few lone individuals. Only after hearing from us at length about the founding of Pesta did it become clear to him that this was no institution but a project of work that had grown organically out of the interaction between internal and external needs and that was still very much in progress. It is a project of a highly personal nature, closely linked to our own personal life histories and to a process of maturing familiar to all who, in dealing with their own children or others, have come to question the meaning of education. In order to fill in the background of our experiences and clarify just how the connecting of inner and outer worlds became an orientation for us, I will turn back the clock to the year 1959.

It was a sunny September morning in southern Germany, at the end of the summer vacation season, during which I was earning a bit of extra money to help finance my German philology studies by working as an impromptu tour guide. On that particular day I had been assigned to a tour bus going to the Bavarian castle of Neuschwanstein with forty visitors from all corners of the globe looking forward to a pleasant day. While the tourists took in the rococo wonders of the architecture, the guides from the various buses lunched on prosaic cheese sandwiches. Among them was a young man who had already shown himself to be looking for some fun and games and now seemed intent on disturbing my peace on this Sunday. Slightly annoyed, I was trying to fend off his unpleasant advances when a somewhat foreign-looking young man of about my age whom I had not seen before among the guides suddenly appeared at my side. I have since forgotten what it was he said but not the effect that his quiet voice had upon the obnoxious tour guide. There was a particular authority about him that made my tormentor unsure of himself and caused him to back off. I gave the stranger a look of thanks and felt suddenly touched by his presence: this was a man who, in an unusual way, was simply himself. His facial expression, his bearing, his tone of voice, and his choice of clothing all indicated harmony and a natural, easy way of evaluating situations.

We met again down at a lake called the Alpsee. Given the splendor of this lovely late summer day, we decided to row out on the lake and leave the tourists to admire the castle on their own. We spent a pleasant hour indulging in small talk and laughter. Before we returned to our respective buses, the new guide, who in the meantime had introduced himself with a foreign first name and a German-sounding last name, invited me to go to the cinema with him and succeeded in taking my telephone number. This subsequent date to go to the movies turned into a three-hour walk through the streets of Munich. It was then that I learned that Mauricio Wild was born in Ecuador of Swiss parents and had come to Switzerland at the age of twelve for further schooling but had never been able to adapt himself completely; thus, six years later he had begun traveling around Europe. He took on odd jobs when his money ran out and learned several languages, but above all he was in quest of an identity that, after the contrasts of his childhood in Ecuador, his youth in Switzerland, and his years of travel, had eluded him and demanded to be found.

It was already during this first walk together that we talked about "learning to be oneself" and "seeking authenticity, the true self" or "being honest with oneself": terms that might seem overly philosophical for twenty-year-olds but that corresponded perfectly to our frame of mind at the time. My childhood during the war years had taught me to live every day to the fullest in spite of fear and insecurity. My school years, however, often obscured the need for an authentic sense of life and hindered more than promoted true understanding and clarity in thinking and feeling. During my studies at university, Romano Guardini's lectures on Plato had more meaning for me than my required courses in philology. In those few weeks Mauricio and I enjoyed together during that sunny Indian summer, I was impressed over and over again by his clarity and certainty in thought and feeling, quite in contrast to the uncertainty of his external circumstances. My own conviction of being exactly sure of what I wanted in life was considerably shaken by our encounter. And suddenly the idea of a journey leading both inwardly and outwardly into the unknown seemed to me more real than my previous goals.

Three weeks later, when the tourist season came to an end, we parted ways. Mauricio wanted to commence a long hiking trip through Italy to Africa that autumn, while I returned to my studies of German philology, which soon occupied my full attention—save for the unforeseen distraction offered by regular letters from Italy. The letters, full of travel impressions and personal reflections, entailed no response, since the writer had no fixed address and could not be reached by mail. Then, however, shortly before Christmas, Mauricio suddenly interrupted his travels and returned to Switzerland. A friend of his who was paralyzed—and who painted with his mouth—had asked Mauricio to undertake his care for a few months to replace his father, who had injured his back with the constant lifting. And thus it happened that letters began to arrive with a return address, enabling me to write back, and in the following winter months we were able to visit each other a number of times.

During this period of time, our plan to venture a life together in Mauricio's native Ecuador gradually took on clearer contours. We thought that perhaps there we would find more freedom of movement and opportunity, freedom to make our own decisions, than in Europe, and that these circumstances would help us in our common quest for an authentic life.

In 1960 Mauricio returned to Ecuador. I went to join him there in July 1961, to embark on a journey into the unknown, a journey that is still in progress today. Whoever has traveled to South America has surely experienced the feeling of arriving in a country where everything is different from what one has known at home: from things such as the air, the smells, the sounds, the language, the food, and the feeling for time to the sense of what is important or unimportant, what is cause for laughter or for tears, how one walks or dances. There is such a different feeling for life that many tourists, after having seen the obligatory sights and snapped a sufficient number of pictures, withdraw in exhaustion back to the neutral atmosphere of a hotel.

As I mounted the watch one long, sunny tropical afternoon on the deck of a banana-bearing steamboat that had come in on the Rio Guayas to see if Mauricio—whom I had not seen for a year and a half—would finally appear from one of the many docked boats, I was still floating between two worlds: on the one hand, the spotless white German steamer that had all the elements of my familiar and comfortable world, and on the other, not far away, this strange land that was supposed to become my home in the future. Now and then a ship's officer or steward would come by, gesticulate toward the brown river and nearby Guayaquil, which boasted few modern buildings at the time, and exclaim, "You'd be better off coming back with us. This is a filthy country. The people here are just primitive rabble. You certainly won't adapt to it!" The idea was not far from my mind, as Mauricio still had not shown up. The explanations that usually come to mind in such situations of waiting could take no clear shape, since I did not have the slightest idea under what circumstances, that is to say, how and when he would finally appear in flesh and blood. In the letters that had arrived frequently and regularly in the long months of our separation, he had made only passing mention of the external conditions of life in Ecuador, just enough to create a backdrop for his inner preoccupations. He wrote in one letter, "If you expect to find anything that is beautiful and familiar here, then stay where you are. Expect nothing but my love and the hope that, together, we will be able to accomplish something that, as yet, remains unknown." Of course, at our age of twenty-two, we had only a vague notion of what the reality of this would be; however, we assumed that the way that lay before us would have both an inner and an outer direction. Our ideas were rooted in the Christian tradition and the mystics as well as in the wisdom of the East and the psychology of C. G. Jung. Even if orientation was difficult for us in this apparent chaos, we were confident that unexpected doors would open for us.

Our first encounter after this long period of writing letters and speculating about our common path was less festive than (characteristically!) turbulent. Mauricio had inquired about the arrival date of the *Perikles* in good time and even driven the two hundred kilometers from Quevedo to Guayaquil one day earlier to have his less-than-new Volkswagen van overhauled in the garage. But the *Perikles* had arrived a day ahead of schedule, in time for a planned harbor celebration for banana shippers, which was to be held onboard the ship. Mauricio, still dusty from his long drive, had just left the car at its repair shop and was making his way along the docks back to the hotel for the evening when he noticed the newly arrived ship in the distance. He counted the number of letters in the ship's name, and they agreed with the name of the *Perikles*. He began to run until he could read the ship's name clearly and immediately hailed a boat. On the ship's ladder he ran into the duty officer on watch, who did not want to let anyone on board at that hour, but he managed to win the argument. As for me, with the onset of night I had given up my wait on the upper deck and invited an Englishwoman with whom I had become friendly during the three-week crossing to open a bottle of wine with me. Just then I heard my name being called and started to run toward the ship's exit. For fear of thieves, all the doors onboard were carefully locked. I had to beg someone to open every door for me, which was then shut tight behind me again. Mauricio was going through the same thing on the lower deck. What a miracle it seemed when, after this endless opening and closing of doors and before the eyes of the astonished steward, we finally fell into each other's arms!

And then we were in a hurry to leave the ship. When I set foot on land, a welter of sensations and impressions of the most unusual kinds assailed me. In those few days in Guayaquil, we went shopping to buy what we believed to be the essentials for our young household. Our purchases were rather modest, yet they made quite a load for the VW van. Finally we were ready to leave for Quevedo, which was to be the location of our first domicile. At that time it was a small town, center of export for the banana trade and surrounded in all directions by jungle.

For the first time in my life, I drove past broad rice fields, fields flooded by the rivers all year-round, where cows and horses stood up to their fetlocks in water, looking for fodder on small green islands. In every village, we were overwhelmed by a noisy avalanche of merchants wanting to sell us provisions for the rest of the trip. Other than hard-boiled eggs, none of the dishes offered were recognizable to me as edible. The trip went on through plantations with mixed produce, the plants of which I saw for the first time: mango trees, coffee, cocoa, tapioca, and then the first bananas. After four hours we reached our destination; Quevedo had a population of just under seven thousand inhabitants at that time. From the height of the road, one had a view overlooking the whole town.

The first thing we noticed was a small water tower, which was supposed to supply the town with drinking water; however, it did so only once in a while. I could compare the whole appearance of the town only to pictures of the Wild West, the only difference being that most of the houses were built of bamboo, which gave them a tropical look. Among these bamboo huts were a few houses of brick and wood, and a very few cement houses. The streets were unpaved, and since it was the dry season, every vehicle raised huge clouds of dust, against which pedestrians tried to protect themselves by means of handkerchiefs pressed to their faces. In the rainy season this dust metamorphosed into—as I was later to learn—thick mud that required of pedestrians feats of Olympian proportions in jumping, leaping, and evading. In these surroundings the small half-naked children of Quevedo were obviously and surprisingly quite at home, together with pigs, dogs, and chickens. They ran away in all directions only when a banana truck or a jeep disputed their right to the street.

Our first apartment was located on the second floor of one of the "better" houses in Quevedo. Below us on the ground floor was a small store where the necessities of life could be bought. There lived the proprietor of the store as well, a friendly grandfather, with his children and numerous grandchildren. They seemed to be a happy family, even though their worldly possessions consisted of a few beds, a wobbly table, and two hammocks. On the upper floor they had constructed the simple apartment where we lived; Mauricio had paid a pretty penny to have running water installed, which worked only sporadically.

Our first supper in the only Chinese restaurant in Quevedo and a short walk around the town, which awoke to noisy liveliness in the evening, were soon finished. The apartment furnishings were simple enough and the move into our new home quickly completed: a table and four chairs and a comfortable hammock, a shelf of simple wood hung on the wall with chains to provide a place for our books and the record player, on the wall some pictures that had been wedding presents from our handicapped friend in Switzerland who painted by mouth. A bed, a wardrobe, and a chair furnished the bedroom; its most attractive decoration was a large white mosquito net. In the kitchen were more handmade shelves for the basic necessities in the way of household utensils, a kerosene stove, and a washing trough made of wood. In these plain and simple rooms, our modest wedding festivities took place, with a few friends. We did not regard our circumstances as poverty because we felt ourselves to be rich, and no one was bothered by these homely surroundings, since, with only a few exceptions, everyone in the country lived like this.

When we think back to our first year of marriage, it seems like a year of vacation to us. It was our ideal to get along with the absolute minimum of external luxury. This minimum was covered by the income from a wood business that worked in the following way: Every once in a while, Mauricio went off into the jungle with a group of young people in order to locate and estimate the volume of certain woods that a lumber dealer in Guayaquil who was a friend of his had promised to buy from him. The young men then made a trip into the jungle every day, loaded as much as they could onto their antediluvian vehicle, and came back into Quevedo with their load of wood around four in the afternoon, making a great commotion. Then we went down to the nearby river by bicycle to measure, appraise, and pay for the logs before they were unloaded at the edge of the broad river and tied together. And so, in the course of days of work, we had an impressive float, which could be taken downriver to Guayaquil when the rains set in, an adventurous trip lasting several days.

In the early sixties, life in Ecuador was unbelievably cheap. We spent the equivalent of one or two German marks (about a dollar at the time of this writing) a day for food; equally cheap were our rent, gasoline, and travel. A bus ticket to Guayaquil two hundred kilometers away cost about one mark at that time. This simple life was exactly what we wanted. We felt free, free to spend our days just as we liked. At sunrise we rode our bicycles upriver, where the water was still crystal clear and deep, and bathed and swam to our heart's content. Back at home we did a considerable number of yoga exercises. Then we had a simple breakfast consisting of fruits, oatmeal, and roasted barley. While I put my limited school Spanish into practice at the market and made my first independent attempts at cooking on the kerosene stove (which kept blackening the pots), Mauricio devoted himself to his autodidactic studies in the field of comparative religions and learned to type as well as to play the flute. The afternoon was reserved for reading and learning Spanish. After our daily work at the riverside measuring logs, we often bathed in the river again under the hot afternoon sun. After supper we frequently had long conversations in the hammock, visited friends, or had them to visit at our place. Occasionally we went to a movie at the only cinema in town, in which the loudspeakers hummed so loudly that it was impossible to understand the spoken word—one had to depend on the subtitles.

We did not worry about the future, we lived from day to day, as only seems possible in the tropics, and enjoyed a life without the pressures of responsibility that was devoted entirely to our own personal interests. The idyll was interrupted only by occasional explorative trips into the jungle and short journeys to Guayaquil on business. And yet, little by little, we began to feel a certain uneasiness, a slight disquiet. The avoidance of "worldly tumult" or the necessity to earn more money no more brought us to the "inner way" that we longed for than did the daily yoga exercises or the reading of books describing such ways, it seemed. No baby was on the way, which would have demanded greater responsibility from us. Gradually our breakfast granola began to lose its flavor, and we began to droop more and more, from doing almost nothing. Or was it just the hot rainy season that was robbing us of our strength? But in what direction were we to seek meaning and enrichment? In the course of time, we took on a bit more work: private lessons in English and music for interested villagers. However, in reality we waited, without knowing what we were waiting for.

Around this time we became friends with a Dutch family who lived not far from Quevedo on a large farm that consisted of—in the typical style of the Dutch in Indonesia—several tasteful houses with tropical gardens around them. The farm was completely surrounded by jungle; on approximately thirteen hundred hectares (a hectare is just under two and a half acres) were planted bananas and cocoa. During one of our visits, our Dutch friend cautiously inquired of Mauricio whether he might be interested in taking over his position in the management of this farm so that he would be free to accept an interesting job offer in Surinam. This friend could only terminate his contract in Ecuador if he found a successor. We were full of objections: Mauricio had no idea of tropical agriculture, pesticides, export, or the administration of a plantation. But our friend brushed aside all our doubts. He himself, as he told us, had studied agriculture, but his real learning had only begun when he left theory and got into practice. In addition, a friend of his, a biologist, could fly over from another farm once a month and give Mauricio an introduction to the most important techniques of plant protection.

This is typical of Ecuador: only two weeks later we accompanied our friend to the airport and moved to the farm with all our paltry possessions from our first household. The spacious house there was equipped with all the necessities, and suddenly we found ourselves in a "larger" world—our horizons had broadened. At twenty-three Mauricio was suddenly a man with much responsibility. With great enthusiasm, we learned about everything that now was part of our new field of work: the planting, cultivation, and protection of one thousand hectares of bananas and three hundred hectares of cocoa, then the supervision of the harvests (consignments of thirty thousand to fifty thousand bunches of bananas of different degrees of ripeness were shipped to Germany, the United States, and Japan every month) and the organization of the transport by truck to Guayaquil, 250 kilometers away, over roads often washed out by tropical rainfalls. For all these tasks, including the care of the still young cocoa plantation, Mauricio had about one hundred workers, who lived in three camps. One of the most serious responsibilities was the daily estimate of the bananas to be harvested, which had to be made to our agent in Guayaquil by shortwave radio; on this estimate depended to a great extent the financial success of the farm.

All these responsibilities had the heady effect of an elixir of life on us. We felt so much more alive. There was work of all kinds to be done. Every day we learned something new. We came to like our very social life with our Dutch neighbors. Often came cars full of unannounced visitors who wanted to spend a nice day or even a week of vacation with us. Fortunately for us, it was not a problem to feed all these unexpected visitors, because when they went around the plantation, they stuffed themselves so full of our wonderful bananas that they could eat only small servings at meals. During this time we had innumerable celebrations on the farm: at the birth of a child, weddings, all kinds of occasions and festivities. There were typical dances, loud music, cheers called out: the festive party atmosphere that is only imaginable in South American countries. And even on the quiet evenings that we spent alone in the farmhouse, we were surrounded by the natural sounds of the jungle that began close to our house and stretched far up to the beginning heights of the Andes.

After work or on the weekend, we often saddled the horses and rode through the thick jungle on a path that had been opened by a tractor to "our" waterfall, which united all the waters of the area into one gigantic and deafening fall. After the long ride, we refreshed ourselves in the icy cold water of a natural pool between bamboo shrubs and tall ferns, and returned home when darkness fell, exhausted and happy. When we had enough of lush vegetation, we took the Land Rover and drove through the banana plantations to Quevedo to drop in unannounced on old friends, in keeping with local custom. Or we went to the cinema to see if any film worth seeing was playing. Now and again we took a few days off and went to Guayaquil, so as not to forget how it feels to be in a city with paved streets, stores, and streetlights.

Thus we lived every day, our senses and thoughts attuned to the external, with no financial worries and also without preoccupying ourselves with a search for a deeper sense of (our) life. We did not bother our heads about whether we would spend the rest of our lives among bananas, cocoa beans, and the jungle. However, we reserved one hour for yoga exercises every morning, and by so doing gave our personal life a definite place in our timetable of hours, perhaps more out of habit than conviction that a particular goal would be reached. After a year and a half, we noticed that the humid climate of the jungle was beginning to have ill effects on our health. Just as we became conscious of this, a young Swiss man appeared one Sunday morning and offered Mauricio a position in an import firm in Guayaquil. Again we had the same objections: Mauricio had no experience in business. But we had the opportunity to speak to the head of the company, and we were assured that the best method was "learning by doing" if a person had enough interest in the work.

Not long afterward we moved into a modern penthouse apartment directly on the quay of Guayaquil. Mauricio became a typical businessman who changed his white shirt twice a day and worked in an office with air conditioning. I accepted a job as a trilingual secretary at an export firm dealing in bananas—after all, experience can be gained by practice. . . . A maid saw to the household. We were now living a life considered normal by innumerable people all over the world: work, leisure hours, weekends at the seashore, a good book every now and again, interesting conversations with friends over a cool glass of wine: a life without great personal involvement and without great consequences.

It took only a few months for us to feel that this lifestyle did not correspond to our expectations of life, to what we wanted out of life. We gained sufficient insight into the business world to recognize that we were not doing a great service either to ourselves or the country that had become our home. Because of business interests, over and over again we had to act against people for whom our feelings were as strong as for our fellow Europeans. And so we drew closer and closer to a state of consciousness, a level of comprehension that enabled us to see clearly that our ideal—a personal realization of self—must be consistent with, indeed must be directly connected to, the needs of our environment, the world around us in which our lives took place. Looking at the day-to-day operations of a business that, located in an underdeveloped country and thus surrounded by poverty, discrimination, hopelessness, and self-disgust, sees only its own profit, it becomes clearer and clearer that there is a strong necessity for social responsibility. We spent more and more long evenings on the roof of our penthouse with its view of the Rio Guayas, where perspiring and shouting carriers could be seen loading the banana boats night after night, and discussed what we should do in order to achieve harmony in our life and unite all the internal and external needs for fulfillment. Friends came to us and we had long nights of discussion. But only a few of the young people who were employed in the business sector were willing or prepared to reflect upon the effects that their work could have on themselves and on the well-being of others.

We became friends with an Anglican pastor who was doing good work in a poor quarter of Guayaquil and gradually reached the decision to begin studies in social work and then come back to Ecuador to apply our new knowledge and experience for the benefit of the country where Mauricio had been born. There followed five years of study in the United States and Puerto Rico, then a year of practical work in cooperation with the Anglican Church in Colombia and in Ecuador. Later came a project for organic agriculture with production of biogas in an impoverished region of the Ecuadorean Andes. After all of this, the experiences of more than a decade, we reached the conclusion that from then on our work would have to be done within the framework of our own initiative, working and thinking freely and independently, in reference to the contexts and needs of this country. This meant doing without a permanent job and thus personal security in many ways. So finally, after going many ways and taking various detours, we arrived at the project of which this book will tell the story: an alternative school, the origin and growth of which is to be seen and understood in the combination of our own needs and the needs of our environment.

Our son Leonardo had been born at the end of our first year of study in New York. We were completely and absolutely fascinated by this event, although it did not fit in with our earlier plans. To get away from the huge city, which seemed all too inhospitable for a child to grow up in, we decided to continue our studies in Puerto Rico. By means of a scholarship as well as teaching private music lessons, we were able to finance ourselves. I had a great deal of time to devote to our child. However, after all the years in which we had been living according to our own adult interests, we found out something that innumerable couples around the world experience, namely, that this small child was capable of turning upside down all our habits, all our attitudes and ideas, as well as all our plans for the day's work. This situation reached the proportions of a small crisis when the sweet little baby who still took a nap every day became a very active toddler who never seemed to quiet down or tire and who also developed a very clear will in regard to his own self, which did not always agree with our own needs or desires. At that time a girl-friend of mine put a book by Maria Montessori on the table. After reading this book, we took leave of two things: first, the idea that the child was a sort of intruder infringing upon our private rights, and second, the notion that we had the task of bringing him up in such a way that his urge for movement and investigation could be regulated in a systematic and timely way, using fixed or established attitudes of adults, and thus directed into safe channels.

One day we made the decision that it was not the child who had to adjust to us but rather the other way around, and this put a new face on everything. We felt light and exhilarated; the scenes and rows with which our son tried to assert himself became fewer and fewer and finally disappeared altogether. Without any ado the legs were cut off the high crib so the little boy could climb out as soon as he woke up and go to bed by himself when he felt sleepy. We paid increasing attention to what attracted him and found much enjoyment in putting many things within reach that seemed to in-terest him. He was so busy that it was very seldom necessary to forbid him any of our personal treasures. This was how we became aware of the initiative of a child when investigating the world. We no longer attempted to anticipate him, to beat him to something, to show him everything, to explain, to interpret, to let him feel our greater experience of life at every turn.

Although very little had changed outwardly—an unknowing visitor would certainly have noticed hardly any difference— everything was different within a very short time. Our son, as small as he was, noticed the change right away and without any doubt or hesitation swung himself around to the new course, which is called normalization by Maria Montessori. He now exhibited obvious pleasure in us, as did we in him.

Here some readers will doubtless be thinking that this book is now going to talk about antiauthoritarian upbringing. Therefore I wish to say at the outset that the method we have developed, which we call "active education," is not to be compared with what has become known as antiauthoritarian upbringing in Europe or the United States. Perhaps it will be possible for me, in the course of this book, to make it clear that between the traditional form, dominated by authority, and its counterpart, which strictly refutes it, there lies a huge territory of innumerable possibilities. This is a territory in which an adult learns to respect the quality of life as well as the structures of thinking and feeling of a child in every stage of growth and where a child can personally feel—in its own body—what respect is, and thus learn from this experience to respect itself and others, including adults. The following chapters of this book will have this as their subject: How can we achieve it? How can we shape the environment of our children in such a way that they remain full of curiosity and grow up full of confidence in themselves and their world, that they are permitted to experience and to modify their world to make it significant and full of meaning for them, without the necessity for adults to disappear from this world so that the new generation feels comfortable in it?

This work—to see to it that our children have an acceptable environment—is no simple enterprise for us grown-ups. Perhaps we ourselves have experienced so many changes that we do not really feel at home anymore in our own world and seek security by raising our children in the old tried-and-true fashion. But maybe it is in fact just this discomfort that we already feel, as well as the thought of an unimaginable future, that will cause us to look for new methods of education. This is where the active school comes in: it adheres neither to the models of antiauthoritarian education nor to the examples of the traditional schools based on discipline. In the active school the activity of children is just as important as that of adults.

However, in the active school an adult undertakes to learn to become conscious of the authentic needs of the children at all times and to do all in his or her power to fulfill these needs as much and as far as possible. This leads to a mobilization of forces and strengths in both adults and children through which these two groups of persons—as well as their environment—will be metamorphosed. During this process the present will become so meaningful that we no longer need to wait until the releasing school bell rings or school vacation begins in order to feel ourselves free and alive.

Out of the unpretentious experience with our first child, a project of work grew, gradually and at first almost unintentionally, that began to correspond to the ideals of our youth: to live our own lives fully and in authenticity, and at the same time to touch the needs of our immediate surroundings as well as of the country in which we lived and to help in the fulfillment of these needs. The reading of the first book by Maria Montessori was like a stone in the water that incurred ever widening circles. A chain of events followed. I signed up for a Montessori course for preschool children at Saint Nicholas Training Centre in London, purchased some basic Montessori material, organized a small group in our home in Puerto Rico for our son Leonardo and some neighbors and then, when Leonardo reached kindergarten age, opened a kindergarten in Cali, Colombia. Despite my lack of practical experience, the results here with an increasing number of children were so convincing that both the parents and we ourselves were very surprised.

There was, for example, one girl—small, fat, and very spoiled—who for three months did nothing at kindergarten except sweep, mop, and wash dishes. One day I was asked by her very distinguished and elegant father, a serious expression on his face, the following question: "Can you perhaps explain to me what you do with my daughter here?" Because of my lack of experience, I immediately felt insecure, driven into a corner, as it were, and I tried to give the gentleman a short lesson in the Montessori system of pedagogy. But he shook his head and informed me that it did not interest him. "You see," he told me, "before my daughter entered your kindergarten, she cared nothing at all for me and now she loves me. I just wanted to know how you managed to achieve that."

Another child, a little boy of four years of age, comes to mind. For a long two months he only sat or stood around, apparently not interested in anything; he did not touch any material, took part in no group activity. Even when a ball rolled against his foot, his only reaction was a bored look. Moreover, he had the odd habit of calling himself by the name of his brother, two years older, and calling me by the name of his brother's teacher. My mostly theoretical knowledge about "spontaneous activity" of a child was put to a hard test by this boy. I often had to bind my hands behind my back, figuratively speaking, in order not to make an attempt to move him in the direction of some activity seeming sensible to me at that point. He had apparently sworn to himself to nip in the bud my belief in the ability of a child to educate itself, as impressively described in the books by Maria Montessori. So as not to make things all-too strenuous for myself, I gave him a period of three months in which to do nothing. A few days before his time elapsed, he shot back for the first time a ball that rolled toward him. On the following day he literally threw himself at every material that lay ready for use on the shelves and in the cupboards, proving by every move he made that he knew very well—from his "inactive" or "indifferent" observations—how to use each object. A week later he was the organizer and initiator of all group games, and every day one could hear his clear shout *"Yo, yo, yo quiero"* ("I, I, I want . . .") many, many times. At the end of the school year his parents invited us to dinner and thanked us. In their opinion their small Paul had made such great progress in those last ten months that he had by far overtaken his older brother, a pupil at one of the best schools in Cali, in self-confidence, initiative, cooperation, and faculties of reaction and observation.

In spite of many positive and surprising experiences with the children in Cali at that time, I did not really get down to reflecting on, that is to say dealing with, the problem of education in any depth. The year we had planned to stay in Cali came to an end. We moved to Quito, Ecuador, and left the first kindergarten in the care of a woman with whom we were well acquainted. Leonardo, now five years old, was registered for the kindergarten of the Colegio Alemán—the German School—which knew nothing of Montessori principles but was intended to bring him into contact with the German language and culture.

If we had been more attentive at that time, we would have noticed very soon that Leonardo was becoming more listless and insecure with every week that passed. His frequent headaches and stomachaches, his wanting to sleep late every morning, and his daily resistance against putting on his school uniform, getting on the school bus—we would have recognized all of these as clear signs of "school fatigue" if we had known a bit more. But our own wishes and myriad activities made us turn a blind eye to the unmistakable alarm signals of our child.

When Leonardo was of school age, we were just starting our project for organic agriculture. We moved to an upland farm that was sixty kilometers away from Quito. Leonardo was put into a Salesian school in the next village, ten kilometers from the farm, and attended classes together with sixty red-cheeked mestizo and Indio children in a classroom filled to bursting. A resolute teacher kept his pupils in line, if necessary with a stick. In this group there were few reprisals for Leonardo—other than those coming from his classmates, who often teased him about his blond hair. But there were also enough backs for him to hide behind when he wanted to be left alone. So he enjoyed an advantage, which he had in common with many children in Ecuador who still go to school today under completely inadequate conditions: a teacher who had to cope with fifty to eighty children in a class did not even try to keep every single one of them under complete control. Neither teacher nor pupil doubted that the hours at school were a very unpleasant matter, just as recruits in the army are not under the illusion that they are spending "the best years of their lives" there. In these overcrowded and absolutely primitive schools in Ecuador, no secret is made of the fact that reading and writing are painful—there is a saying in Spanish that goes as follows: *"La letra entra con sangre"* ("Learning the alphabet draws blood"). The children arm themselves, so to speak, with equanimity in this situation, and go their own way in the rest of the time.

In the almost five years that Leonardo was in attendance at this school, we saw alarm signals of a school neurosis very rarely, in spite of the long school hours. Already in his first year there, he insisted on going to school by bicycle—this was a distance of ten kilometers one way, twenty kilometers there and back, on a road that was quite steep in places. He woke up long before sunrise and left the house at six in the morning, no matter what the weather—and it can be very unpleasant in the Andes, especially in the rainy season. He spent his afternoons playing on the farm and had fun with the cows, horses, and chickens as well as with the tractor and the trucks. He learned how to do production checks of milk and eggs, helped with the dissection of dead cows, stood by the cows when they were calving and the horses when they foaled, and slept in a tent at the edge of a ravine on the weekends, together with his friends, to watch the condors and the mountain foxes when it got light.

The farm bordered on a typical Andean village that in former times had eked out a living with a small Panama hat industry that had since moved away. With its houses made of clay, the mostly defective waterworks and electric lines, its deserted square, and the rundown school building, it was a sorry sight. The farm provided work for fifty families in the village and thus represented a certain source of hope for the inhabitants. The headmistress of the village school asked me to assist her in the establishment of a kindergarten in one of the empty classrooms. I jumped at the chance to apply the knowledge and experience I had gained in Colombia in such different circumstances. I introduced the Montessori system to a young female assistant. The most necessary furnishings were made in the carpentry shop of the farm. Each child brought a few bricks that were to be used together with plain boards to make shelves for the Montessori material. This material was supplemented by all sorts of handmade toys and utensils. In this simple kindergarten, which was attended by barefoot and uncombed children with eternally runny noses, we could see a reflection of Maria Montessori and her first "*casa de bambini*" in Rome. We experienced the slow transformation of fearful, ungroomed, and taciturn children into happy, self-confident personages. A year later they were the first children who, when they moved up to first grade, were able to build an unexpected bridge between the teacher and the Indio children just starting their school careers. For those children who did not even have knowledge of Spanish, they made signs with their hands to communicate. They helped the ones who had not seen tables or chairs, paper or pencil at home to learn the use of all these objects. As a rule, Indio children come to school in the beginning with the illusion that they can become part of or at least link up with the "other Ecuador" through schooling, but they drop out of the race in most cases and go back to a life without the alphabet. The Montessori children took these children under their wing spontaneously, helped them with their schoolwork, and established friendships with them.

When this farm project was at an end after five years, our second son, Rafael, was just two and a half years old. In the peace and quiet of the farm, we had had time to read new things about child psychology and issues of child rearing as well as education, neurological research, and other such topics. In addition our work had brought us into direct contact with the social problems of Ecuador. We had often had the bitter experience of discovering how difficult it is to do any kind of basic work with adults that gives them—more than just their daily bread—true self-confidence and thus facilitates the possibility for self-help. In contrast, it had become clear that small children quickly seize the slightest opportunity to restore or re-create their environment and to make the best out of everything. Therefore, if we wanted to do something positive for our environment and at the same time make use of our particular talents, everything pointed in the same direction: we had to create a real Montessori kindergarten for our small second son. And this kindergarten should not only cover its own costs but also those of a parallel kindergarten for poor children. The first, Pestalozzi I, would integrate children of different economic and social backgrounds from Quito and the surrounding neighborhoods. The second, Pestalozzi II, would serve those who lived too far away to get to our place every day. In Pestalozzi I, they paid as much as they could afford:

at that time we had set aside around thirty percent of our school budget for scholarships. At Pestalozzi II, the parents contributed voluntary work or some garden products for the children's breakfast.

Again we had furniture made in the farm's carpentry shop. In Quito we went looking for a large house that could accommodate not only our family but the kindergarten as well, which was to take in twenty-five children. After our years on the farm, we were, of course, searching for a house with a large yard, but such houses had skyrocketed in price in the meantime—they were unaffordable. Ecuador had meanwhile become an oil country. As a result of the increasing stream of dollars, every house of better quality could command four times its previous rent, while poverty became more and more blatant.

And so we threw ourselves into the adventure of locating our planned kindergarten in a rural area. We were especially taken by the valley of Tumbaco, which can be reached in thirty minutes from Quito, on a road with many curves. Until then there had been idyllic country estates with subtropical fruits of all kinds and weekend houses in the valley, some of which were available for rent or purchase. Just at that time, however, more and more families had ventured a move down into the valley in order to get away from the disadvantages of the increasingly metropolitan Quito. However, places of work and school were still in Quito. We were the first to think of establishing a kindergarten out in the country. This idea was contrary to all accepted practice, and so it was no wonder that we had only three children on our first day. Gradually, though, the number grew, as more and more people recognized the advantages that rural surroundings could offer to their children: an ideal climate, a landscape with mountains and eucalyptus trees, clean air, and—as we became aware only much later—a new system based on freedom and nondirectivity with a large supply of materials.

CHAPTER TWO

The Prevailing Myth of Education

In his book *Celebration of Awareness*, Ivan Illich speaks of a myth of education to which we have been doing service for two hundred years, in much the manner of paying court to a sacred cow. In Ecuador this myth has just come into full bloom.

At regular intervals the papers are full of articles about a "dramatic failure of the educational system." They report on the fact that only about 27 percent of the first-graders who start school actually finish the six-year elementary program. This catastrophic situation is attributed to overcrowded classrooms, to insufficient teacher training, and—once in a while—to an unsuitable system of education as well. Such articles often go on for pages, lamenting that even high-school graduates seem to comprehend only very little of what the school faculty has tried to teach them over a period of at least twelve years of school attendance. In spite of these and other complaints, one still must not dare to doubt that school or—more accurately put—attendance at school is the only way to social recognition, economic success, service to one's country, and last but not least, self-fulfillment.

The law provides for compulsory school attendance. In earlier times this comprised six years; it has now increased to a period of nine years. For the last three years, since 1979, kindergarten has been compulsory for five-year-olds. However, in Pichincha, the province with the highest level of development and where Quito, the regional as well as national capital city, is located, there were only one hundred insufficiently trained kindergarten teachers available at the time the law was passed. This proportion is much less favorable in other provinces of the country, as most cultural advantages are already and intrinsically concentrated in the capital.

The legislation of the country stands in great contradiction to the opportunities that are actually available to acquire a school diploma. Those of the rural population are the first to drop by the wayside in the race for this hotly desired certificate. The greatest number of dropouts is to be found in villages. In the public schools of towns and cities, there are battles to gain entrance to a classroom, and when a place has been acquired, the last thing one wants to risk is its loss because of undesirable behavior. It is an art in itself to gain a place at one of the prestigious private schools, which protect themselves by various means against undesired pupils. Selection is done by means of social standing and "pull" and high tuition fees, as well as considerable investment sums "requested" of parents, psychological tests, and the demand for absolutely perfect behavior.

No one wants to lose advantages once they have been gained, and so great sacrifices are made for a recognized school education: in rural schools these include long distances on foot for the children as well as regular contribution of agricultural products to teachers, and in urban areas it means long rides on buses. On the so-called Teacher's Day that is celebrated in Ecuador, on name days and birthdays, at Christmas and just before grades are given, expensive gifts are the rule. At schools of prestige, great importance is attached to the attendance of parents in elegant wardrobe at social events, their participation in the organization of bazaars to raise money for improvements in the school's physical plant, equipment, and so on, as well as their regular contact with teachers and school psychologists to be informed about their children by these experts. By fulfilling the school's demand for this ideal parental behavior, parents can spare their children a good deal of trouble. Most important is that they attest over and over again to their complete and unlimited trust in this highly paid institution as regards questions of upbringing and education.

It is an unwritten law that the school is the last instance for the judgment of children, and only it possesses the exclusive right of perfect education. Parents often promise in writing to use their own authority to support the school and its high aims. In practice, what is seen is that parents feel responsible for homework getting done. They often assist until late in the evening so that everything is completed as desired and the teacher can be satisfied with the work on the following day. Thus, as a matter of course, the atmosphere at home is often tense, but there is never the slightest doubt that the children bear full responsibility for this situation. Even the most loving parents tend to blame their children for not being able to comprehend their own homework. Only a very small percentage of parents entertain a doubt as to whether so much cramming and writing makes sense at all. And if they do, such doubts are put aside with the remark that "life is not always a bed of roses and it's best if the children get used to discipline and a hard life very early on."

In Ecuador the external symbol of order, discipline, and affiliation to a particular educational institution is the school uniform. The children often hate it after a short time. Who would not, wearing the same colors and the same style day after day, year in and year out? On the other hand, it is an important symbol of their status for the pupils of the prestigious schools, at least in the beginning, and they are not averse to appearing in public in this dress. All schools attach the greatest importance to a complete and correct uniform every day. Parades are held each day, with spot checks to see if a pair of brown instead of black shoes or even the wrong color of socks has caused the honor of the school to be debased. Moreover, the best schools differentiate between everyday and dress uniforms. But even in the most rural of schools, a uniform, albeit simple, is absolutely necessary to offer the proper framework of dignity for learning the basics. Long daily examinations are undertaken to check if hair has been brushed, handkerchiefs ironed, shirts starched, and shoes shined. At times children are even obliged to stand in front of the whole class while the teacher scrutinizes their underwear.

The belief in the power of institutionalized education is almost and for all practical purposes unshakeable on the part of adults, and thus it is systematically transmitted to the new generation. Should there be any doubts, the following argument is inevitable: "I can see in my own case how good school was for me. Look at me, I turned out all right."

Only recently a mother took her four-year-old son out of our kindergarten. It was her opinion that the time had now come for the boy to be prepared for the entrance exam at one of the prestigious schools in Quito; otherwise he could jeopardize his place there. She complained that her son had been much further along before his kindergarten year with us: he had already learned some letters of the alphabet at that time and had been able to count to twenty. The free system had obviously done damage to him, as she said; now he only wanted to play and not learn anything. Particularly scandalous, it seemed to her, was his great love of sand and water. And this is not an isolated case—it illustrates par excellence the widespread fear of losing one's connection to the miracle of education.

Let us direct a more careful look at this myth: what is behind it? What is the real aim that lies hidden behind the urge, the pressure to acquire higher knowledge, high morale, and culture? In this country we experience modifications and improvements in the curriculum, change after change in the plan of studies: foreign experts are consulted, teachers are given course after course in further training, new textbooks and statistical forms are printed, and new model schools with methods never seen before are opened with great ceremony. Yet the "hidden" syllabus remains untouched. It is threefold and tolerates no contradiction: the school trains our children to obey (you have to know that someone knows better than you do in regard to what, how, when, and how much you have to learn), it trains punctuality, and it trains children how to work by routine. For gaps in knowledge, solutions can be found: tutoring or the possibility of improving a bad written grade by a good oral mark. But a child who does not demonstrate by his or her behavior a readiness to adapt and fit in is soon out of an Ecuadorean (or other) school.

Most recently, a great deal of talking and writing has been going on about the fact that educational methods are indeed antiquated, that too much is dictated that should really be learned by means of better pedagogical systems, that the main focus unfortunately lies on learning by rote and on answering oral questions on the material learned this way. But no one dares to confront a teacher in the flesh who uses such antiquated methods. In fact, children beg parents who inveigh against what they feel to be a senseless piece of homework: "Don't talk to the teacher—the teacher will treat me even worse then!" And so the myth of "a good school education" remains much stronger than the concrete proof of its opposite. Who would dare to inflict a wound on a sacred cow?

What are the visible consequences of this situation? Children of kindergarten age already begin to display the signs described in manifold form by American home schooling pioneer John Holt: the "smart ones" learn all the tricks that serve them well in giving adults—teachers and parents—the impression of an educational success. An intelligent ten-year-old girl who came to us half a year ago from a prestigious Colombian school put it as follows: "The teachers all believed that I was good in arithmetic, and I believed it a little bit, too, because I had good marks. But now I know that I really hadn't understood anything at that time. Because I calculate everything now using materials, I see when I really understand something."

Those who are the fastest to learn how to deal with words, with mathematical symbols, and with logical conclusions are the ones who experience the most recognition and attention. The more sensitive children feel in some way deceived, even swindled, and indeed, sooner or later someone will have to pay for this deception. Yet external pride in knowledge, which often enough is not real knowledge, frequently wins out over the more refined feeling of knowing that one does not know something or other.

Some children—often the ones with the more honest natures or the emotionally weaker—lose out in the race at an early stage. Since there are no, or almost no, alternative educational tracks in Ecuador, many simply disappear from the general educational program. Others experience a painful disintegration of their personality, become accustomed to living in a state of fear, and start to hate any kind of learning. Some begin to stutter, some become bed wetters or suffer from headaches or stomach ulcers. Many turn to drugs.

When, at the age of twelve, our eldest son showed clear signs of personal insecurity and a school neurosis (this was at a time when he was treated with great cynicism by a teacher at a prestigious school in Quito, who boasted that only half of the students were able to follow in his classes), we provided him with security at home, telling him that he could leave school without any fear, should he decide to do so. Which in fact he did—for more than a year. During this time he regained his old self-confidence; he was interested in everything going on in the world and made the decision to return to school in order to get his "piece of paper."

The long-term consequences of the Ecuadorean school system are detrimental not only to the individuals but to the entire country as well. It creates the right conditions for a monstrous bureaucracy that provides work for all those who can solve all problems by means of words and paper and pencil, more recently with computers, even if they, by so doing, create additional and more difficult problems. The widespread personal dissatisfaction leads as well to the kind of consumer society that burdens a country like Ecuador, which already suffers from its own problems as well those imported from abroad. But what kind of education would we like to see for a country like Ecuador? Keeping in mind that it is a country attempting to open new doors for itself, yet finding itself in danger of being caught between the values of yesterday and today, its own values and the values of foreign countries, we would like our children to come into contact not only with wonderful words but also with concrete reality; we would like them to become people who dare to make decisions, even when the possible alternatives contradict generally accepted expectations.

In *Memories, Dreams, Reflections*, C. G. Jung offers an assessment of our situation in the following words:

As a rule, however, the individual is so unconscious that he altogether fails to see his own potentialities for decision. Instead he is constantly and anxiously looking around for external rules and regulations which can guide him in his perplexity. Aside from general human inadequacy, a good deal of the blame for this rests with education, which promulgates the old generalizations and says nothing about the secrets of private experience. Thus, every effort is made to teach idealistic beliefs or conduct which people know in their hearts they can never live up to, and such ideals are preached by officials who know that they themselves have never lived up to these high standards and never will. What is more, nobody ever questions the value of this kind of teaching.[1]

---

1. Jung, *Memories, Dreams, Reflections,* 330.

The primary school printing press gives many opportunities for practical work—and for learning writing, reading, and cooperation at the same time.

CHAPTER THREE

First Experiences with the
Pestalozzi Kindergartens

It was time to create a kindergarten for our two-and-a-half-year-old son, Rafael, that could fulfill the fundamental conditions that corresponded to our feelings about life and our convictions, and that would allow both the external and the internal to develop in harmony. What we were acquainted with and what could be reconciled with our feelings as compatible was based on the Montessori system. I had meanwhile completed a practical as well as a theoretical course in London, and this opportunity enabled me to bring a quantity of concrete learning materials to Ecuador. There was no lack of criticism and well-meaning advice: wasn't Montessori long since out of date, and shouldn't one look for modern reformers? For South American progressive pedagogues, only the newest methods are good enough, and these come directly from the laboratories of behaviorism. Such methods achieve astonishingly good results by taking into account human imperfections only in terms of their external effects while ignoring—as far as possible—the uncomfortable or "troublesome" inner processes not so easy to deal with. Through a methodical and completely scientific singleness of purpose, everything in the individual that cannot be measured receives no attention, is left out. And it is a proven fact: the results of these methods (which make use of rigorous conditioning techniques based on input and output or work with teaching machines rather than with people) are much more positive than those of the old "blackboard-and-chalk" system, in which teachers again and again fall victim to the temptation of listening to their own voices and, as beautifully described in the impressive and well-known study *Pygmalion in the Classroom*, influence the progress of pupils through their own mind-sets, sometimes positively, all too often, however, in a negative way.

The main difference between these methods and the active method we prefer is that for us the primary purpose of education is not to get desirable knowledge into the head of an individual as quickly and painlessly as possible. For us the most important thing for children and young people is that they can grow into a rapidly changing world in such a way that their being and thus their ability to make a positive adjustment to new conditions and situations in life is not weakened by the educational process but rather strengthened. In his reflections on our contemporary problems, Jung emphasizes that it is the lack of knowledge about our own psychological powers and our inner world that makes us susceptible, even dangerous beings. Our fear of the unknown processes going on inside us largely unobserved makes us easy prey for those forces that promise us security and relieve us of responsibility. Thus we sacrifice our autonomy in favor of an external authority if, by doing so, we can spare ourselves the suffering of becoming conscious of our own self, the pain of our individual inner growth, and the burden of our personal responsibility.

So we withstood bravely the temptation to take as a basis for our kindergarten the most modern of techniques. In spite of the danger of being looked upon as "unmodern" or "unscientific," we trusted our own feeling, which advised us not to place too high a value on direct and fast results.

A kindergarten that intended to serve small children in their processes of becoming conscious about their own being and conquering the world into which they would grow—what should it be like? How ought it to be? For us there was no doubt that the Montessorian idea of the development of a child was in harmony with our concept of an "education for being" or "learning to be." From the very beginning, Maria Montessori respected the natural powers that guide the child from inside in its process of growth. She entrusted to the child the steering of its own little vehicle, by means of which it gets to know and practices its abilities in mastering its own life situation. She showed how nature leads the child through all the "sensitive periods," in which the child gradually learns to try its strength against the conditions of the environment. She showed how the senses become the "window to the soul," enabling the child to take in effortlessly all that is needed for its own growth. In the "darkroom" of its own unconscious, the child processes what is useful. In doing this, the child seems to exhibit no interest in things that at that moment do not correspond to its inner needs. The language of Maria Montessori, in her early books, is often more mystical than scientific. Long before the time a scientific discipline systematically studied the growing understanding of a child and the gradual structurization of its brain, she recognized, often intuitively, some of the most significant phenomena of human development of consciousness. For example, she proved how important a suitable environment—adapted to the child—is for its growth. She gave the child the right to individual activity, to free choice of activity, and to his or her own personal rhythm. She showed the value of a self-critical attitude on the part of adults truly interested in the development of the child, adults who learn to set aside their own personal need to control every situation, attempting instead to fulfill the needs of the child for sensory experiences, movement, and attention—without setting conditions.

When a small child no longer has to fight for the fulfillment of these needs, the transformation, or normalization, as Montessori calls it, is inevitable. The child becomes active, without being hectic. Movements become orderly, the personality shows harmony. The child begins to become more deeply absorbed in its activities, often for a long period of time, and without tiring. The child respects others as well as the objects of its environment and seems to feel comfortable and good in its own person, which is even manifested in a stable state of health. The books of Maria Montessori move us deeply time after time in their loving descriptions of such normalization processes. On these pages, however, I would like to describe our own experiences in Tumbaco and try to tell a bit about the processes of the children who have shared their lives with us during the last few years.

We began to work with a method that had been known in Ecuador only by name five years earlier. Our kindergarten became known by word of mouth. From the three children we had on the first day, fifty children filled our prepared environments already at the end of the first school year. Two young female teachers, whom we ourselves had introduced to the method, worked with us in the first year. In the afternoons and sometimes on the weekends as well, we worked at other jobs in Quito in order to earn money for our own living, and used the proceeds from our work to build another large room for the kindergarten. The fees that came in from the children whose families were in a position to pay them covered the costs of rent, teachers' salaries, and the parallel kindergarten. One of the teachers took over the children's transportation from Quito to us, and Mauricio went out in the car every morning to pick up all the children from the Tumbaco Valley. We built a carpentry workshop and hired a carpenter, who since that time has constructed all our buildings, furnishings, and materials, in addition to many things for other kindergartens. Thus the two kindergartens survived the first year.

Right from the start, it was clear to us that "Montessori in Ecuador," in spite of the high costs involved, was not to become a model of education only for the wealthy. It was for this reason that we made personal sacrifices and looked for paying jobs outside the kindergarten project; we were thus able to operate the parallel kindergarten as well as offer numerous scholarships for Pestalozzi I, which led to social integration. However, after the experiences of the initial year, we recognized that despite financial difficulties we would have to concentrate all our efforts on the work in Tumbaco. The construction of new materials, talks and discussions with parents and educators from other schools, the training of our teachers, and therapy hours with disturbed children took up more and more time.

The second year began with seventy children in Pestalozzi I and twenty children in Pestalozzi II, which was now moved to serve a closed commune at the other end of the Tumbaco valley. Everything pointed to the fact that our work had begun to touch a real need in the society in which we lived.

Perhaps I can give my readers a bit of a taste of the experience as a whole that we—both children and adults—had during the first two years of the Pestalozzi kindergartens, which in the end led to the desire to make the same experience of an alternative education possible for older children of school age.

A typical morning for the preschool children looked like this: As of 7:30 in the morning, three buses bearing the name "Pestalozzi" drive through the streets of Quito and along the bumpy unpaved roads of the Tumbaco valley. The children of Pestalozzi II all live in the same rural village, and they are able to reach their kindergarten on foot over safe paths. At 8:30 we greet the children at the gate. The small personages climb out of the buses, often with considerable difficulty down the high steps but always with great circumspection and very mindful of their independence. There are loud greetings to be heard everywhere. Some children jump at us and want to give us a big kiss, others prefer to be tickled, while others have apparently been given an overdose of parental love in the meantime and enjoy being left in peace, content just to wave hello at us. The teachers, most of them having come by school bus themselves, immediately go to their areas of work assignment, rotated among them each week according to a schedule.

The children bring along their *lonchera*, Spanish for a snack or sandwiches for in-between times. Some, having found the bus ride very long or having left home without too much breakfast, find themselves a nice place on the grass, at the picnic table, or up on top of the climbing platform where they can partake of their second breakfast. This is an opportunity to exchange the latest news with their friends or trade a hard-boiled egg for a mango. Others quickly stow their things in the places provided for each child for this purpose and settle down to work or play. But who tells them what they should do first? A large range of possibilities is open to them. Every morning they have this assortment of choices and must decide on an activity, stay with it until their interest is exhausted, and then choose something else, something new. The first decisions are made already on the way from the gate to the kindergarten building. Should the child stay outside? The morning sun, almost always shining here in the Tumbaco valley, offers wonderful warmth outside in the yard. Or maybe one should first have a look to see if the dog has already had her puppies, or whether the burro is squabbling with the lamas, or whether the seeds just planted yesterday have already begun to sprout.

A few children can be seen in the sandbox. Others are digging tunnels in the big pile of sand in front of the building, while others, their clothes protected by huge rubber aprons, are carrying buckets of water away from the water table with great enthusiasm, in order to beautify the sandbox by adding rivers and lakes.

Or how about the seesaw, or the trampoline, all the climbing apparatus, the slide or the little stream, on which a few children are already sailing their small handmade boats? Should the child play alone, join a group, or invent a game and invite others to join in? Two teachers are on duty outside, but neither of them seems to be organizing the activities of the children. What are they doing there, then? Although they apparently do not take over the initiative for the children's activities, they can be seen in different places, at different times, always with undivided attention and never passive. One of them looks after children who are just arriving, either on foot or in the car of their parents, and who must be checked off on the attendance list. Both keep a constant eye on the entire yard and feel responsible for the observation of the house rules: no child may hit another child or disturb another in his or her selected activity, aprons must be worn for games involving water, and waste materials or garbage must be put into the pails provided. They look to see if any children are sad and need comforting, help to get desired equipment or materials, talk to individual children or play with them, if that is what the children want. They are often to be seen in the middle of all the various activities, watching, writing something down every once in a while.

A like situation is to be found in the various rooms open to the children. In the "old house," which also serves as our domicile, there are three rooms equipped with small tables and chairs, mats, and shelves full of inviting materials. All the well-known Montessori materials are available—for daily life, to exercise the senses, as preparation for reading and writing: calculation materials of all sorts, games of skill and dexterity, round games, games requiring logic, Lego and other construction games, all kinds of natural materials that can be sorted, compared, or simply admired and touched, a typewriter, colored pencils and paper, a cozy and comfortable library corner that gets the morning sun, and a small living room with a sofa, armchairs, a harpsichord, and blooming plants. In each room there is a "teacher" who asks in a friendly way if help is needed and who shows a child a new game or how to use one of the materials, if desired and, if necessary, reminds the child that all things must be returned to their place after use. It is not always easy to discover this teacher in the room. She is almost never standing up to her full height. Instead, she is squatting on the carpet with a small group of children, or she is sitting beside a child on one of the small stools and looking, together with him or her, at the work in progress. Her voice is never raised above the voices of the children in the typically didactic tone of a teacher; she is always careful to make herself as invisible as possible, so as not to disturb with her presence the atmosphere determined by the children or to steal the initiative from them.

In the "new house" the atmosphere is similar. This is a sextagonal building made of wood with large windows on all six sides, through which our mountain landscape, the sun, and birdsong can enter the room. A number of low tables and stools in the center of the building are for all types of handicraft activities: cooking or baking, ceramics, plasticine, working with glue, cutting, weaving, sewing, painting. This is where the "dirty" work takes place, and many small and nimble hands move with great alacrity and agility.

Around the tables along the walls of the various rooms, different interest centers invite children to participate in a variety of both games and serious occupations. One offers building blocks of all sizes, shapes, and colors plus model trains and cars. The next has a big dollhouse with all its accessories. Then comes a play store in which the children can "do business" as shopkeepers and customers, buying and selling with great concentration. There are cupboards and shelves with numerous materials for making things, and a "family corner" with a dining room, iron and ironing board, dishes, a kitchen sink, cutting boards, and knives to chop vegetables. Almost hidden is a corner with dolls, dolls' beds, doll clothing, bed linen, baby bottles, telephone, and so on. Here the children can act out in play, undisturbed, all that they have taken in from the world around them. Next to the doll corner we find a puppet theater, easels for painting, and an indestructible workbench with hammers, saws, nails, and balsawood. Outside, a little playhouse provides a place for secret games and undisturbed conversations in an atmosphere of privacy.

What is it that regulates all this activity, and how do small children of three to six years of age get to the point where they are able to decide what to do, how long to do it, with whom to make friends, whether help is needed or they prefer to solve their problems alone, or whether they might even prefer to do nothing for a while and just watch the others at their activities? In such a prepared environment that offers many stimulating attractions but excludes the possibility of any pressure exercised by adults, it becomes surprisingly clear that each and every child, provided that it has no severe disturbances owing to disrespectful or inattentive treatment, possesses a clear inner direction or guiding force, as it were. This is what leads the child in its choice of activities, makes it possible for the child to find its own rhythm, and allows the child to achieve a new balance with each new activity. If permitted to follow this inner directive force, the child is able to act and react as a self-confident, happy, and helpful human being, despite its tender age, and to enjoy each day to the fullest. Of course, not all children—in fact perhaps only a very few—come to our kindergarten in such an "undamaged" state. Even at only three or four years of age, many have lost confidence in their own inner direction as a result of the constant intervention and know-it-all behavior of the adults who love them. Some may not even have had the complete love and attention of their parents when they came into the world, the purpose of which is to enable them to have basic trust and confidence in life itself.

Before a child can deal with the difficult task of making autonomous decisions, it must fulfill its old needs exerting pressure from inside. Then—but not only then—it is our task to respond to the child when we recognize such needs. If, for example, the child has had to go without the all-encompassing love of its mother, it is possible that the child will cling, quite literally, to one and the same female teacher for weeks or months and perhaps accompany her faithfully from room to different room, from week to week, as she changes her particular work assignments according to the schedule. The child will take every opportunity that presents itself to sit on her lap and will prefer being close to her above any and all other activities. Our teachers know that such needs must be fulfilled as far as possible, in keeping, of course, with the myriad other responsibilities of the area of work. Experience has shown us that even the child most hungry for love and affection gradually begins to let go, becoming independent as well as enterprising and interested in activity, if given enough time to fulfill these old needs.

Another version of the typically insecure child expresses the insecurity through aggression. We will never forget how Laura, a small two-year-old girl, came to us. She hit out at any child who came close to her. We soon found out that since her birth, her parents had been trying to decide whether to separate or to stay together for the sake of the child. They had begun their marriage on the mutual understanding that they would both retain their personal freedom. After Laura was born, the mother soon noticed that this agreement was no longer valid in her case and felt herself decidedly let down by her husband, who had not allowed his lifestyle to be cramped by the arrival of his daughter. All Pestalozzi teachers agreed that Laura was to be given additional security. The therapy that worked wonders on her was this: everywhere Laura appeared, she was touched lightly by an adult, then caressed, taken onto the lap of the adult, and held there in a warm hug for as long as she herself wished. Although her home situation did not improve in any way, Laura's aggressivity disappeared after a few weeks.

In the case of four-year-old Eric, we were unable to understand what made him so aggressive and insecure. He came from a model family. The mother, a university graduate like the father, had given up working outside the home in favor of her two children and was devoting herself with great dedication to their upbringing. In the beginning Eric was accompanied to kindergarten by his mother. It was easy to see how attached to her he was and how coordinated they were as a team of two. The mother looked around carefully to see what, in her opinion, could interest her son and then called out to him, for example: "Look, Eric, what a lovely butterfly! Do you see the colors? Look, it's yellow and blue with a little bit of black. Do you see it fluttering and how it glitters in the sun? Isn't the butterfly beautiful, Eric?" Eric beamed and confirmed, "Such a lovely butterfly. Blue and yellow. Glitters. Is beautiful!" Then he waited to see if his mother would show him something else. His hope was not in vain. She had already found a nice game for him, then some interesting handicraft. And so it went the whole morning. As soon as his mother no longer came with him to kindergarten, Eric did not feel good anymore. He stood around in misery, found nothing to do, and refused to take off his lined windbreaker the whole morning—his mother had put it on him because it had been a cold morning in Quito. When another child approached him, he hit out. Then he realized what he had done and burst into tears.

Another type of insecurity was exhibited by children from poor families. They are sent to kindergarten with the instruction to be good, not to touch anything, to do everything that Miss Teacher says, and not to make any noise. With these admonitions still ringing in their ears, the children of Pestalozzi II enter their kindergarten, where all the playthings and materials are displayed invitingly, but they do not dare to touch them at first. In Pestalozzi I as well, there are enough children who have heard the following innumerable times at home: "Leave that alone," "Stop that," "Don't touch that!" "What have you done now?" These are children to whom we must give special attention. We let them look around and watch what the other children are doing, perhaps putting an arm around them so that they can feel close to us, and we describe in a low voice the things or activities that they see. At first we avoid recommending this or that game to them. We try to get a feeling of whether they enjoy this looking around and watching and thus will be able to decide on an activity in the course of a bit of time. However, if making a decision is obviously painful for them—this is reflected in most cases very clearly on their face and in their posture—we give them a choice between two alternatives. We estimate their age and gauge what they could possibly be interested in, then we show them two different things with which they can play. This may be their first experience with a situation requiring a clear decision.

For children coming from well-off families who have no lack of toys yet suffer because their real needs are not respected, it often takes a long time to be able to become deeply absorbed in an activity and gain true benefit from it. They touch this and that, pull a lot of things off the shelves and out of the cupboards, then refuse to put them back. In the end they cannot decide on anything. Their movements are unorderly, the expression on their faces one of sadness or boredom. However, if one lets them be, not failing, however, to point out the house rules (what you take out must go back on the shelf; what another child has cannot be taken without permission from that child), and they are not forced into an activity of any duration, there is a good chance that they will come upon something that, even if only for a moment, really captures their attention. This is an important moment for them. Quite unexpectedly, they have the experience of how a person feels when inside and outside, that is, external activity and authentic internal need, coincide for one moment. At this moment it is of the greatest importance that the child can be sure of the respect of an attentive teacher. All small children still possess an accurate feeling for the kind of respect that accepts them as they really are. This feeling provides them with the necessary security that enables them to find their own way. It is therefore one of the most important tasks of an adult to protect a child at such a moment—when there is such an experience of real concentration. This experience is so positive for the child that he or she will always strive for it, again and again, from then on. The occasions, the favorable moments, become more and more frequent, the duration and the depth of concentration greater and greater, until the child no longer needs the protective presence of the teacher. From that point on, the child can even concentrate if the world seems to be coming to an end right then and there. This state is accompanied by a feeling of peace and harmony that now allows even the child who caused disorder and discord before to interrupt the activity voluntarily in order to help another child.

More difficult than the disorderly or hyperactive children are those who, already at such an early age, have given up doing in favor of talking. There they sit, not lifting a finger in the middle of all the assiduous activity that is going on, and talk—not about what they see but about what their aunt did yesterday or what their grandfather says about this or that, in short, about everything save their own experiences. These are the same children who still cannot find their respective places for personal belongings after months of attendance at Pestalozzi, never get themselves dirty, do not get out of the way when they see another child coming with arms full of materials, do not notice when the buses come to take them home, and always forget their things at kindergarten.

The picture would not be complete if I did not describe as well the difficulties of the children who spend many hours in front of the television set at home. It is hard for them to orient themselves in space and time, to perceive the stimuli offered by a prepared environment, and to make sensible use of them. We recognize them by their facial expression and their movements. Some of them even ask, as their very first question, where the TV is! As soon as these children grasp the freedom offered to them here, they do precisely what nature dictates, namely, to create a balance between outside and inside, the outside and the inside worlds. When watching television, these children are bombarded with stimuli that enter only through eyes and ears, whereas the rest of the child's organism remains understimulated. So they utilize the possibilities of the free environment to provide their bodies with the necessary compensation. The huge number of insufficiently "processed" images, pictures that had just been "taken in" that bear no relation to their life experience with their physical being, must be "processed on the outside" as well, and this occurs in the form of "playing it out." As no one forces them to do or learn any particular thing, they spend most of their time searching for a balance that is bearable for them. They act out Batman or Superman and transform letters and numbers, blocks of wood, in fact everything that is available in the prepared environment, into the elements of television shows.

Our worst case was little Andy. At his house they had five television sets and at least one of them was always on. Andy needed one hour of free play for every hour of watching television. He would stand up on the top of our climbing apparatus every day and replay all that he had seen the day before, including the numerous commercials, which he was able to imitate brilliantly. Andy soon turned six and still "had not learned anything." Six weeks before the end of the school year, his mother came in and urgently requested that we teach him English, as he would have to pass an entrance exam for the Colegia Americano, or American School. Here I must explain that at our kindergarten we speak the native language of each child with him or her as much as possible; thus the children hear other languages all the time and often ask how to say this or that in English, German, French, and especially Spanish. Sometimes they also listen to a story in another language. However, on principle we do not give formal lessons in foreign languages, as is the practice from kindergarten on in the "better" schools.

So we reminded Andy's mother, "We warned you at the start, when you registered Andy for kindergarten, that we do not teach any foreign languages. You have also attended various meetings for parents at which we have discussed our method." But the frightened mother asked us to make an exception. His acceptance at the American School was extremely important to her. So we made a pact with her: "Okay, you see to it that Andy doesn't watch television, and we will teach him English." As we had expected, the parents were not able to keep to the agreement and Andy continued to play Superman until the end of the school year. They hired a private English teacher, and his mother was angry at us. And then, in the middle of the following school year, she asked us to accept her second child. We were astounded: "You were very disappointed, weren't you, that we let Andy play as much as he wanted to?" She admitted it, but then went on to say that she now had a different opinion about the school. Not only was Andy the best pupil in all the subjects at the school he attended now, but everyone noticed and remarked upon his team spirit and helpfulness, his independence, and his creative streak.

The problem of "television kids" is by no means limited to the children of Pestalozzi I, who come from families with greater financial means; the effects are also to be seen in Pestalozzi II. Even in the mud huts of the poor, frequently lacking the most basic of household things, often with only one bed in which the entire family sleeps, where guinea pigs, rabbits, and chickens share the one room with members of the family, a television set is to be found. If there is no electricity, it can be powered by batteries. All the attractive and expensive illusions of a strange world far from the reality of such houses are broadcast to these families, who often do not even have running water. Long before the family is provided with the necessities of life, television propagates the newest mixers and vacuum cleaners, automated toys, deodorants, and other luxury articles as well as industrially produced foodstuffs, which are unnecessary or even detrimental to health.

In spite of this, the effects of television on the children of the poor rural population are not as fatal as can be seen in cases of the more spoiled children of urban areas. Their constant contact with nature as well as the visible and tangible daily activities of their parents, in whose life they have a direct participation, plus the small responsibilities that they take on at an early age inside and outside the house, give their organism support and a stable foothold in reality. Their reaction to the offerings of the carefully prepared environment of the kindergarten is a healthy one, as soon as they have overcome their initial timidity and fear of touching the objects offered as stimuli.

At one of our monthly parents' meetings, we discussed *Four Arguments for the Elimination of Television*, the controversial book by

Jerry Mander. This book is the result of years of research on the effects of television both in the life of the individual and on society, and has made a significant contribution to the drastic limitation of television consumption in a number of Pestalozzi families.

I could go on with many more variations of problems that can rob even small children of their spontaneity at the start of their time at kindergarten. But it seems much more important to me to show how an open form of education need not suppress or try to hide these difficulties or "preconditions" with which the child may come to us. Rather, it can give the child an opportunity to "let out" what is deep inside, in a way that is permitted and acceptable, and thus gradually gain confidence in his or her own activity.

In practice the first one and a half hours at kindergarten are reserved for free activity, on a regular basis. During this period the children are faced with the task of feeling, on their own, what corresponds to their most inner or deepest interest. Adults "stay down," leaving to the children the control over choice and configuration of their activities. The children are meant to learn how to take on a tangible reality and what difficulties they have to overcome while doing this. The adult gives the child the materials for the task, demonstrates some small or preliminary techniques, and provides for the security that guarantees that all activity of the child takes place without risk or danger.

It is our task to learn how important our restraint is, how important it is for this process that we "hold back." Our lessons in the use of materials are very clear in terms of movement yet are accompanied by few words: "Let's put the block on this table. Now we take out all the cylinders" (the child follows with its eyes the movements of the adult, who takes the cylinders of various dimensions out of their cavities and places them, as silently as possible, on the table in front). "Now we mix them" (the child helps with mixing). "Now we put them back where they belong" (the hands of the adult try out the dimensions of each individual cylinder as well as the depth of the holes; they put a cylinder into a hole, correct an error if necessary, and continue until all cylinders are once again in their places). "Do you want to try it yourself?" Not one word was said about the kind of differences to be found among the cylinders, about thickness, length, depth. What is important is the activity of the child, who practices with sharp senses how to experience the world directly, with its own body and soul, as it were. Not until later, when the child has completely absorbed the experience and begun to discover parallels to this specific material, does the teacher take the opportunity for an informal little "lesson": "This is high, this is low." And so it goes, with all the materials that stimulate the child into new experiences, which not only coordinate the child's movements through the utilization and refinement of all its senses but also help the child to put in order and to organize its small world. By means of this, its own understanding is structured, together with its environment, and becomes the basis for intelligent actions.

Blindfolded, Monica had shown great interest in putting the small fabric samples together into pairs. After this work she skipped out into the garden. Through the window I could watch her moving about outside. She began to play with the bushes growing along the wall. She touched the leaves and then started to pull off a great many of them. An uninitiated spectator would most likely have called out to her, "Stop tearing off the leaves!" After a while she proudly returned to her previous place of work with a supply of leaves. She got out the fabric samples again and began to touch the surface of the leaves very carefully with her fingertips. Then she compared them with the fabrics. While doing so, she discovered differences and similarities, happily inviting the friends nearest her to share in her discoveries.

It would, of course, be impossible for me to describe all the materials that are used like this, or in a similar manner, every day by the children. However, I would like to emphasize that these materials make sense only when the child has had the opportunity to store up innumerable and unstructured sensory impressions and experiences before making use of them. A child who, because of an impoverished environment or the ignorance of adults, has never had the chance for free experimentation with a quantity of objects, above all with natural materials, will not gain much benefit from handling structured material. Because of this, we are careful to keep on hand many new unstructured materials for our children, which we offer regularly: seeds and pits of all kinds, bottle tops, crates, cartons and bottles of all shapes and sizes, strings and cords, wires, flowers, leaves and roots—the list would be endless if I kept on adding everything that has passed through the hands of our children over the years.

With the structured materials, a presentation that appeals to the senses is important. The same importance must be attached to a built-in "error check" that enables the child to be independent of the eternal corrections by omniscient adults. The unstructured materials, on the other hand, have a "surprise effect," their most significant factor. These appear in the surroundings in unexpected ways, showing a new face each time, offering new possibilities for discovery and play over and over again. No one is angry when they are used for all sorts of unexpected purposes. Anyone who has small (or older . . .) children can testify to what happens when a few old cartons just happen to be standing around: The children may first try to see whether the top opens and closes, if and how the cartons fit into each other, whether they can be stacked up to build a tower. Perhaps they climb in and out for a while, experiment to see how many children fit inside at one time, how they feel when sitting inside if the top is open, if the top is closed. After that, they may try to pull the cartons around and play automobile (this is often painful to the ears of adults). After a certain time, the cartons will serve as hurdles to jump over, ending perhaps in a battle of cartons. Other children may make them into beds for dolls, or transform them into a castle, a hospital, or a rocket launchpad, with the help of paints, glue, and all kinds of other additions and trimmings.

Who can dare to make the determination whether a child learns more if it sits at a table in an orderly fashion and works diligently with structured materials or if it coaxes out of a few old cartons all imaginable and unimaginable possibilities of use for the whole of a morning? Regardless of where the child begins in its activities, most important is that the child really "gets into it," that the activity is a complete act. For us this means that the child can feel itself in a given situation and then, out of this feeling, decide on an activity, carry out actions with full dedication, and end the activity when he or she so decides. All of this serves to satisfy and contribute to the growth of the child's personality. In addition, consideration for its environment also requires that the child put back in order what it needed for its own satisfaction and enjoyment. Thus the consummate action includes as much responsibility as the hand of a child can grasp. However, this true responsibility comes from the free choice of one's own activity and, as such, is quite different from the situation in which a child is forced to tidy up after having been persuaded to take on a particular activity in the first place. In children's faces, it is easy to read what mixed feelings are created by such tactics.

With this we have come to the problem of discipline, which is, of course, part of any discussion about questions of education. "But how should they learn discipline in a free system?" is the fearful cry of all adults. It is true that from the very start, we avoid a form of discipline that is arbitrary and based on the authority of adults; we even consider it harmful. However, in an active school such as this, the child is confronted with firm house rules of quite an unbending, that is to say, uncompromising, nature, which have their origin in the necessity to create a safe place for all. It is only consideration for the rights of others and the safety of oneself and the others that sets the limits for the freedom of the individual. Observance of these rules is overseen at first by the adults but quickly taken over by the children themselves. They experience, themselves, directly and personally, the necessity and the sense of these "limitations of freedom." They are soon to be heard reminding each other: "At this school you mustn't take anything away," "We don't hit here," and so on. From this functional discipline necessitated by the general good and well-being of all comes the possibility of true self-discipline. Just as an adult who works creatively, that is to say, in one of the creative or freelance professions, often works much more intensively and much longer than the salaried employee of a firm, the "creative" child "creates itself" through its activity, in the words of Maria Montessori. This self-discipline, which comes about through every autonomous act, makes out of the child a human being who can later take real responsibility for his or her world, because this child is already permitted to take over the responsibility for its own actions today.

This functional discipline often meets with the disapproval or—at the very least—incomprehension of educational specialists, as does the fact that in the "open" system, children with age differences of up to three or sometimes four years play and work together, rather than being put together into homogeneous groups corresponding to their age and level of intelligence. The structural material, however, does have the tendency to attract children according to their abilities and experience, thus leading to a certain grouping effect. The sensory materials are preferred primarily by the smallest children, whereas the materials dealing with reading, writing, and arithmetic attract the older ones. The advanced arithmetical materials, which allow calculation up to ten thousand, are normally seen in use by five- to seven-year-olds. Frequently, however, older children can be found playing with the early materials, as though they were making a little digressive excursion back to their "youth." They often offer themselves as teachers to the little ones, or they happily blend in with them in a game for all. The little ones can be seen again and again watching the older ones in their activities and drawing who knows what conclusions from this observation. The open system, therefore, makes use of the great dynamics created by a vertical grouping of children: small children learn much more easily from older ones than from adults, as the difference to them does not seem so insuperable. Hasn't everyone heard, at one time or another, a mother asking one of her children if it understands what its small sibling wants to say? The older children, on the other hand, can grasp how far they themselves have come by means of comparison with the little ones. They practice consideration for the weakness of the smaller children and can also be "small" again themselves, if they feel like it.

It is true that in this form of vertical grouping, there is little room for the well-known competition: wanting to be better than one's neighbor, to receive more praise, to get better grades. But because of this lack, the early trauma for the weaker or slower children of not being "good enough" or "good for anything" is avoided. Yet the healthy kind of competitiveness is not checked or thwarted: each and every child can compete against itself, every day, trying to better itself a little bit with each day that passes. Every year we accept a small number of children with various handicaps for both kindergartens. Their number will have to remain small until we can offer them specific therapy at some point in the future, but for each of these children, the possibility of free activity and use of tangible materials as well as the association with healthy children is in fact a therapy in itself. Some of them, having been through specialized therapy previously, soon show rapid improvement after entering kindergarten. In some cases parents have decided to break off these therapies outside of school entirely.

For healthy children a school life together with handicapped children means valuable practice in consideration of others. They are often able to feel—much more closely and accurately than an adult—what the handicapped child can do for itself and when it will need help. They ask in a very serious manner about what type of handicap it is and how it occurred. We have never seen a handicapped child made fun of or treated badly—clear proof of the fact that a child who is respected in turn respects others.

We often remember my small fellow countryman, a little German boy whom we will call Hans here. When he was three and a half years old, he and another child ran into each other, and he fell into the empty swimming pool of a hotel in Quito, landing on his head. After several operations fraught with risk in an American clinic, his life was no longer endangered, but a transplant of brain cells could promise only shaky success and offer just the *hope* for a complete recovery, only to be seen, however, after a long period of therapy, as the parents were told. Hans was in Germany with his mother for ten months; after that the family was reunited in Ecuador. When he entered our kindergarten in Tumbaco, he had regained only a limited vocabulary. He had only limited use of his right arm and his right leg. He limped around unsteadily and could not go up or down steps. He could move his right arm only by swinging it from the shoulder joint. His right hand curled inward and felt cold and lifeless to the touch. To protect the hole in his skull that was about the size of a man's fist, he had to wear a padded helmet. According to the doctors' reports, his ability to concentrate was limited to one or two minutes, only going up to a maximum of five minutes if he was offered rewards.

From the first day on, Hans had an ardent interest in the water table, heroically refusing to put on a rubber apron, however. In order to avoid a battle, we allowed him to get wet. It was unbelievable with what concentration and perseverance he poured water from one container into another, inventing new difficulties for himself in this operation through the use of funnels, sieves, small openings, and hoses, and using his almost completely crippled arm in new and different ways. In one month his concentration span at his water games had increased to one hour. He chased away anyone who wanted to distract him before the time he had set himself was up. After all his work was finished, Hans was willing to sit on the lap of an adult and allow his crippled arm and cold hand to be stroked lightly and then massaged. He laughed and cried and became talkative. Later he began to play with sand and many other materials, in addition to the water. When, after the end of the school year, he went to Germany for further examinations and therapy, the doctors there could not believe that this was the same child they had discharged some months before. Hans had not only made a dramatic increase in his vocabulary, he was also able to use his arm in a variety of ways that the doctors had deemed impossible. In the following year Hans learned to distinguish between those with whom he spoke Spanish and those with whom he needed to speak German. He is an impressive example of how nature gives a child new and unexpected opportunities for development if we only give the child the freedom to determine how, how much, and how long—according to its own feeling.

The main focus of practice in the kindergartens is therefore the many self-chosen, in fact often self-invented, activities of the children in a well-prepared and orderly environment. It is only in the second half of the morning that group activities are offered by the adults. On the occasion of regular school inspections, we often see the confusion and bewilderment of the officials who are accustomed to strict order and inflexible planning. At our school they look for something familiar, something they can recognize as a curriculum or plan of study. When they discover our group work, they are visibly relieved: "Oh, you do have a schedule! I'm pleased to see that!" And then they note it down eagerly in their books.

At ten o'clock Mauricio goes through the various rooms and the garden, announcing the juice break in singsong. Every child who is finished with its particular work gives up table and chair, helping to carry them outside on the grass. Those who prefer to continue their work retreat with their materials to a quiet room. The children carry out pitchers of juice and cookies from the kitchen through the living room, then down a few steps and through the next room, down more steps and through the corridor, and finally out into the garden. In the first few weeks there are spills on the floor, but with every day that passes, the children show a greater mastery of the art of carrying pitchers of juice, until at last there are hardly any accidents. We are used to the sight of this juice procession. Many visitors, however, who know small children only from their destructive side, are so astounded that their mouths remain open. Recently one woman was completely overwhelmed by the sight of one of our smallest children, not even potty trained yet. This little boy, clad only in his disposable diaper (he had stowed away all his other clothing in the proper place allotted to him, a sort of pigeonhole that each child has at Pesta), climbed up on a chair, took down a full pitcher of juice, and went on his way outside, showing complete control of his movements and not spilling a drop.

After the break for juice, the start of the "project" is announced, also in singsong. In the "new house," careful and dedicated preparations are made for a well-planned project in the fields of handicraft, painting, sewing, or advertising. On this occasion all children work with the same technique and use similar materials; most of the teachers place themselves at the disposal of the children for help and assistance, as needed or desired. If the children wish to take part in the project, they must adhere to the technique and the materials on offer for the particular project of the day. What they produce, however, is not determined beforehand. Participation in the project as well as in other work groups is voluntary. Most of the children join in with enthusiasm, but others do not respond to the invitation, not allowing themselves to be interrupted in the work they have selected. Some first ask about the project of the day before they make a decision.

A little later a new activity is offered: it is music or dance time, depending on the day of the week—singing and playing an instrument according to the Orff method, free movement to music, body expression, or folk dancing. This is structured group work. Those who want to participate must accept the discipline of the moment, without which the group would not be able to function. The morning at kindergarten comes to an end with a story, which is told in various locations for the various language groups. Most children speak Spanish, but we find it a nice custom that the children with a different mother tongue also have the chance to hear the story in their own native language.

That is the end of the morning for the little ones. Some have difficulty tearing themselves away from their activity when the call for going home is heard. Unwillingly they get their belongings together and climb into the bus. All the teachers help to make this difficult moment as free of stress as possible, so that the happy atmosphere of the morning is not lost.

Though sitting close together, the youngsters mostly work with math materials on their own, each following his or her own process of interaction and understanding.

CHAPTER FOUR

Effects on Adults

U p to this point I have attempted to give an idea of the beginnings of the Pestalozzi School: how we personally experienced
our first impulse to become interested in questions of education, out
of the direct necessity to find practicable ways for our own children.
In the philosophy and methods of Maria Montessori, we found our
first alternative; our work was built on it, work that promised satisfactory solutions not only to us but to others as well. Soon, however,
we discovered that a process had begun, not only for the children
but for us, too, which in the course of time revealed new needs time
and again, caused new disquiet, demanded a search for new answers
and new forms of balance. Indeed, this process may still be in its
beginning stages at this moment.

To our kindergarten teachers and the parents of our kindergarten children, we showed a Dutch documentary film on Montessori
(which can be borrowed from the Ministry of Education and Culture here) a number of times. For all those who saw this film, it was
always impressive, time after time, how tasteful, orderly, attractive,
and harmonious the environment and the people in such a Montessori atmosphere are. One feels a great incentive to do just as well,
not only to create a truly attractive environment but also to become
the perfect example, the very embodiment of an always properly

55

dressed, always calm, friendly, and secure Montessori teacher, gathering around oneself a multitude of clean, quiet, and friendly children every day who continue on their path to perfection and higher knowledge without missing a step.

One of our teachers, a woman who was already more than fifty at the time, had felt an urge, after twenty-five years as a senior secretary and the raising of five intelligent children, to at last do something that could really fulfill her from within. After her first year with us, she admitted to me that she had tried for months to imitate my way with the children. It had caused her great conflict to admit to herself that this was not only impossible but also detrimental to her own relationship to the children. Only after she had come to the point where she could truly be herself did the children begin to show real trust and confidence in her. That point, however, represented the start of the actual process about which we are speaking here: namely, that adults begin to observe themselves—as they are to learn how to observe the children—and then ask of themselves, "Am I being myself now, or am I acting according to an ideal, an image I have set up, a model or example I have seen?" More and more new questions soon follow: Why does this child interest me more than the others? Why do I have days on which I take pleasure in being with the children and others on which it is hard for me? Sooner or later we have always found ourselves, together with our teachers, facing the necessity of being authentic with the children. This, however, has required us to deal with ourselves first, with our own unconscious impulses, feelings, urges.

Intuitively at first, later with a greater degree of consciousness, we recognized the importance of giving our teachers regular opportunities to speak about their daily experiences. In the first year it was an informal thing. We had lunch together once a week, and after we had eaten we discussed the practical aspects of the work, planned projects as well as transportation and so on, exchanged ideas about other technical matters. Soon the behavior of individual children as well as our own reactions in critical or incomprehensible situations began to worry us. An unquestioning application of the Montessori method did not always seem the right thing. Rather, we began to see the necessity of opening ourselves up to new experiences, of doing our work in a creative way. Over coffee and cake a spontaneous discussion about personal insecurities and fears of making a mistake came about, including as well the positive discoveries that were made. These talks led to the desire to establish a study circle dealing with questions of education and upbringing, child psychology, and any other topics that might become important for those taking part, in relation either to their work or to their own personal process.

At the beginning of the second school year, two regular work sessions per week had become a tradition and were accepted as such by newly arrived teachers. We felt ourselves to be a true working team. Many lunches and cups of coffee together contributed to our growing interest in talking about the results of our studies and applying them to both the children and ourselves. Constant comparison of the work in the two kindergartens with their different types of needs gave us food for thought. The study group was soon joined by a group of parents who showed interest in the development of a primary school based on the kindergarten. Therefore we went deeper and deeper into the general practices of elementary school in Ecuador, comparing them with the findings of modern child psychology as well as proven alternatives in other countries, and these once again with the particularities of the situation in Ecuador. Later on in the book we will come to how these studies finally led to our own alternative primary school. Here I would like to talk a bit more about the large and small crises of the adults, who were beginning to grapple with the problem of an alternative education with growing dedication. As the kindergarten grew, and later the primary school, so did the number of teachers who shared the responsibilities with us. In the last school year (1981/1982) there were twelve of us as teachers, not counting Mauricio, who acts as director, chauffeur, therapist, and father to all, depending on the current need or necessity of the moment. For two years now, an introductory course on the active school system has been held during the summer vacation for about twenty-five interested persons. Lately our new junior teachers have come from the ranks of these participants. The course provides for 120 hours of theoretical and practical instruction, discussions, introduction to the Orff method, and preventative medicine. (The Orff method is based on the natural sense of rhythm of small children, their need to move and to create their own melodies with just a few notes, and their joy in experimenting with simple instruments.) After the participant has undertaken a two-week internship of practical work in the kindergarten, the training is recognized by the Ministry of Education in the form of an official diploma.

During the course we have a great deal of opportunity for close contact with the participants. The papers handed in, contributions to discussions, handling of the didactic material, and private talks help us to gain insight into the personal aspects and ways of working of the different aspirants. It can still happen, though, that after a few weeks a teacher notices that it can be very painful to "be yourself" every day. Some unexpectedly find themselves in an existential crisis and need help then. In direct proportion to the increase in the team of teachers, we felt the growing necessity to take over a certain responsibility for our staff members, especially when they showed signs of a crisis. A one-to-one conversation, dinner together, or an excursion could often keep open the channels of communication that do not always open spontaneously in a larger group, such as at a teachers' meeting. Thus we were able more than once to prevent a teacher from giving up on himself or herself and the children.

The sessions of the study group have also undergone changes in the meantime. Out of the spontaneous desire to keep ourselves abreast of the latest research and developments in connection with an open method outside the borders of Ecuador, we developed a course of formal study, for a time, with written papers and later discussions. In the third year there were teachers who felt this to be too hard. So we tried to organize all studies in an open system and left it up to each teacher whether he or she wanted to turn in a short summary of every book read, so that the group could decide on what book we would all discuss. However, this "free system for adults" was condemned to failure because only a very few were able to work without pressure from outside. After only a few months, we regretfully returned to the old "cramming system." The results, understandably enough, were not as satisfying as if everyone had contributed to the studies out of real interest and a hunger for knowledge. Last year there was a turn for the better, an upward swing, as it were: contributions to the discussions were more influenced by personal interest and much more lively. This year some of our teachers visited a number of public and private schools, bringing back with them not only impressive experiences but also valuable material for comparison in the studies.

Despite all these efforts to make this work with young children significant for the teachers as well, on their adult level, thus preventing them from becoming mechanical in the performance of their duties because of lack of understanding, the difficulty still remains: how to relax sufficiently every day, and day after day, to be able to coincide with the wavelength of the children. We notice again and again that we equate work with strain or tension, albeit unconsciously. As soon as we relax, we can feel our own unsatisfied needs come to the fore. A teacher in the free system is therefore involved in a reeducation process: teachers must learn to put the needs of the children before their own, and this while in a relaxed state.

The picture would not be complete if I did not also report on the effects on the parents who have registered their children at a Pestalozzi kindergarten. What are the motives of parents who send their children to a kindergarten that, for many, is quite some distance away along roads that are by no means free of risk, where there is no school uniform, no drill, and no school bell, from which the children often come home dirty, with wet socks, sweaty hair, and no homework? These children answer the eager question of "Well, sweetheart, what did you do today?" either with the word *nothing* or by replying laconically, "I played." In the case of the children of Pestalozzi II, things are easier: this kindergarten can be reached on foot, even by the smaller ones, and the parents do not start thinking about an alternative—they gratefully accept the opportunity offered. However, they do make sure that behind this good fortune there lies no new sect or missionaries of another religion, let alone communist agents of some sort.

At Pestalozzi I there were various stages in regard to the motives of the parents. The "first wave" brought above all children from Tumbaco, whose parents wanted to spare them the long trip into Quito. Parents from Quito, on the other hand, found country life for their children a healthier kindergarten alternative and considered it absolutely idyllic. Some parents had placed their trust in us personally, partly because many Ecuadoreans are still fascinated above all by what comes from abroad. Some were our personal friends and had become interested in our ideas a long time before.

The "second wave" brought us parents with new motives. For some, Pestalozzi was the new "in" kindergarten, and they wanted to keep up with the Joneses. Others had heard that children in the Montessori system learned reading, writing, and arithmetic at a particularly early age. For certain social classes in Ecuador, these are the best guarantees for a successful career; here, that means becoming either a lawyer, a doctor, or a manager, thus holding the key to a respectable, secure, and relatively comfortable life. Yet in the second wave there were also parents who in their youth had suffered from an authoritarian system themselves. Perhaps they had learned to hate religion in schools of Catholic orders, or, as a result of being beaten, they had learned to hate learning rather than to take pleasure in it. Some had learned something of psychology and thus began to wonder why their otherwise happy and well-balanced children became listless or mistrustful after a year in kindergarten. And there were parents who just followed their intuition and perceived that their children in Tumbaco could simply be children and at the same time gain worthwhile experience for life. In this connection, a number of household servants must be mentioned: they saw the changes in the children of the families they worked for (these children cleaned up their rooms, maybe wanted to help in the kitchen, and treated the servants and family members with respect), began to be interested in this form of education, and then came to us to request a nonpaying place in Pestalozzi II for their own child.

And so we can see that our children, who come from such different homes and are influenced by so many different types of parents, bring with them all sorts of customs, interests, and attitudes to life. Some of them have never seen a bathroom, since there is none at home, and so they relieve themselves in the garden or the yard until someone explains to them how to use the toilet. Others have a great fear of getting their freshly starched clothes dirty. And some have never done anything for themselves, because the maid does it all. There are children who come to kindergarten with a folder full of exercise books and insist on filling them up with written exercises in order to satisfy their parents. Every once in a while we have children who trip over every little thing on the ground and do not even know what a grasshopper is. Some come burdened with grave conflicts and quarrel in the sandbox over such issues as whether God exists or not: "My grandma says I have to pray every day. My father says I shouldn't believe anything she says, because there isn't any God. What does your family say?"

Toward the end of the first year of our stimulating work with children, it gradually began to dawn on us that with every child we dealt with, we were also dealing with the parents and that we would have to make conscious efforts to include them in our work. So we began to hold monthly meetings for parents at the only respectable restaurant in Tumbaco. Parents were offered short introductions to the basic principles of the open system, which was totally unknown in Ecuador. In the discussions that followed, many parents showed a great need to talk about their own problems. They were often not in a position to draw the line between purely personal matters and what was of general interest to all. The following year we drew up information sheets, copies of which were distributed before each meeting, serving as the basis of the discussions. Occasionally we invited speakers from the university. Another year we gave parents the opportunity to get to know the didactic material and use it themselves, so as to get an actual feeling for how the children learn. Sometimes the parents themselves had topics that they wished to have explained and/or discussed.

All these methods succeeded in bringing the parents into the process to a certain degree, the process that their children were going through every day in an unaffected and natural way. These parents frequently found themselves compelled to think a great deal about all these things, and they asked for private talks in order to get our advice in regard to their insecurities, cares, and difficulties in dealing with their children. All of a sudden we found ourselves in the path of the proverbial snowball effect. Even on Sundays we were often unable to ward off the rush. We tried to manage these talks by doing double duty, so to speak: one of us spoke to parents in the office, the other in our living room, while the waiting troop of children had great fun in the kindergarten and then no longer wanted to go home. We had suddenly become confidants, confessors, marriage counselors; our house, in addition, was the destination of Sunday excursions for an unbelievable number of people. Even when shopping in Quito or at the weekly market in Tumbaco, we were taken aside for improvised consultations or asked to come to a particular home because the family, including grandparents and aunts, had worked itself into a crisis over the children's upbringing or education or both.

When our young son Rafael, for the sake of whom we had started the kindergarten in the first place, went to the school secretary to make an appointment with his father, reserving one hour of play therapy per week, we knew we had made a mistake—we were "doing too much good." From then on we parked the car on the weekends where it could not be seen and introduced definite office hours for parents, which admittedly could not always be adhered to by all but did serve to stem the more or less uncontrolled tide of parents invading our private life.

How can this phenomenon, which must be well known in other open schools as well, be explained? Perhaps the most important reason for this need to talk lies in the fact that in our modern world, there is too little opportunity for personal conversation. How many visits to the doctor or how many psychotherapy hours only satisfy the need for an opportunity to speak about oneself, and in which someone finally listens patiently, even if it is done for a fee? The talks with our Pestalozzi parents exhibit a great deal of this need, yet they also bear witness to the insecurity and confusion our own children can cause us when kindergarten provides them with an environment in which their needs are taken seriously, whereas at home they often live with people whose own needs are far more important. In the words of a three-and-a-half-year-old boy to his teacher, "You know, at home I go in my pants, because I have to get back at my mother. Here I'd rather go to the bathroom." This little boy was once hit in the face by his mother and screamed back at her, "At my school they don't hit!" On the following day he was taken out of our kindergarten. His mother was not prepared to give up her right to treat her child as she wished. Today this boy goes to a military school.

Despite our efforts, many of our kindergarten parents do not notice that the "active system" offers personal enrichment not only for their children but for themselves as well. They throw the information sheets into the wastebasket, never have time for a parents' meeting, and send their children to a traditional school as soon as they are old enough. Others do see the danger that they could come into conflict with their own upbringing, with their families, and with the values of their friends, and soon get themselves and their children out of the danger zone—often with a "good" excuse: "You can't send children to kindergarten on this dangerous road" or "My child always gets sick because of the change in climate," or even "Mauricio hits the children" or "I had hoped that my child would get a socialist education, because you are alternative, aren't you?"

Still others get drawn into the process almost before they realize what is happening. They begin to utilize the opportunity of living together with a new generation in order to feel like a child again, to see life through the eyes of a child, and to look for new possibilities of a life together with both young and old. These alternatives do not always correspond to the advice of the respective grandparents (who play a very significant role in Ecuador), parents' own ingrained habits and confirmed convictions, or the opinions of friends of the parents. One mother expressed it in very drastic words when she said about the situation, "Since my children have been going to Pestalozzi, we have had to find new friends."

What great and terrible thing is it that at times "derails" the parents of Pestalozzi children? Through all the studies and discussions we conduct, using Montessori, Piaget, Janov, Bettelheim, and similar great names, we simply try to make it clear to parents that their small child is a person deserving of respect, even if he or she is often hard to understand, and that they are only hurting themselves and the child if they insist on their own parental authority to protect themselves against this "intruder." Equally negative is the transfer of responsibility for the well-being of their children to specialists—be they teachers or psychologists.

We try to awaken their consciousness, make them aware of what it is that really causes the frequent conflicts between adults and children, namely how adults live under the pressure of a modern, often hectic world with its inflexible schedule of hours; how they must save time and work under this pressure in order to survive in competition with others; how they give short shrift to everything, even in their thoughts and emotions, and solve their problems theoretically before they undertake anything in practice; how logical thinking has largely replaced feeling; and how each one has to battle his or her own worries and fears, rarely finding satisfactory solutions.

In contrast, the world of their child: a rhythm of life largely without a feeling of time, completely focused on experiencing the moment; the need to be constantly in motion, to touch things, to make noises, to try out something new; a doing not earmarked for any particular purpose, simply out of the urge for activity, which seems in itself to be the objective; an inexplicable repetition of seemingly useless actions; the frequent inability to perceive the needs of others, especially adults. Add to this the strong will of the child to achieve that which seems to be an inner necessity, however incomprehensible this may often appear to adults.

Even the tools that adults and children know how to handle are very different in the first few years: an adult works with symbols that the child cannot comprehend. By comparison, the child expresses itself by means of play: through games seldom understood by adults, games that seldom attract an adult to such an extent that an entry into the child's world of play would seem interesting. The adult has mastered the handling of many objects and operation of complicated machines, the use of which is often dangerous or incomprehensible for children, yet of great attraction for adults. The child, in contrast, still feels at home in a world of fantasy and imagination, which seems to the adult childish or even dangerous. Adults feel comfortable with abstractions and logical explanations, often given at great length to their children. But children need opportunities to discover the secrets of things through their own activity, to make their own discoveries.

And thus the generations often live in conflict. Adults have the advantage of being able to control the situation by virtue of their greater size, power of decision, authority, and range of experience—at first. But it does not take long at all until even the smallest children find ways and means to defend themselves and their own little world. One group specializes in obeying and pleasing, another group in rebellion; some attract the attention of the adult world to themselves by means of constant demands, by lies, tears, or fights with siblings; some refuse to eat, others eat too much. The list could go on and on.

What we offer for this well-known situation, which occurs "in the best of families," is cooperation, the willingness to oblige on the part of parents. We advise parents to take their children as seriously as they themselves would like to be taken by others, first to try to understand the needs of their children, without neglecting their own rights, and then to attempt to fulfill these needs, as far as possible and in accordance with the common good of all. Thus parents, when they start to take our often very practical suggestions, become involved in a process that more and more allows them to combine thinking with feeling. Gradually they are able to approach an understanding of their child's secret world and thus of their own life, back to their own childhood, often buried deep inside yet ever present in the form of their own unconscious reactions. In the practice of our suggestions in everyday life, they soon notice that even with only small changes in favor of the children, they can achieve great successes, creating a shared milieu, an environment for themselves and the children in which both—parents and children—respect each other and feel comfortable.

"Since I started announcing meals to the children ten minutes in advance, having meals together has become much more harmonious. The children come to the table in a good mood, eat without complaining, and enjoy the time we spend together in eating and talking." One good habit leads to another. Almost unnoticeably, the "battleground of the generations" is transformed into a family in which everyone, including a visitor, feels good.

Nevertheless, we still have to expect that doubts will not cease and that parents who felt secure in the "new system" and able to give good advice to their neighbors will find themselves in an unexpected situation with no answers for the problem, and then show up anew during the Pestalozzi office hours for parents. One worry that never disappears is how children from the free system will survive the switch to the traditional school system. We try to calm parents' worries about this, because experience has shown that children from the free system are flexible and quite capable of adjustment, managing this transfer without difficulty. In most cases they have even become model pupils. However, there are parents who have lost their confidence in the traditional school or had such negative experiences themselves that they wish to spare their children a repetition of the same. They were and are a great support in building up our alternative primary school.

Before I go on to speak about this new experience, though, I would like to report on some research that has been very helpful to us in our work with children and parents in the last few years. These findings have allowed us to understand our own experiences better, see connections more clearly, and explain them better. I have included some of this research, which became known to us only recently, in my second book, *Sein zum Erziehen* ("To Be in Order to Educate"). I would now like to report on some studies that greatly helped us to expand and clarify our concept, after our first experiences with the Montessori system of education. Looking back, we see that the understanding of correlations we were able to gain in the course of these readings was of great service to us as well as the Pestalozzi parents and in our discussions with school authorities, and contributed greatly to the survival of the school.

CHAPTER FIVE

Education and Emotion

O n the following pages I would like to recount the story of how the concept for our work gradually crystallized. But first I wish to emphasize in particular that for us theory never came before practice; on the contrary, out of our practice developed the many questions to which we looked for answers, and in order to find these answers, we obtained various types of information. We noticed relatively quickly that any and all development is connected to needs that must be fulfilled if the child is to develop in accordance with its own inner precept. But how could we define these needs, learn to distinguish between those that are truly authentic and those that are not? When must we "go with the child," when should limits be set? Being able to answer such questions is of great importance, not only for the well-being of the child but for that of the parents as well.

Among the first authors who helped us on our way were Arthur Janov and Michael Holden with their book *Primal Man: The New Consciousness*. Janov had worked as a psychoanalyst for many years, then developed a technique that became known as primal therapy. Later he was head of the Janov Institute, which included a division for neurological research under the direction of Michael Holden, as well as president of the Primal Foundation for Education and

Research. Through the cooperative work of these two physicians, valuable knowledge in regard to the maturing process of brain structures could be gathered; from their observations and published findings, it becomes clear to what degree childhood experiences determine the feeling for life, that is, the thinking and feeling of adults—in the last analysis, in fact, many of our tensions, fears, and unsuitable behavior patterns are connected to childhood experiences, or even to experiences we have had before birth, a phenomenon that is by no means rare. In their description of cases in therapy, we recognize with consternation and dismay that these "cases" constantly repeat themselves before our eyes today, in our own children, for example, and in the children whom we meet and come in contact with every day: at the supermarket, in the waiting rooms of doctors, at the homes of our friends—everywhere children have experiences, unnoticed or unremarked upon by us in most cases, that will then have an effect on their lives. It becomes clear to us that it depends on us whether our children will grow up with the same burdens that lie heavy on our own lives. The point, therefore, is how we bring our children into the world, how we treat them, what we expect of them, and what environment we create for them.

In the work of Janov and Holden, the focus is upon experiences of early childhood and how they influence the maturing process of our tripartite brain. As far as the information presented in their book is relevant to our work, I will make short mention of it. However, before we go any further, I would like to say that these two represent only the first impulse for us to take a look at the development of the human being from an understanding of our biological reality and by so doing gain a new point of view on the life situations of a child.

The thought is simple: every child is a complex being and confronts us with riddles over and over again, but as an organism, the child's most elementary needs must correspond to those of all organic life on earth. If we do not respect these basic principles, we cannot expect that an organism will develop without any problems and have a "good feeling for life"—and in life. A systematic disregard for the basic needs of life, of living things, threatens not only the life force of the individual but that of the entire species as well.

In the book *Der Geist fiel nicht vom Himmel* ("The Spirit Did Not Fall Down from Heaven") by Hoimar von Ditfurth, we found what we consider to be the most impressive presentation of these correlations. He goes back to the primitive cell in order to show how organic life on earth could develop and maintain itself. In the long history of the earth, the appearance of the primitive cell had come about through the cohesion of a large number of giant molecules. Here rose the curtain on the first drama of organic life. The primitive cell was tiny, microscopically small, and did not even have a cell nucleus, not even distinguishable centers. But its protoplasmic body contained a molecule that was able to store its own construction plan and copy it, thus enabling reproduction. With this the first form of organic life set itself off from the predominance of the chemical and physical reactions of the environment—it became independent, so to speak, and followed its own inner plan.

And this led to the first need of organic life—the primitive cell had to set up borders against the outside world, put up protection against the outer chaos from which it had come, but which at the same time threatened to destroy it again. Thus the first conflict came about: in spite of all the dangers, the primitive cell could not close itself off completely from its environment, because that would have meant the end of it just as surely as opening up too wide. Without contact and exchange with its environment, however chaotic this environment may have been, it would die out by virtue of the basic principle of entropy, which is valid for closed systems.

Therefore it was absolutely necessary for it to open up to the outside world. This conflict was solved ingeniously by nature, a solution that still serves all organic life today: a semipermeable membrane saw to it that the primitive cell could maintain the necessary energy exchange with the world around it. This membrane let in only that which served the inner structure of the cell for its survival and its development.

And so there was now an inside and an outside, and the first principle of life had been established. Since then, life has been possible through the interaction of an organism with its more or less chaotic environment. Thus we come to the next principle that became necessary for maintaining that first life: regulation and control of the interaction lay, from the very beginning, not outside but inside the organism. It was the cell that determined what was allowed to come in from outside and what not. And only the cells that completed their development could survive in order to tell us their story. For this survival there were three abilities at its service: the cell had to differentiate, in the outer chaos, between the many varied substances and things it came in contact with; it had to evaluate them; and finally it had to choose what to let in and what was to be excreted again later. As early as this stage of development, it can be seen that intelligence is not the final result of a well-planned curriculum but part of organic life since the very beginning.

After great accumulations of single cells had put themselves together as organisms, all taking over particular tasks, the necessity arose for an organ that could serve as the coordinator for all the already manifold functions, very different even at this early stage. Thus the reticular nervous system gradually took shape, which achieved a high level of perfection in the reptiles and still regulates the automatic functions of all complex living things, including the human being. Biological research has found out that the reticular system reacts and functions only in direct contact with the environment. We see this principle in worms, for example, which roll themselves up only upon being touched or change their direction only after they have encountered a direct obstacle. In the reticular system of warm-blooded animals, there is, for example, a monitor that continually measures blood temperature. Should the central control room for such measuring functions get a message of "too cold" or "too warm," a number of mechanisms will be set off, by means of which the organism tries to protect itself from too much heat or cold.

Although the reticular system with its distinct and polished regulatory functions provides the organism with valuable services, it has come to pass, in the great interplay of evolution, that such a way of reacting to the environment is not always appropriate or expedient, and can, in fact, even be a danger. The organism reacts only after it is already involved in whatever is happening. A moth, for instance, can react to the heat of a candle flame only after it has come into direct contact with the flame—the moth cannot recognize the danger in advance of the event. So nature invented an additional system, one that does not just react upon direct contact but is able to "foresee" dangers or events from a certain distance, before the fact, as it were. This is the limbic system, developed to its greatest perfection in mammals. It can react to signals, receive indications, and take action before the organism is directly involved in something.

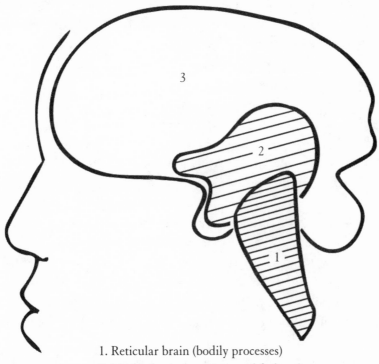

1. Reticular brain (bodily processes)
2. Limbic brain (emotions and feelings)
3. Cerebral cortex (cognitive level)

Development of brain structures and levels of consciousness
(schematic illustration)

It is extraordinarily fascinating how the coordination work of the limbic system is set off and how its program runs. The most important signals for the survival of a species are already contained in its genotype, that is to say, its DNA material, just as are completely preprogrammed plans of action that have apparently proved themselves to be practical and functional over a period of generations. These combinations of signals and their corresponding actions determine, above all, the vital behavior patterns of a species, such as mating, care of the young, body care, and defense. Such inborn behavioral patterns, which pass on the collected wisdom of a species, gave the species a very much greater chance of survival.

But development and evolution did not stop there. These automatic control systems, because of their almost 100 percent efficiency and exactitude, can also mean danger if the outside circumstances no longer agree with the original stimuli that caused this original program to be developed. The giant sea turtles on the Galapagos Islands, for example, learned to lay their eggs in the warm sand of the beaches at a certain distance from the water. However, this program of characteristic behavior was set up in their species before there were seagulls in this region, and now the seagulls fall upon the hatching turtle eggs and devour a high percentage of the baby turtles before they can reach the safety of the ocean.

If their living conditions suddenly changed, many species had to exit the scene on the stage of evolution as a result of such strategies that were no longer suitable in the new circumstances. Slowly something new started to emerge, the most successful beneficiaries of which are we ourselves. It was an astonishing response to the problem of adjustment to a changing environment, although the building blocks for the new development—as is the case with all life processes—came from the previous structures. A new structure was put on top of the first two nervous systems, namely the cerebral cortex or "new brain," also called neocortex or the higher brain center, as Janov terms it. This term is quite correct: with this part of the brain, nature invented something entirely new. The cerebral cortex is not preprogrammed, other than being divided into certain areas, and even this general division is not definite; things can be moved about if the necessity arises.

Therefore the cerebral cortex, in contrast to the lower brain center, in which automatic control systems are stored, is open and waits for its programming—received in the form of experiences had by the individual from the womb on. Thus the individual human being is free to learn to use, by means of will, the programs stored in the old brain, to not only react to situations by instinct but to analyze them from many sides and find alternative ways of acting and reacting in his or her personal life. The cerebral cortex is the most ingenious structure of organic life since the emergence of the semipermeable membrane. Thanks to it, every human being, in the short life span granted to our species, can learn to find new solutions for unexpected situations.

Yet this instrument has its own dangers as well. Because it is so open, it can be directed and programmed from outside instead of from inside, through the wisdom of its species that can be transferred from the old brain to the new one. Thus the owner of a well-activated cerebral cortex can function in circumstances that do not respect the basic principle of interaction, namely "from inside to outside." Homo sapiens, because of predisposition, is above all susceptible to conditioning when the connection to deeper structures is in some way disturbed or damaged. The history of our species gives us many tragic examples of this, and today we are close to destroying our own natural habitat—proof of the fact that in the cultivation of our intellect, we have neglected or abused our inner life-preserving intelligence.

It should not be hard for us to draw the parallel between this excursion into human biology and our own concern—a respectful association with children. The point to be made here is that we must provide environments for children in which their "human plan" can realize itself. Our question is therefore how we can avoid conditioning from outside and promote an optimum process of maturing from inside. To achieve this, the connections between the various structures of the brain, which work according to the same principles as the semipermeable membrane, must experience as little blocking as possible. And this is possible only when the environment is free of dangers and there is no interference with the inner functions of the organism from outside.

The human plan—that means learning through personal interaction with the environment as directed from inside—sees to it that the inner balance of the organism is not endangered, and thus that the balance in the outside world is not disturbed. In a form of learning that is programming from outside, these sensitive networks of systems, all interconnected, are inevitably put into disorder. The aim of such learning is, after all, not a harmonious process of maturing; it is directed at the various expectations of the respective society, which does not hesitate to utilize conditioning techniques in order to make an individual conform to its values. Therefore it is no wonder that learning controlled from outside goes against nature and leads to problems sooner or later. Joseph Chilton Pearce goes into these issues in a particularly impressive and enlightening way in his book *Magical Child Matures*.

In our practice we have very much learned to appreciate the information gathered in the course of the years about the structurization of the three brains. It has helped us to understand and to respect the processes of children and adults. Arthur Janov and Michael Holden point out that the reticular system is completely developed already in the embryonic state. This seems to prove that at least from the sixth week of pregnancy on, the embryo is able to register the experiences of a developing human being. Of necessity, these experiences are themselves influenced by the way its mother experiences, physically and psychologically, the state of pregnancy. All the positive experiences are fully integrated and promote the healthy development of the new organism. Negative experiences, which could be damaging to the new organism, are blocked, forcing the organism to undertake maneuvers of evasion and substitution as solutions. These negative experiences are responsible for all psychosomatic illnesses. When the development of the first structures is completed and the reticular system is fully functional, it takes over the control of all vital bodily functions such as blood circulation, respiratory system, digestion, and so on. At this moment the new organism gives the body of its mother a signal, and this signal starts the process of birth. This is the first act of life—if nature is allowed to take its own course—that the new organism itself "desires." And at this early moment in its life, the new human being can experience its first disappointment if the birth—whether out of true necessity or not—is introduced by initiation from outside.

The act of birth itself is known to be critical for the new organism. If it takes a natural course and has the willing cooperation of the mother, it can be registered by the baby as a strong and positive experience. In the birth canal the child experiences a strong stimulation of skin, muscles, and inner organs, extremely important for its later life, and reaches its new environment with alert senses and in a state of very high receptivity. The second brain structure, namely the limbic brain, having remained latent until now, is called upon to function by means of this powerful experience. It is now ready to take over responsibility for all experiences that bring the child into contact with its outside world: the child's sensory perceptions, its unlimited number of possibilities of movement, its experiences of feeling and mood. It is easy to understand that in the case of a difficult or unnatural birth, this newly functional brain learns to take its first precautions. A child who becomes entangled in the umbilical cord will try to save itself by pulling back or holding still and will unconsciously repeat this reaction in all the difficult moments of its life. Another child, unable to get out of its dangerous position fast enough because of a delayed birth, has to push forward with all its strength and thus might very well exhibit a reaction later in life opposite to the first child's, hitting wildly or hectically running away, rather than going rigid.

For such reasons, more and more women are choosing—and more and more doctors are advocating—a natural practice of birth. The mothers-to-be, and often both parents, prepare for this important event, which can be of such great significance for the basic attitudes of the child, for weeks by means of informative talks and presentations, breathing and relaxation exercises. The mother learns how to make this event a positive experience, albeit hard, for the child and for herself as well, through her active cooperation. The doctor is prepared to do without some of the advantages offered by a modern delivery room. The child is born in a warm room with subdued light. Loud noises and brusque movements are avoided; before the umbilical cord is cut, the baby is placed at its mother's breast. Mothers who have experienced such a natural birth confirm to us time and again that these babies show a positive difference compared with those born under the conditions of a modern clinic. They do not sleep with clenched little fists but with open and relaxed hands; they are less fearful, suffer less from colic, and regulate their daily rhythm more easily. In France it has been observed that all children who came into the world according to the natural childbirth method (advocated by French obstetrician Frederick Leboyer in his book *Birth Without Violence*) use both hands with equal skill; they do not have the characteristics of either right- or left-handed children. We have made the same observation with Indio children in Ecuador, who as a rule are born in a dark mud hut.

Depending on the stage of development, the processes of maturing take place primarily in one of the three brain structures. But we must not imagine these structures to be separate from each other. Rather, every experience at a certain level of maturity includes the other structures as well. In the first seven or eight years after birth, it is the automatic control systems of the limbic brain, those that are specific to the respective species, that are activated while at the same time the cerebrum is prepared for new possibilities of experience. From birth on, the limbic brain, which we share with the higher mammals, registers all experiences of the child, coordinates new experiences with the old, and thus unites three things in one structure: feelings, sensory perceptions, and movements. If the child does not experience enough love, this lack can be reflected in uncoordinated and tense movements and reduced sensory perception. Seen from the other side: if the child's desire for movement is suppressed or if the senses do not receive suitable stimuli, the lack of these can lead to a disturbed emotional life. The limbic brain thus becomes functional in the course of time through the manifold and constant association with the environment. This development is not complete until the seventh or eighth year of life. For as long as we live, its ability to function, together with the undisturbed functions of the reticular brain, responsible for bodily health, gives our actions the necessary energy as well as direction and depth.

The cerebral cortex, the third brain and the "new" one, which makes us thinking people and enables us to deal with abstractions such as language, symbols, and logical inference, enters on the scene only slowly and gradually, functioning above all in the service of sensory perceptions and feelings up to about the seventh or eighth year. The stage of its most intensive development lies approximately between the eighth and the fourteenth year, and it is this stage to which we will turn our attention in the following chapter.

In our association with children, the importance of the first seven years cannot be overemphasized. We must remember, consciously and as often as possible, that the structures of a child have not yet matured. Our attempts at "upbringing," therefore, can have only one aim, if we are prepared to fulfill the needs of the growing organism and avoid disturbances as well as developmental deficiencies. No one doubts that the needs of the growing body for healthy food, free air, and cleanliness must be fulfilled. In Europe, babies in their cribs can be seen out in the fresh air at an early stage of their lives. Sometimes they are brought inside only to be fed or to have their diapers changed. Everyone knows that sick and undernourished children do not make progress in school. Undernourishment in the Third World has long since been one of our deepest concerns, and we see it as our duty to help prevent or otherwise relieve this affliction.

Yet there is little awareness of what the second brain structure actually is and of the needs connected with it. Here lies the overwhelming significance of the findings of Janov and Holden, which we were to utilize for the enrichment of our relations with our Pestalozzi children. In essence the connections are simple but significant. Every growing organism has needs that must be fulfilled if later problems are to be avoided. Every unfulfilled need gives rise to pain, which in turn leads to a state of danger alert in the entire body—secretion of hormones, increased heartbeat, rise in temperature, changes in brain waves. The effect is the same whether it be a case of physical or psychological needs (it makes no difference if one has been physically or emotionally hurt). Should the pain be too strong or continue for too long, the organism must defend itself against it, even though pain in itself is a necessary warning signal in life. So it blocks this pain precisely in that part of the brain that is responsible for the registration of the respective experience. The original need remains unsatisfied but becomes unconscious.

The organism now sees to it that the access to the painful experience is blocked, so as to prevent a repetition of the dangerous bodily reactions. If further experiences of pain accrue, they are all kept in a common "well of pain" and sealed off (but this well can run over in especially critical situations). By means of this mechanism, the organism goes on living, all in all apparently undisturbed—with some changes, however, that remain unconscious for the affected person, often for the rest of his or her life. The purpose of this strategy is, of course, to make the pain "unconscious" so that it need not be felt. To maintain the blockades, the organism must expend energy—energy that would be better used elsewhere. This energy causes tension, which perhaps only comes to the attention of the "blocked" person when it makes itself noticeable in the form of bodily discomfort, back pain, feelings of pressure on the stomach, headaches. It is often easier for us to discover such tensions in others than in ourselves. We notice the shrill voice of our neighbor and wonder why he talks all the time or makes jokes about everything. Many of these little signs of inner tension are considered part of the "typical" character of a person. This tension, however, is in fact what causes certain changes in our original personality or being, and they often remain unconscious for us and for those around us, as long as they do not take on pathological forms. All unsatisfied needs, the accompanying pain having been "encapsulated" to enable us to "store" it without having to suffer, are still present, still with us, whether waking or sleeping. Since the original satisfaction has been denied to them, they crave a substitute form of satisfaction at every opportunity. Such unsatisfied needs make out of our children people who need more and more new sensations, which take the place of well-integrated feelings. They make out of us people who always need something new, who always need more, and still are never satisfied. Wherever we are, whenever we observe ourselves and our fellow human beings, everywhere we look, we discover typical signs of a certain dissatisfaction that craves substitutes—in "normal" as well as "neurotic" people. For us these observations often remain subjective impressions, and in most cases we become aware of them only when they cause irritation.

But what are the real and original, the true and authentic needs of a young child that we must fulfill in order to avoid later tensions and promote an optimal development? For us as parents and teachers, who make every possible sacrifice to bring culture to our children from the time they are very young, it is not easy to accept that up to the seventh or eighth year of life, the most important needs of a child are of a very "primitive" nature. It seems shocking that we have these needs in common with the primates: the need for bodily contact, for movement, and for a rich variety of sensory impressions. We as human beings often have great difficulty in fulfilling these needs of our offspring. In this connection, our higher intelligence often causes us much bewilderment. How often have we seen intelligent mothers put their babies out for fresh air, only to leave them screaming there so long that they finally cry themselves into an exhausted sleep!

When we say at our kindergarten that a child has not received enough love from its mother, this does not mean that some mothers do not love their children but rather that they deny them the necessary bodily contact when the children most need it. This unsatisfied need for physical contact often remains for a lifetime. The small child whose mother does not hug it or puts her arms around the child at the wrong moment, whose mother gives it physical affection but only against certain conditions, will in time transform this need into "substitute needs" that the mother is more able to satisfy. It may become a "smart" child that carries on wise conversations with its mother; perhaps the child learns to capture the mother's attention by means of beautifully painted pictures, learning to write early, or playing piano. But none of that will help: the actual need for bodily contact remains. During adolescence the child may experience the

satisfaction of this need for the first time with a boyfriend or girl-
friend and confuse it with "true love" or "great sex."

In South America it is still easy for mothers to give their small
children the necessary physical contact, if they are not all too modern or warring with their own emotions, because the culture gives
support to this. Indio women carry their children with them on
their backs throughout all their daily activities and put them to sleep
next to them in the bed. More progressive Ecuadorean women are
most careful not to cultivate any Indio customs, but they do not find
anything wrong with picking up a child to provide the comfort of
its mother's arms if it screams, at any hour of the day or night.
An entire family organization—grandmothers, aunts, older siblings,
friends—sees to it that a baby is carried around, cradled, caressed,
cuddled. Everyone sings and talks to the baby, laughs and plays with
it, and when one person tires, the next is ready to take a turn.

But if we remember that the same early structure of the brain
is responsible for emotion, fine motor control, and the senses, we
realize that such untiring affection and attention is not all the child
needs. Here an interesting comparison can be made. The educated
white parent, who often does not give the child sufficient close physical contact, fosters, however, the development of its motor independence and often encourages early self-reliance as well as exploration
of surroundings. These little persons do not always demand so
much freedom of exploration, since a sense of personal security has
its origin in the arms of a mother. We can often see how these
children are propelled into conquering the world, so to speak, and
prompted to prove their initiative and bravery. This situational correlation is proven to us in kindergarten every day, exemplified by
children who are indeed incredibly active but aggressive at the same
time, more easily breaking out in tears and hurling accusations in
critical situations.

For traditional Ecuadorean mothers, grandmothers, and aunts,
on the other hand, it is not easy to give the cute little baby the
necessary independence. An Indio baby remains tightly wrapped up
in shawls and bands, even long after it can crawl and wants to grasp
at objects. Everything is done for a mestizo child that in fact it could

do for itself: it is fed, up to the age of five or more, and carried although it would prefer to walk by itself, and when it reaches out for something, the object is quickly put into its hand. When these children come to kindergarten, they do not make such great demands to be close to a teacher, but they also do not show much enterprise or pleasure in discovering the world. In a stress situation, however, they are much more likely to remain calm and collected.

Thus there can be no doubt that the true art of dealing with small children lies in giving them, at the right time and in the right way, security and physical contact as well as independence and freedom of movement. How can we mothers manage, though, to do or not do the right thing in each and every situation if we hardly understand our own feelings? An interesting experiment was recently carried out in Mexico with a number of mothers and their newborn babies. In different variations, they were left together after the birth or separated. It was found that the most critical period of time was the first twelve hours directly after the birth, not only for the child but for the mother as well—in a very specific sense. If a mother has bodily contact with her child in this critical period of time after birth, a specific form of sensitivity in her is facilitated, through which she can understand the needs of the child in a natural way. She can, for example, distinguish more clearly if her child is crying because of hunger, cold, a stomachache, or some other reason. It is much easier for her to fulfill the needs of the child without losing time. In comparison, the mothers who were separated from their children during these first twelve hours lost this special sense for the most part—similar to a mother animal that no longer recognizes her offspring if the little one is taken away from her after birth. How difficult it must be for "modern" mothers like us to respond to our children spontaneously and naturally, and how great is our need to be advised by specialists!

And so at last we come to the following important question that demands an answer: How can parents who are themselves full of unfulfilled needs and tensions summon up a direct feeling for the needs of their children, if all that they feel when they open up is their own pain? Using many examples, Janov shows to what a great extent parents, often with the best of intentions, project, in reality, their own unfulfilled needs onto their children. In the lower social classes of Ecuador, it is a whole society that wants to make the school education possible for their children that they themselves did not enjoy. Every year at an elite school in Quito, a fifth-grade class is put together out of the most intelligent children from the less prestigious schools in the city. Here, after many examinations, tests, and trials, the selected children are given a first-class school education up to and including a high-school diploma, plus the hope of going to a university abroad. More than once I have been an eyewitness to scenes like the following: A group of ten-year-olds is waiting for the start of their entrance test. Around all the frightened and nervous children stand batteries of relatives who deliver a torrent of words, final advice, and excited admonitions to these children. Their hair is combed once again, they are given a clean handkerchief, the sign of the cross is made over them. How many expectations of the adults weigh heavily on these small shoulders!

We see variations of the same scene day after day in our association with parents and children: parents who were not loved and accepted as they were, who were not permitted to be small beings in need of love and experience, with many possibilities to become themselves; children who did not want to be instructed and corrected in everything they did but desired to experience the world through their own activity, their own forms of trial and error. These same parents now change their own children into little human beings who deserve their parents' love only under certain specific conditions.

A year ago a little boy named Pedro was sent off from Pestalozzi to a traditional school. His mother cried at his farewell party. There had been many differences of opinion between her and Pedro's father in regard to the right education for the child, and she had finally decided to give in to her husband in order not to endanger her marriage any further. Pedro had come to us as a four-year-old with an obvious muscular disability of the legs and an unpleasant rasp in his voice, which was more pronounced after every weekend at home than after the five days of the school week. According to Pedro's mother, his father made great efforts with him each weekend. He did not want to admit that his son had weak legs. He himself would have liked to play soccer in his youth, but his parents considered the sport unsuitable for a boy of their social class and gave him music lessons instead. So it was important to him to play soccer with his small son on a regular basis, though they didn't make much progress. At kindergarten, where Pedro had a choice, he never touched a ball. He was soon sent to swimming lessons by his parents, although he was having problems with ear infections at that time and had to wear earplugs and a bathing cap (unusual in this country), to the great amusement of the other children. Pedro learned to swim "correctly" there and was the only six-year-old who swam across the pool when he entered preschool, even though his movements were stiff. But while the Pestalozzi children had fun paddling around and enjoyed trying out all kinds of things one could do in the water, Pedro enjoyed sitting on the edge of the pool and not being forced to get into the water. Had he not been found to swim before he had time to play at leisure in the water, he would probably have joined the happy group in the pool.

At the beginning of the last school year, after long discussions, we accepted the ten-year-old daughter of our neighbor into our primary school because the parents were becoming more and more dissatisfied with the effects of her former school on the character of their otherwise vivacious daughter. They described to what an extent she had lost her enjoyment of learning and even of play. Her piano lessons were now the only thing she still showed interest and pleasure in, according to the parents. After several weeks in the free school system, Sarah declared to her parents that she "never wanted to play piano again." It was a black day for the whole family. The fact that her parents were so upset showed us how important these piano lessons were for them, apparently seen as a confirmation of their qualities as good and generous parents. It took a year before Sarah felt respected enough as a person to be able to take the risk of playing the piano again.

An important aspect of the kindergarten work is, perforce, allowing the unsatisfied needs of the children to come to light and, if possible, satisfying them. In consultations with parents it is never an easy task to make clear to them the difference between authentic needs and substitutes for such basic needs. They try to defend themselves: "You can't expect us to give our children everything they want!" We try to show them the difference: the small child who kicks and screams and wants to have everything at the supermarket would not be satisfied even if it ate every single thing that the money of its bewildered and annoyed mother could buy. Its behavior simply shows that it is not getting the love it needs or not being loved in accordance with its real needs.

Some parents who have taken our advice make it a habit to let their children sit on their laps a great deal, to cuddle them or allow them to make decisions. Often, however, it remains simply a technique. If it does not come naturally, out of real feeling, the child will find it insufficient or even manipulative. Nothing is good enough for a child except real feeling. As we ourselves feel, we feel, and have feelings for, the child. Feeling, true emotion, is an all-encompassing force that cannot be divided. For many reasons it often takes a long time until parents who truly want to establish a good relationship with their child can come into contact with their own emotions. To those who ask us, we give simple and realistic suggestions. We explain, for instance, that laughing and crying are the keys provided by nature that can dissolve old blocks and set free the energy tied up in them. Crying is frequently "not accepted," especially in the case of boys. We quickly comfort the child to get it to be quiet: "Let me see it . . . look, nothing has happened . . . it's all right." Or: "You're too big to cry." We have no idea that the present small accident or hurt has caused the "well of pain" inside this small child to run over, and the child is crying for all the pain that was stored inside this well. If we let the child cry as hard and as much as it wants, holding him or her in our arms, offering acknowledgment of the pain in the form of a "Yes, I know it really hurts," the well could finally run dry and the tensions of weeks, months, and years could perhaps be dissolved.

When our second son, Rafael, was six years old, Mauricio and I had an experience that made a very great impression on us. We were both busy at work in kindergarten and school. Suddenly Mauricio, who was working in the office, heard terrible screams and recognized Rafael's voice. Before he could jump up and run out of the office to ascertain how bad the accident was that had obviously occurred, Rafael was carried into the office in the arms of a teacher. He was screaming at the top of his lungs and holding out his hands in front of him. Mauricio tried to find out what had happened. The teacher was at a loss for an explanation. He had only fallen on his hands on the cement floor in front of the house. Judging from the screams, it could have been a broken hand or wrist, yet nothing could be seen upon careful examination. The hands were slightly red, but not even a scrape was to be found. There seemed to be two possibilities: either drive into Quito and have X rays taken or assume the best, since no injury could be found, and calm Rafael down. Mauricio chose neither of these. Instead, he sat down with Rafael on his lap, put his arms around him in a firm hug, and confirmed with every new scream, "It really hurts, it really hurts." This went on for half an hour. It was a huge outburst of screams and tears that would have had a deeply unsettling effect on anyone present. At last Rafael could catch his breath—and then he stammered, "I burned myself! I burned myself!" And it was as if the scales had fallen from Mauricio's eyes. When Rafael was four years old, he had had a terrible accident with boiling water and a red-hot immersion heater. His stomach and right upper leg were covered with second- and third-degree burns. At that time Rafael had been extremely brave. Had he not blocked the pain, it surely would have caused him to go into shock. The wounds had long since healed, and sometimes Rafael even recounted his accident with noticeable pride. The burning feeling in his hands had suddenly brought him into contact with his blocked pain. Now older and more stabilized, he was in a position to experience the painful situation again. When he was just drying his eyes, I came over from the school, and Mauricio explained to me, "Rafael has just had a terrible experience. He burned his hands in a fall." And Rafael added, "Yes, and it hurt much more than when I burned my stomach. But my stomach really was burned, and my hands aren't hurt."

In the following weeks, Rafael hung on us, although his independence is very precious to him otherwise. Once, when Mauricio had put aside a book to play with him, he began to cry for no apparent reason. The first reaction of an adult who had wanted some time for himself would have been the following, of course: "I play with you, and you start to cry. I didn't do anything to you!" But Mauricio had noticed that the crying began when he touched Rafael's stomach. So he continued massaging the same place very lightly, causing Rafael to cry over and over again. As soon as he went on to another part of the body, the crying stopped. This went on for almost an hour. After this experience, Rafael was a completely different child for the next three weeks. Seldom had we seen him so relaxed, happy, enterprising, and creative. But after this period of time, he looked for similar opportunities to cry. A small touch was often sufficient to set off the process. It took several months, but each time the crying was a little bit shorter.

Janov maintains that only parents who have had primal therapy themselves can truly be feeling parents. In his book *The Primal Revolution*, he states that he himself finds it remarkable that many of his former patients have such great awe of their responsibility toward children that they prefer not to have any, for fear of not being able to do right by them. Mauricio and I have often had discussions about this dilemma, coming to the conclusion, for ourselves, that a therapy as described in Janov's books is certainly appropriate and recommendable in many cases but that it remains an artificial situation. We are much more in favor of a "reality therapy" that each of us can apply in his or her daily life. Every tangible situation in life, all our associations with our family, friends, and colleagues—these give us plenty of opportunity to feel ourselves in each particular situation, in all honesty and sincerity; to recognize our secret motives, hidden fears, and expectations; and to find alternatives for our habitual reactions. The children who are in our care are waiting for the opportunity to try out new ways. They are still in close contact with their feeling for life, not surrounded by the walls of defense of logical constructions, as we are.

A few months ago the parents of Andres came to speak to us

during office hours. They wanted to express their worry about the fact that their five-year-old son, in his second year with us, showed so little leaning toward "serious work" at kindergarten. We tried to calm the parents, both university instructors, telling them that the child would know best what he needed. In fact we had long since noticed that this child, in absolute contrast to all other children, looked only for wild games in which to take part. If someone wanted to grab him and hug him in play, he pulled away as fast as possible and showed great resistance. At the end of our conversation, which had gone on for an hour, the parents wanted to know, in a manner seeming almost incidental, whether the frequent nightmares that Andres had been suffering from for months, causing him to crawl into their bed in tears every night, could have any significance. They were unsure whether to send him back to his own bed or let him stay with them. At the word *nightmare* we pricked up our ears and proceeded to ask the parents questions about Andres's life at home and his early childhood. We were told that his mother had had a very difficult pregnancy, forced to lie still in bed for months. The child was born with the help of forceps and had had his first operation at the age of two weeks. In the first two years of his life, Andres was operated on three times. Fortunately, however, his health quickly began to improve. His mother was able to go back to work, and the family, in particular a very dominant grandmother, took over the care of the boy. It was very noticeable that Andres got along especially well with the members of the family who did not waste any time on expression of feelings, whereas he avoided the more emotional relatives. The parents were a bit worried, as an old wound of Andres's had opened up again a few weeks earlier, festering since then and discharging pus. However, as they told us, Andres never complained about it—he was a brave boy and never cried.

At first we could not believe what they said about the open wound. Andres jumped off our climbing platform and got into fist fights with his friends without ever complaining about a blow. The next day we examined him, and he did indeed have an open wound the size of a man's hand on his side. We tried to make it clear to his parents that their son was in danger of becoming an intelligent but unfeeling person and advised them to caress him at every opportunity and give him every chance to cry. A week later the mother returned in a state of shock and fright. Her little Andres was crying all the time now. Once he had asked her, "Mommy, why don't you love me anymore?" In tears, she had assured him that she loved him. But his answer to that was, "Every time you touch me, you hurt me!" Through the help of his parents, Andres had come into contact with his own pain that had been bottled up since his birth. Every feeling, even the caresses of his mother, caused him to feel his old pain. His parents, only interested in their careers up to that point, began to look for alternatives for their life together, for the sake of their son.

As I sit here, busy with the final version of this chapter, the new school year has long been in progress. The number of primary-school children has doubled this year. We have again taken some new children from other schools, about whom I could fill a whole chapter with interesting observations. However, I would just like to add one more story, one that particularly wrung our hearts.

An American family had left the United States this past summer in order to begin a "meaningful and more fulfilled" life in Tumbaco. Included in that was the possibility of an open education for their children, which had been impossible for them before coming here, for financial reasons. The move was particularly hard for their oldest son, more difficult than they had imagined. This ten-year-old boy, who had to leave his friends, change to a new school system, and learn a new language, all at the same time, has felt completely lost and depressed since his arrival in Ecuador. He does not want to do anything, drags himself through the day, does not even want to make friends with the other English-speaking children of his age at school. In short, he is miserable, and anyone who sees him can do nothing but feel sad as well. I really began to feel sad, however, when I heard that his parents had offered him a reward of ten sucres for every day that he put on a happy face! Poor John, you are learning early that your parents cannot accept you in your present state, the way you really feel. In principle we all want smiling, intelligent, strong children. What are we supposed to do with them when they are depressed and crying, when they show us their anger and resistance, when they don't want to see, hear, or understand anything, and seem to us to be weak and useless?

Ample space is reserved for handicrafts of all sorts—and serves as an important meeting place for young people of different ages.

CHAPTER SIX

Comprehension Means Invention

The studies of Janov and Holden have meanwhile been accorded great significance in our daily contact with preschool children. In our work with older children, they are of constant help to us in recognizing unsatisfied needs and in facilitating therapeutic measures. The very extensive work and numerous publications of Jean Piaget, however, have become of critical importance, especially for the foundation of the primary school, although, of course, study of his work not only enables our preschool teachers to gain valuable understanding of their daily work but also gives them satisfaction on their own adult level.

Jean Piaget himself repeatedly emphasized that he was not an educator but a psychologist researching the development of thinking in children. His life's work is of such richness that it may take generations for all his possibilities of application to be recognized in full and made available to a general audience. Piaget has expressed his thoughts and ideas on the subject of education only occasionally in the form of concrete advice and suggestions, such as in his published work *To Understand Is to Invent: The Future of Education*. Some thoughts from this little book may give an indication of the conclusions drawn by Piaget himself from his considerable research for the general practice in the field of education.

Piaget put an end to the idea that children come into the world with thought structures similar to those of adults. We cannot content ourselves any more with the old idea that children are made into full and complete members of human society by means of a process of education during which we fill the already existing but empty "vessel of the human mind" with the necessary contents and knowledge. A normal five-year-old child is not capable of understanding what are for us plain and simple correlations or an unequivocal context, even if we explain these things in a clear and loving way. If, for example, two receptacles having differing shapes (receptacle A and receptacle B) contain the same amount of water, and a third receptacle of a completely different shape (receptacle C) contains the same amount of water as B, then A must contain as much as C, logically enough. This logical conclusion can be grasped by a normal eight-year-old child, but doubts remain up until the eleventh or twelfth year of age as soon as new factors, such as weight of the receptacles, appear, or if such argumentation is carried out verbally without the use of tangible materials. In his work Piaget has proved again and again that logic, as it is understood by adults, does not begin to form until the age of eleven or twelve, and that this process is completed only in the fourteenth or fifteenth year of life.

Such proven facts must of necessity have far-reaching consequences for our work in education. In Article 26 of the United Nations' Universal Declaration of Human Rights, we read that every human being has the right to education. Unless we are prepared simply to put aside this research on thinking processes in children and how these processes develop, as though it belonged on the shelves of a university library, this right to education cannot just mean that all over the world children sit at desks in a classroom and learn from textbooks, using exercise book and pencil and with the assistance of a teacher, how to read, write, and do arithmetic. If we make conscious use of Piaget's studies, for example, in our actual school practices, new perspectives open up to us everywhere—not only in a Third World hungry for education but also in progressive nations with their old pedagogical structures.

Piaget shows that the intellectual and moral structures of a child are qualitatively different from those of an adult, yet the child is very similar to the adult in its most important functions. Like the adult, the child is an active being, and its activity is subject to the principles of interest and internal and external needs. Piaget illustrates this point with the famous example of the tadpole and the frog. Both need oxygen, but to breathe it in, the tadpole uses a different organ than the frog. Similarly, the child does the same as an adult, but with a mentality of childlike structures that vary according to its age. In this context, Piaget poses a serious question: Is childhood only a "necessary evil" that one has to get through as quickly as possible, or does it have a deeper significance that the child can show us through its spontaneous activity, and that the child should enjoy to the full, in as much richness as possible?

Piaget insists that the right to an ethical and intellectual education means more than just the right to gain knowledge, to listen and obey. Much more than this, it is the right to develop certain valuable instruments for intelligent thought and action. For this a specific social environment is needed—not, however, subservience to a fixed system. Piaget speaks of the right to the most effective use possible of the latent powers of the individual, with which he or she can later be of service to society. Yet in the course of the process of education, these powers can be not only developed but also destroyed or left dormant, not utilized. Piaget suspects that the traditional school exercises the same function as the initiation rites of primitive societies, which have as their effect the complete conformation to collective standards. The traditional school with its expectations of absolute submission to the moral and intellectual authority of the teacher and absorption of an apportioned amount of knowledge that is necessary to pass exams—does it not indeed play a similar role to the rites of initiation, which pursue a similar aim, namely to pass on generally accepted truths to the next generation and thus guarantee the unity and coherence of a society upon which are impressed common values and standards as well as its continued existence in as unchanged a form as possible?

In contrast, according to Piaget, education should be directed at the full development of the human personality. It should bring forth an individual who is both intellectually and morally autonomous and who respects the autonomy of others, by means of the principle of reciprocity, as indeed this principle is used by others toward the individual. This goal of education takes us directly to the central questions that represent the basis of the movement for an active school.

The traditional school offers its pupils a carefully apportioned quantity of knowledge and gives them the opportunity to apply it in many forms of "intellectual gymnastics." Should this knowledge be forgotten with the passing of the years, we still possess the satisfaction of having had it once. Our reply to this is that it is not the size of the educational program that ought to be given so much importance—such a large amount of learned knowledge is never really put to use anyway and thus is quickly forgotten. Rather, we should pay much greater attention to the quality of the learning. We know very well not only that knowledge gained through personal exploration and spontaneous effort is remembered much better but that the method acquired in the course of such learning can be useful for the rest of one's life. Natural curiosity is aroused anew each time by such a method, whereas methods of passive assimilation cause it to become indifferent or disappear altogether. Through personal participation in the learning process, pupils train their own powers of thinking and formulate their own ideas, rather than strengthening the memory or doing cognitive exercises prescribed by an outside force.

Not even the founders of active schools can imagine how important a radical reform of intellectual learning and teaching in fact is. It is hard to understand what factors have been able, for such a long time, to prevent or limit a sweeping and effective application of well-known research to the development of rational operations and the formation of basic ideas in educational practice.

In his observations contained in *To Understand Is to Invent: The Future of Education*, Piaget devotes a great deal of space to the problem of mathematics in education. For him there is no doubt that its true significance lies in the intelligent use of tangible objects, long before the utilization of symbols. He shows that even persons who have long since blocked themselves off from any comprehension of the mathematical field are able to carry out such operations when their actions are motivated by personal interest and need. Piaget goes as far as to say that nothing can be understood if it is not "invented" and discovered by the individual, through repeated actions that always receive fresh impulses from new forms of stimulus and new contexts, through new and active experimenting. "To understand is to invent," as he formulates it, the indispensable principle of a learning that takes place through activity that is self-determined, if our children are to be capable of personal productivity, not just the repetition of spoon-fed facts and figures. The process of abstraction of such experimental actions into concepts follows its own natural course, as well as its own rhythm in the case of each individual. An intelligent handling of such abstractions, meaning definite concepts, can be practiced successfully only after the onset of puberty, that is to say, after the formation of the relevant cognitive instrument.

This necessity of free action and experiment is by no means limited only to mathematics, logic, and similar areas of knowledge, all of which have always required of us a certain amount of time and effort "under a thinking cap." Piaget expressly points out that it is impossible to bring up human beings who think in ethical terms if, in their intellectual learning, they are not allowed to discover truths on their own.

Likewise, it will be impossible for a person to be intellectually independent if this human being's personal ethics consist of submission to the authority of adults, and the only social intercourse that enlivens classroom learning takes place between pupil and teacher. An active school could in fact set everything up so that a pupil acquires his or her knowledge about things through the use of tangible materials, yet at the same time shrink from the idea of allowing this activity to take place in a free, spontaneous, and unchecked exchange among pupils.

For Piaget an active school deserves the name only when free living and working together in it is not only permitted but consciously and deliberately promoted. In his book *The Moral Judgement of the Child*, he shows in a variety of ways how one-sided respect toward an authority fosters egocentricity, thus making truly ethical behavior, which recognizes the viewpoint of the other person, impossible. Only through free and spontaneous working—together and on one another—is it possible for an individual to "see the side of the other person" and so grow out of the egocentric stage and become a "person."

From this comes the necessary counterargument to the frequent accusation that a free system of upbringing and education leads to "individualism" and would result in the destruction of society were it put into general practice. If we believe Piaget and give it a try in practice, we discover that in fact it leads to exactly the opposite: a democratic society is made possible only through free forms of education but is endangered as long as authoritarian methods stay in place in the system.

In *To Understand Is to Invent: The Future of Education*, the small book already mentioned above, Piaget gives his impressions of a visit he had made to a reformatory for adolescents in Poland between the two world wars. At this school the headmaster had dared to place the responsibility for daily life there, with all its ramifications, in the hands of the adolescents, these disturbed young people and teenage criminals that society wanted to see in custody. Thus the adolescents were not dealing with guards and custodians but with each other. As in A. S. Niell's famous experimental school, Summerhill, the adolescents set up their own rules, saw to it that these were followed, and administered punishment to those who broke the rules, if it was deemed necessary. Piaget describes how these young boys achieved their own reform in an impressive change for the better, something the experienced persons of authority in their former environment had not been able to do. Can it be true that such self-regulation and the practice of mutual respect is possible only among criminals, while our good, well-behaved children from normal families continue to bow to authority and compete against each other for good grades, praise from the teacher, or other gains and privileges that can be had?

From Piaget's comments on the subject of education, we can draw a double conclusion. First, it is inadvisable to force children into an obligatory school situation without at least having found out as much as possible about the nature of the child and the nature of the material that one wishes to teach. (A theoretical study of child psychology offers only limited help. It can never replace attentive observation of children in their spontaneous activity with tangible objects as well as fellow pupils.) Second, we should reform our teaching methods in such a way that they do not work against the laws of a child's nature. These methods should have as their goal the awakening of the child's latent abilities, preventing at the same time any necessity for the child to build up various tactics of defense in order to maintain integrity in an unjust or unsuitable learning situation.

These remarks would be of too general a nature if we did not come back to the well-known stages of development that may be the most important aspect of Piaget's work. David Elkind's book *Child Development and Education* establishes valuable and helpful connections between these studies and modern education. Very early on, Piaget himself declared himself in favor of a "vital structuralism": instead of examining the object of his studies with the help of a narrowly circumscribed and sharply defined scientific discipline, he united from the start a great variety of apparently unconnected elements into a type of interdisciplinary method and came to unexpected insights, which are beginning to influence the school system all over the world. Elkind gives us important guidelines on how educational practice and research in the field of psychology can arrive at a dynamic mutual exchange, instead of having only an inadequate connection, as has been the case up to now. Probably one of the most important perceptions we owe to this living structuralism is the concept of the integrity of the child. Whatever stage of development a child may find itself in, the child is and remains a complete and organic unit. The child's experiences and the way in which he or she encounters and explores the world are valid at all times and worthy of the greatest respect. This organic unit goes through continuous and sustained transformations that are set off by the dynamic reciprocal influence and effect of a growing human being and its environment on each other, through which both, individual and world, are constantly transformed. In this process of constant transformation, new forms of balance must be achieved; older forms of balance are reorganized by each new experience and raised to a new level of understanding.

This process goes through the same phases on each new level. The first of these phases is always characterized by adaptation. The newborn baby, for example, learns to adjust the position of its mouth to the breast of the mother in order to obtain nourishment. The second phase is that of assimilation: the child sucks on all kinds of objects, adjusting the environment to its urge to suck. In this way the newborn child constantly learns new possibilities of using its mouth and comes into contact with new shapes, temperatures, surfaces, dimensions, and so on, which it learns to distinguish from its mother's breast. Through this perceiving of differences, the young child becomes an intelligent being.

In this process there is always a new balance established between the organism and its environment. New stimuli and the process of organic maturing that is going on lead the child time and again to the necessity of leaving its established balance in order to make adjustments and assimilations on various levels. Through this unceasing activity in its environment, it gradually forms patterns; it finds out early, for instance, that an object that it touches with its mouth is the same object it sees with its eyes or feels with its hands, hears with its ears or smells with its nose. Various patterns formed through activity are then set into relation, correlated with each other, leading to an initial recognition of the environment and to the first intelligent actions.

In this manner the small child, by the end of its *sensorimotor stage* of development, has become sure that there is a concrete world, not to be confused with its person. Through its growing possibilities and powers of movement and its physical strength, it learns to orient itself in this world and has its first experiences with periods of time.

The *preoperational stage* (lasting approximately from two to seven years of age) is characterized by the growing use of language and the creation of symbols. The child not only learns to call objects by their names but also takes the liberty of calling a piece of wood an airplane, for instance, and using it as such. During this stage, free play full of imagination and fantasy comes into full bloom. The child not only works through, in the form of play, significant experiences it has had, thus integrating them into its life, but also achieves, by means of this play, new reorganizations and levels of mastery of the elements of its environment. Thus play full of fantasy is as important for emotion as it is for the growing intelligence of the child. In this stage, however, the child sometimes suffers from nightmares, inexplicable fears; it lives in a fantasy world filled with fairies and witches and assigns every object a life of its own. For the child at this stage, the name of a thing or a person is identical with the object or human being. (This is an important reason for the well-known phenomenon that a small child can hardly give up a toy because, in a certain sense, it feels at one with the toy.)

The egocentricity of the child is very pronounced at this stage of development. It is still impossible for the child to follow rules of play, since it does not yet have the ability to generalize patterns of behavior. The child still needs the security of performing certain acts accompanied by a certain ritual. By doing so the child is gradually able to form generalizations.

The *concrete operational stage* can be recognized in definite form only around the seventh—in some cases not until the eighth—year of life. It lasts until the start of the *formal operational stage*, between the ages of thirteen and fifteen. In this connection the concrete operational stage is particularly important, because it coincides with the elementary-school years. A characteristic of this operational stage is the beginning ability of the child to understand situations and objects having several factors—for example, color, shape, and texture simultaneously—that play a role. This occurs, however, only if it has the objects at hand or knows them from earlier experience. At this stage the child begins to incorporate the concept of a definite mass, weight, number, length, and space. These concepts are learned exclusively by means of tangible materials and concrete situations.

If one tries to base the learning process on symbols, no matter how vivid, graphic, or "scaled down" to "child size" they may be, the child is forced into a form of defense maneuver: it will use its memory in order to be able to remember and "summon up" the information on demand.

An especially interesting aspect of this stage is the "inventing" of rules. During progress through this stage, the child has a spontaneous tendency to put all its many individual experiences together into an orderly and understandable whole. In doing so the child gradually approaches general truths and methods, which it continues to compare with the truths and methods of its environment. This is a never-ending process that leads the child to new forms of equilibrium between itself and its environment, over and over again, which should not end when the years at school are over.

It is impressive how much time is spent in elementary schools here in Ecuador on the dictation and learning by rote of rules: grammar rules, spelling rules, rules of arithmetic, rules of behavior, and so on. Dr. Edouard Claparede formulated the law that everything one learned by heart at one time is much harder to understand later. It comes as no surprise that we see time and again how such a practice of learning rules makes a later intelligent application of such rules more difficult. In the many critiques of the educational system in Ecuador, this point is always recognized and brought up repeatedly, yet the real reasons for this lack of intelligent application are seldom understood.

At the concrete operational stage, the child learns more and more how to master its environment, weigh factors against each other, compare the results, see the other side of things, notice ever finer differences. The child learns to blend and to separate, to measure as well as to write down what was measured, and to adjust its own behavior to constantly changing circumstances. But the child's ability to draw logical conclusions from its experiences and formulate them is still limited. If the attempt is made at this time to spur the child to produce such inferences or deductions at the wish of an adult, one gets astonishing answers—unless the child switches over to reciting answers learned by rote. The studies of Piaget are full of such observations made by children before the age of fourteen, and they illustrate this lack of ability for logical verbalization of activities and life situations.

But how can we make sure that children, out of their concrete activity, finally get to the point of being capable of abstraction, without which they cannot become full members of our society? This question causes fear in many parents. According to Piaget, this process of "learning to think" and to symbolize, meaning to develop the power of symbolization, can be as much as three years behind the first appearance of a concrete intelligent action, if we do not hurry it along artificially, that is to say, "push from outside." For us adults it is usually immensely difficult to wait so long, and we tend to equate intelligence with early symbolization. At Pestalozzi we try to make it clear to the parents of our children that this process of formation of intelligence is in fact similar to the organic assimilation process: in order to give our children sufficient nourishment, we can only offer them good and healthy food, but we cannot teach them how their bodies are supposed to digest this food. The understanding of reality follows a similar natural course. We can only bring our children into contact with it, not instruct them how to assimilate it. The best that we can do is to allow them continuous and manifold activity in real-life situations. Understanding is a natural function of the growing organism, combining and abstraction a natural function of the cerebral cortex, which, however, becomes fully functional only toward the end of childhood—by means of this variety of activity.

In his book *The Dragons of Eden*, Carl Sagan refers to certain things of importance in this connection. He describes how the brain achieves its functionality through processes of bone marrow formation, the strength of which depends upon the intensity of physical activity in interchange with the tangible world. These studies coincide with—and give astonishing support to—the claim of Piaget that during childhood, the structures of intelligence can be formed only through concrete activity, through the use of all the senses as well as the greatest possible freedom of movement. This claim takes us back to an active education, the basic elements of which are described in detail by David Elkind, to follow here in the form of a short summary.

The most important and at the same time most often misunderstood element is operative learning. It occurs through spontaneous experimental activity, constantly changing, constantly starting anew, with a variety of tangible materials, which should be structured as well as unstructured. The child learns to deal with all the difficulties inherent in every material and to come to terms with them in accordance with its level of development. This operational activity makes possible the process of marrow formation in the brain and the development of the structures of intelligence, which lead to abstraction and valid generalization at the proper time. For this activity the child needs freedom, a great variety of materials—always new, always different—and the least possible interference from an adult.

Thus it is not enough to offer the child one single kind of material; the child must have a great variety of materials to work with so that it can gain an active understanding of what the materials can teach, by handling them, by using them. In order to grasp the concept of "oneness" or "unit," for instance, the child needs wide experience with many kinds of materials that it can put into order, compare, set up in rows, and also destroy and create anew, in certain cases. The child must repeat similar actions with many things and in many situations, perhaps with leaves and flowers, designs and patterns, geological shapes, models of houses, clothes, fabrics and surfaces, things permanent and things fleeting or transitory. Such richness of experience can be guaranteed only by great freedom of movement. Exactitude is not so important at the outset. A child who is to learn to swim must feel comfortable in the water first of all, so that its movements do not become cramped. In the same way, every activity demands a long period of free experimenting, which leads to smooth and flowing movements before the best technique is adopted.

Figurative learning comes second in the active school, even though in most cases it takes place parallel to operative learning, just as in real life. It does not have to do with what the child works out for itself but rather with what the child takes over from outside:

imitation, memory, language, habits, and customs. This kind of learning makes sense, however, only when a broad base of operative learning has already been assured and established. If this basis is missing, a predominance on the part of figurative learning can lead to distortion and finally to forgetting, as we know it in the case of knowledge learned for exams, which is most often of a figurative nature. A law that is valid for figurative learning states that the main and most important thing is the learning process and its intensity, not the amount of material to be learned.

The third type of learning in the active school, connotative learning, forms the link between the first two forms, between actions and words, between direct experience and symbols—through the learning of names, terms, expressions. Through association with adults and other children, the child picks up words and terms and learns to repeat them. Only gradually does the child understand what term fits what situation. Thus operative and figurative take turns in practical life, going hand in hand. Through constant trying out and experimenting, the child arrives at the point where, for its personal use, these two areas begin to coincide. Constant correction makes the child insecure and inhibits the joy of discovery. Activities in the fields of handicrafts and art offer great opportunity for connotative learning. The many texts with pictures that are in use here aid and encourage the "connotative connection." The best possibility, however, seems to me to be free play, indeed as determined by nature itself, which allows the child, in the course of time and through experimentation, to bring together words and actions into harmony. This free play will be a recurring subject in this book.

The active school wants to provide an environment for the children that fosters these three modes of learning in the right way. Be warned, however, all who undertake to shape this environment: do not be surprised at the fact that children use it in their own ways. Each and every child, based on its own individual needs, will make its own choice out of all the stimuli offered for learning. An adult will sometimes not be in a position to say, from one day to the next, what material the children will find of interest. We know, though, how deep the priority of these inner needs is and that a true equilibrium with the environment is possible only when we allow the "child organism" to establish this balance in accord with its pressure from within. This principle is more important for the day-to-day practice of the active school than would seem at first, and has a great influence on our behavior as teachers. Knowing about this need for true equilibrium, which comes so clearly to the fore in the free school system, can help us to be less disappointed when we have spent a whole night of preparation setting up a wonderful arrangement of new materials in the classroom—and the children run right past it to get a long-forgotten material down from the shelf.

It is impossible to overemphasize the importance of this "floodgate mechanism." A child who is currently involved in the phase of evaluation of experiences, and who is also allowed to choose out of a variety of attractions those that correspond to its present inner structures, protects itself in a natural way against new or inappropriate stimuli, blocking them out of its consciousness, at least for the time being. Gentle or brusque force from outside can break down this barrier. The child can be lovingly motivated or forced by means of rewards or punishments to give in to outside pressure and direct its attention to things that do not correspond to its real interest. But the child's understanding will be clouded and the subject matter distorted or deformed because to be effective the stimulus must match the real needs of the growing organism, rather than being taken in objectively. On the emotional level, this learning motivated by external pressures causes tensions, from which the children try to escape in manifold ways—a phenomenon that presents great problems to many educators, yet they seldom fully understand it.

Another mechanism of a child's learning that we must consider is the need to store experiences. All the experiences that the child cannot assimilate at the time, because they do not fit into its current structures of emotion or intelligence, are first put aside without being "processed." The task of putting the experience through a first processing is left to the unconscious. This process can take hours, days, weeks, months, or—in some cases—even years. If, for example, as parents or educators, we push the child to express itself openly soon after an experience, or insist that the child tell us what it has experienced at school or perhaps write an essay about the school excursion immediately afterward, we are inviting all kinds of unexpected problems. The following little story may serve as an illustration of this.

On its way into Quito, the school bus had an unusual delay of fifteen minutes because one of our handicapped children had not been picked up on time here in Tumbaco by the respective parents. With other children the bus driver cannot be so considerate; the child goes along for the ride and comes back again, where its parents are then waiting patiently at the bus stop in Tumbaco. This cannot be expected of a handicapped four-year-old, however, and so the bus waited until these parents had come. Then it drove on, very much behind schedule. One mother had become so upset during her wait for her daughter that she let loose a torrent of questions when she saw the child, without first lending an ear to the apology of the staff members accompanying the bus children. The five-year-old girl, naturally enough, could not give a logical explanation of what had happened. To put a halt to her mother's harried questions, she described to her how the bus had been involved in an accident with a blue car. The car had been a total wreck, an ambulance had come for the numerous wounded, and the bus driver had barely escaped being taken to prison by all the police appearing on the scene.

Not all children reply with such imagination to our penetrating questions. Some make it a habit to write boring essays, for example, allowing adults little or no insight into their personality or private life. In *Memories, Dreams, Reflections*, C. G. Jung describes how he was able, by means of mediocre work, to direct the attention of teachers and fellow pupils away from himself, in order to live his own life. And then, in a higher class, he was so interested in a particular topic assigned for an essay that he put his entire intellect into the work. The embarrassing result of this success was that his teacher accused him, in public, of plagiarism, although the teacher could not prove from what source Jung had allegedly copied his brilliant paper.

The need for play, often annoying for an adult, stands in close connection to the natural mechanisms of a child's learning that have already been mentioned. Here I can only indicate in brief form the significance that Piaget attaches to this mechanism.

Although we cannot always differentiate between them—far from it, in fact—let us speak here of two types of play, in the interest of a better understanding. The first is symbolic play, through which the child tries to free itself from inner pressure resulting from overwhelming experiences. With various elements of play, the child stages situations of its life, which may be far away in place and time. What in reality forced the child into a certain position or submission to an authority, to rebel or to cooperate, is relieved of its conflict-ridden character in this symbolic play. The child dominates and controls the situation here at its own discretion and provides for solutions that would be impossible in real life. The child becomes the doctor and gives injections to a doll attempting to resist, or the child becomes the mother who pitilessly shows an undesired visitor the door. This play should be not only permitted in kindergartens and schools (its symbolic character takes on a greater importance in the latter) but encouraged through suitable materials, as well as observed and correctly evaluated by attentive adults. Particular significance is given to symbolic play in the practice of play therapy, which will be discussed in a later chapter.

The second type of play has a less emotional character and is called functional play, or, to use Elkind's term, play of repetitious practices. It consists of three stages. At first the child finds itself confronted with a new situation and adjusts to it, perhaps with a certain timidity or irresolution. Let us imagine that the child is facing, for the first time, the following problem: it has to jump over a small stream. The child hesitates, looks for a possible way around the obstacle, and finally gets up all its courage and jumps over it.

Now the child begins—this constitutes the second stage—to jump over the stream every once in a while. The child practices: sometimes the jump is too short and the child gets wet; sometimes the child jumps too far and loses its balance. Finally the child has conquered this art of jumping over a stream (in the course of which he or she may have forgotten what the original destination was).

Now the child feels itself to be a champion in jumping over streams. Out of pure pleasure in the mastery of this (unfortunately non-Olympic) discipline, the child jumps over all streams that can be found, from now on. This is the third stage, leading to the search for new situations and more and more complicated actions.

According to Piaget, play is the most authentic expression and the most effective learning aid of the child. Regular play enables the child to gain a particularly rich variety of experience in social life with others. The school should value the importance of play highly and not banish it to break times and the almost empty school playground. But even when we consciously integrate play into life at school, we should be clear in our minds about the fact that one of its most important ingredients is spontaneity, and that it should be organized by adults only as an exception and then with great caution, in order not to endanger its self-regulating character.

I would like to make some references to the use of language, to which Piaget has also devoted detailed studies. At an early age the child shows a marked and distinct interest in speaking and listening. By the onset of the concrete operational period, the child has achieved masterly skills in this area. Unless we look at this phenomenon more carefully, subjecting it to careful examination, we could easily come to the conclusion that the child now uses language in the same sense that we do, coming to depend greatly on this mutual instrument in our association with children. As devoted parents, we often give our children long detailed explanations of all sorts of things. The three-year-old child who is fascinated by the sound of our voice and would like to have us close by develops the famous technique of asking "Why . . . ?" and receives from us long and carefully thought-out explanations. At the end of the day we are more often than not completely exhausted and can hardly wait for the moment when we can pack the little questioner off to bed. With an older child, who already uses language with greater fluency, we get impatient: "I've explained it to you a thousand times already. Why don't you understand it?" An entire school tradition has been built on this misunderstanding that a six- to fourteen-year-old child speaks the "same language" as we do. Our language classes make efforts to continue perfecting this "common language." However, Piaget's studies show that this assumption of a common language is based on a misconception. As late as the age of six, the child's language is concerned with information only to a slight degree; it can still exhibit an egocentricity, that is to say, a concern with itself, of up to 50 percent. It is only gradually, through the increasing association with peers, that the child takes on a more social character. Earlier in this book, reference was made to the fact that the necessary mental structures that make our language more or less functional as a means of communication are not fully developed until the start of puberty. But this only happens if the child has continually practiced to match his words with his concrete acts (therefore making it possible to really "express himself," instead of simply repeating what he has heard from other people), which gradually leads him into the new stage of formal operational thinking.

Thus it is not surprising that we are always coming into conflict with our children because we depend too much on a "common" language and not enough on other important factors of communication. A child feels great insecurity when we unconsciously express something, through our facial expression, body language, the tone of our voice, or other nonverbal signals, that does not agree with the meaning of our words. Such nonverbal means of communication are in reality much clearer for the child than our verbal logic and are the determining factor for the child's impression and/or decision.

Anyone who works in an open classroom finds great enrichment in Piaget's studies on the intellectual maturing of children, which takes place in a similar way all over the world. These studies are a valuable starting point for one's own observations, made possible for us every day by the practice of active education. A short reference to the problematics of egocentricity, running like an unbroken thread through the works of Piaget, will bring this chapter to a close.

Each stage of development is characterized by a certain kind of egocentricity. It is particularly visible in early childhood, of course, when the new organism is completely dependent on other people for the fulfillment of its vital needs. During this period it is impossible for a child to be considerate of the interests of others. Its egocentricity is its basic protection, thus important for its survival. Yet even after the child has gradually learned to "help" itself, it still lives for a long time with the conviction that all other human beings have insight into its feelings, intentions, and experiences; that they are somehow one with the child, as it believes it is itself one with its environment. As long as this state lasts, the small child sees no necessity to communicate to us its thoughts, feelings, and experiences in an understandable way.

At school age, egocentricity shows a new face. The child tends to adapt all information to its own view of life in order to maintain the integrity it has built up. Only through constant confrontation with tangible realities and real-life situations is it possible for the child to revise its own worldview and adjust to an objective reality.

The egocentricity of adolescent boys and girls can be especially irritating. The young people are convinced that everyone ought to know how they feel at any given moment. They believe that each and every other human being feels the same as they do.

At every stage, egocentricity has the function of protecting one's own integrity. The baby that wanted to take into consideration how tired its parents are would never find its own rhythm of life. The schoolchild who did not insist on his or her own worldview could never achieve a critical stance. The adolescent who has doubts about the emotions and motivations of adults loses interest in responsibility for his or her own life very early on. We as adults—it does not matter at what stage—contribute to the reinforcement of this egocentricity, perhaps making it a permanent evil, when we prevent or hinder the fulfillment of the specific needs of the individual in its particular stage of growth. The child utilizes a number of mechanisms to fulfill its needs, against our will if that is necessary, even if it only achieves substitute solutions. A child who feels its integrity to be endangered by a false conception of authority clings to egocentricity longer than a child who feels understood, without tension, fear, or reservations, and therefore able to open up to the world and the people who live in it.

CHAPTER SEVEN

An Alternative Primary School

In our educational meetings with teachers and parents, we had collected a considerable quantity of materials about problems of child rearing, the psychology of children, school practices in Ecuador, and legislation governing the school system in the country. The existing necessity for an alternative could be denied no longer. Should we now begin to influence public opinion by means of publications, and thus contribute to awareness of the situation in the public? But then, what path could one offer the parents who would begin to have doubts about the traditional school, after raising their consciousness in this regard? What alternatives were successful in other countries, and was there any model that would allow itself to be adapted to the situation in our country of Ecuador? And was it possible to reconcile and bring into harmony an alternative path, a different way of education, with the demands of the Ministry of Education and Culture?

In the course of our research, we came upon a good deal of material dealing with alternatives that had become known above all in Europe and the United States. Paul Goodman's book *Compulsory Mis-Education* criticized the structure of the modern American educational system with great power of persuasion. In his opinion, many of its evils in fact stem from this existing principle of compulsory education itself, originally introduced for the protection and well-being of the child. Goodman offers a great number of solutions and ways out of this dilemma of "compulsory mis-education." The constellation and the interrelation of forces to be found in Ecuadorean society, however, differ so greatly from the North American situation that we made use only of the most basic insights of the book. One of these insights was a great support for us again and again, namely that a child, taught at the right moment and in the right way, is able to take in the entire subject matter of a six-year primary school in four to six months, with no difficulties. Thus the need to fulfill the official curriculum is no reason not to seize the opportunity to find an alternative.

The members of the John Holt Association in the United States, in their solutions to the American education dilemma, go so far as to offer to parents who take their children out of the general system in order to give them an alternative education at home active support in solving the myriad problems arising from this step. In the United States this has become quite a notable movement. This movement draws its support from the initiative of a growing number of parents who not only have recognized the disadvantages of public education but are also prepared to defend their point of view against all odds and to take over full responsibility in the education of their children, making personal sacrifices as well. How far such sacrifices can go is described in the story of a remarkable family in England. The report about this family was published under the title *The Children on the Hill,* by Michael Deakin. With the greatest amazement we read about how a married couple, for the duration of the formative years of their four children, intentionally and consciously deferred, indeed put aside, their own needs and, by means of consistent and resolute fulfillment of the authentic needs of their children, were able to foster these children's process of development to such an extent that the most unusual of talents appeared and could flourish.

We are, of course, far from recommending to our Pestalozzi parents such complete and extreme sacrificial devotion. Here in Ecuador, perhaps, the despair concerning the public school system is not yet as great, and in most cases the necessary confidence on the part of parents in their own abilities does not exist, which would in turn enable us to recommend drastic measures that would take into consideration an education at home. Our alternative, therefore, was obliged to remain within the boundaries of the familiar school, an alternative within its framework, as it were. Various alternatives in other countries drew our attention: the "open classroom" in the United States and northern Europe, the "integrated day" in England, the "traveling school" in Denmark, Montessori schools in many countries, the Waldorf schools, Celestin Freinet's Ecole Moderne in France, and finally the Schulen zum Denken in Germany, based on Piaget's research studies, all of which aim to direct the early thinking processes of a child in the right direction, using scientific methods.

The model of the Waldorf schools was the first to be eliminated, since we did not want to link our attempt at a new school to an anthroposophist worldview right from the start. The idea of the "school for thinking," as described by Hans Furth and Harry Wachs in *Denken geht zur Schule* ("Thinking Goes to School"), could not completely convince us either. How was a schedule that divided the planned activities of the pupils into units of five, ten, twenty, and twenty-five minutes supposed to strengthen the children's ability to make decisions, take into consideration their individual needs and interests, and lead to an authentic feeling for life, even if it did take into account the general mental structures and logic of children?

Most of the parents and teachers who had already at this early stage shown interest in the project of an alternative school had gone through a personal development process themselves. They were each involved in trying, in their own individual ways, to find the way back to a feeling of wholeness, to relearn how to "really be in the here and now," to dissolve old tensions and blocks, and to face life with new hope and a new openness. For them the question of an alternative school was focused on the basic problem set forth as follows: How can we create a school that does not divest (not to say de-educate!) the child of its natural joy of life, its curiosity, self-confidence, and individuality, plus the feelings of its own worth and the worth of others? A school that does not force the child to block the free flow of its own feelings and that leaves its life undestroyed, so that at some time in later life this child does not have to collect the pieces of its own self laboriously, in order to "find itself again"? Was there a school that left the impulse to learn in the child rather than systematically assigning it to adults?

In our search we soon came upon the works of John Dewey that, early in our century, had already become leading directives for progressive educational methods:

> What is Progressive Education? . . . All of the [progressive] schools . . . exhibit as compared with traditional schools a common emphasis upon respect for individuality and for increased freedom; a common disposition to build upon the nature and experience of the boys and girls that come to them, instead of imposing from without external subject-matter standards. They all display a certain atmosphere of informality, because experience has proved that formalization is hostile to genuine mental activity and to sincere emotional expression and growth. Emphasis on activity as distinct from passivity is one of the common factors. And again I assume that there is in all of these schools a common unusual attention to the human factors, to normal social relations, to communication and intercourse which is like in kind to that which is found in the great world beyond the school doors; that all alike believe that these normal human contacts of child with child and of child with teacher are of supreme educational importance, and that all alike disbelieve in those artificial personal relations which have been the chief factor in isolation of schools from life. So much at least of common spirit and purpose we may assume to exist. And in so far we already have the elements of a distinctive contribution to the body of educational theory: respect for individual capacities, interests and experience; enough external freedom and informality at least to enable teachers to become acquainted with children as they really are; respect

for self-initiated and self-conducted learning; respect for activity as the stimulus and center of learning; and perhaps above all belief in social contact, communication, and cooperation upon a normal human plane. . . .

. . . Even if it be true that everything which exists could be measured—if only we knew how—that which does not exist cannot be measured. And it is no paradox to say that the teacher is deeply concerned with growth, with a moving and changing process, with transforming existing capacities and experiences; what already exists by way of native endowment and past achievement is subordinate to what it may become. Possibilities are more important than what already exists, and knowledge of the latter counts only in its bearing upon possibilities.[1]

The open schools of Europe and the United States, as well as the Montessori schools, maintain and preserve the most important elements of a form of education based on suitability for a child and respect for the personality. Many of them, however, operate at a high level of expenditure for highly priced materials and prefer classrooms with wall-to-wall carpeting. They create the impression that the ideal learning environment necessitates huge investments. Even the schools of the English "integrated day," although less luxurious than many of their American counterparts, count on support from public funds and access to libraries as well as similar aids. In contrast, the experience of the Ecole Moderne in France gives us valuable tips on how an education that focuses on the activity and initiative of the children is also possible in a poorer environment and with simple means. Celestin Freinet, however, attempted to bring this initiative of the children in line with ministerial curricula, and drafted—together with the children—work plans, which then in practice received priority over the spontaneous interest of the children. The impressive movement of this Ecole Moderne has

---

1. Dewey, "Progressive Education and the Science of Education," in *Progressive Education*, vol. 5, 257.

meanwhile been greatly absorbed by the general French school system, and as far as we were able to discover in short visits, there seem to be only a few attempts to apply completely and/or enlarge upon the ideas of Freinet.

Thus we were confronted with a two-in-one question: how could we create an ideal environment for pupils, on the one hand with few means yet on the other hand with sufficient materials? Moreover, this environment should not be just a copy of the models of other countries but should utilize and work with local elements, as far as possible. We could not expect any support from public funds and had to finance this alternative school out of tuition fees paid by parents. It was also important to keep costs as low as possible so that the school could be afforded by people with an average or middling income, and at the same time show how such open methods can be made available to the poorer classes of the population.

Another question that had to be addressed, another problem to be solved, had to do with our relations with the Ministry of Education. From the very beginning, it was clear that we could not expect any financial assistance, as the budget of this ministry is far removed from being able to cover the needs and necessities of the public school programs. The issue in question was how to prevail upon the ministry to permit the existence of an alternative form of school within the uniformity of the educational system. However, when a delegatory commission from our study group consulted with the relevant authorities, that is to say, offices, within the ministry, they received a clear answer: "In Ecuador no school is allowed to exist that does not unconditionally accept the curricula and programs of the ministry. In this country we are accustomed to doing things correctly and well. We do not allow experiments."

But inside the ministry there is an institute responsible for teacher training and continuing education for teachers of all levels and grades. We heard about a small group of progressive civil servants within this institute, quietly, almost secretly, following a new line and certainly not opposed to our plans. An unofficial discussion finally led to the concrete advice not to seek ministerial recognition of our alternative school at present but rather just to begin work and gain experience. In the meantime, as we were told, a favorable constellation in the ministry could ensue, which in turn could result in belated or "after the fact" recognition of the school, without our having to put aside the principles of the progressive methods. This is a South American way of confronting juridical problems. And in fact it took almost three years after this first unofficial decision until—in March of 1982—such a "favorable constellation" did occur and the minister of education gave his signature to the document granting permission for the existence of our Centro Experimental Pestalozzi, with authorization to provide an active education.

But who would dare to register a child at a school that was to start operating without a permit from the Ministry of Education and at the moment only existed in the heads of a small group of people? At the time of year when registration for school is normally done, there was neither a school building nor chairs, nor desks or any other school accessories. A number of parents who had been theoretically interested in the ideas of an active school began to become afraid in view of this still-invisible school and hurriedly registered their child at a visible albeit traditional school. There remained seven couples who wanted an active school for their children, even in this difficult situation. We made a sort of contractual agreement with them: the school undertakes the obligation to create for the children an environment corresponding to the principles of active education and to promote recognition of the school in the ministry. In turn, the parents promised to attend monthly study meetings that would deal with principles of active education and to utilize these principles at home as far as possible, as well as to spend at least one morning per trimester at the school in order to watch the activities of the children and discuss them at the meetings.

Our first classroom therefore had to accommodate only a small group of children. Thus we planned a small addition to the hexagonal kindergarten building. Everything was as simple as could be imagined: a light cement floor, columns of iron pipe to hold up a light slate roof. The walls were of wood panel and the windows were held in place by frames of eucalyptus wood. A small stock of dry wood, the talent and workmanship of our carpenter, plus a credit from the hardware store in Tumbaco made it possible for us to have the schoolroom nearly finished by the first day of school. Only the windowpanes were missing—they were to be purchased with the first tuition fees received. Boards and bricks were substituted for the missing shelves. On the first day of school, the first seven pupils proudly entered their new realm of learning. The kindergarten children were not allowed to enter it, and thus it seemed to them like a forbidden paradise. It was in fact a paradise with lots of fresh air; the chairs and tables had been painted in bright colors, and the temporary shelves were full of new materials. A small and cozy library equipped with straw mats and cushions offered books in three languages. There was a corner for so-called family play, a puppet theater, a large basin of water and a multitude of devices to experiment with, a sand table with toys, scales, and measuring apparatus, and above all, free access to the large grounds and to a bit of garden land that any child could work on as desired—plus the freedom to return to the kindergarten for some hours or days, if that was the child's wish, should any unsatisfied demands remaining from earlier years call for such a return.

This first schoolroom was already too small at the end of the first school year, as more and more children "sickened" by other schools continued to arrive. At the start of the following school year, the number of pupils had tripled. Again we were obliged to wait for the new tuition fees to reach us before beginning to build a larger room. In the first three months the old classroom was crowded indeed. Tables and chairs were set up in the yard. Many activities were transferred outdoors, and many a child suffered a sunburned nose while learning to read and write. Yet, despite the confines of space, the children were not affected in their various doings. With arms full of materials, they climbed over chairs, with many apologies if they bumped into someone else's legs or stepped on another's toes. We watched the new schoolhouse go up before our very eyes. The children helped to pour the foundations; they measured depth, length, and height and paced off the sides, perimeter, and diameter of the room; they estimated and measured, helped with sawing, painting the walls, and putting in windowpanes. And finally all of them helped with moving and decorating. In those three months of construction that were needed for the schoolhouse, it had become a part of their lives.

Again it was a hexagonal building with large windows against which donkeys and llamas pressed their noses. On four sides of the house, the overhanging roof creates a small veranda, as it were, which is used in different ways. On one side there stands a terrarium with lots of room that houses the ever growing collection of plants, small animals, twigs covered with moss, and similar treasures that the children bring back from their informational excursions to mountains and canyons, streams, rivers, and forests. Next to it is a table of unpainted wood that can be transformed into a model city, a zoo of sorts, or an exhibition center.

Another side accommodates a high sand table and a center for water games, together with hooks for rubber aprons and garden tools. Along the sides of the schoolhouse are the lockers of the children, in which they keep their personal things while at school. A further side of the veranda serves as the pottery workshop; the side across from it offers a place for a huge crate in which can be found all the things that most families throw into the waste bin: old irons; spare parts for cars; old engines; parts of clocks, radios, and refrigerators; wheels; cigarette lighters; pipes and hoses . . . in short, a great collection of broken or otherwise supposedly unusable objects that, thanks to the imagination and energy of the children, are transformed into spaceships, submarines, robots, and other inventions as yet unknown to our civilization.

The first schoolroom was then turned into a storeroom, only a few steps from the new schoolhouse. There the children find paper, cardboard, paints, pens and pencils, glue . . . plus an inexhaustible supply of boxes, plastic containers, corks, pieces of wool and other fabrics, bottle tops, empty paper rolls, and other "waste" of all kinds that we ask for and collect from multifarious factories. The nearby carpenter's workshop supplies us with odd pieces of wood and leftovers in all shapes and sizes, shavings and sawdust, nails, sandpaper, and paste.

Outside the actual schoolroom, a large picnic table, a cozy and inviting playhouse, and a huge sand heap lend themselves to various and sundry purposes, all determined and/or transformed through the initiative of the children every day anew. The grounds around the schoolhouse are a bit hilly. The flat areas have been made into "sports fields" by the children: for ball games, high and long jumping, running races, and similar activities. Near the schoolhouse the children have laid out a garden, which they cultivate with a fluctuating degree of reliability. A small meteorological station provides the finishing touch to the "outdoor equipment."

In the schoolhouse itself there are two lavatories on one side, the doors of which have been decorated by the children with the warning—in large letters—*Apestalozzi* (in Spanish the verb *apestar* means "to stink"!). In the center are arranged—in no particular or binding order—chairs, tables, and shelves. All around the sides, following the walls of the schoolhouse, are the "interest centers" with all the available and relevant materials: a completely equipped kitchen; a game center full of board games, games of skill and dexterity, games of reasoning, plus Lego, Mechano, and wooden blocks of all shapes; a center for handicrafts and needlework with all the necessary attributes, including an antediluvian sewing machine and a weaver's loom; a measuring and weighing center with rulers and measuring sticks, scales and weights, plus clocks of all kinds; a center for experiments with a microscope, magnifying glasses, magnets, a small chemistry lab, and ideas for simple experiments; and a Punch and Judy show with a box of puppets, old clothes, hats, and decorative frippery for playing theater. These are followed by a big shelf full of Montessori materials for arithmetic and geometry; a library where the children can make themselves comfortable for reading or listening to stories; a shelf of Orff musical instruments; a cupboard for the Freinet card file with informational material and work cards for natural history, arithmetic, spelling, and geography; an especially comprehensive language center with material in Spanish, English, and German; a shelf with maps, a globe, and material relating to natural history; plus a Freinet school printing press with drying stands for the printed pages, apron stands and a sink, and—finally—a blackboard.

This is the environment for an increasing number of pupils, who live here in their own world, the laws of which are sometimes their own—because these must correspond to the needs of the growing children—and sometimes the general ones of the society into which these children are growing. All age groups from six to ten are still mixed; however, when this primary school has established all grades, the ten- to thirteen-year-olds are to receive their own room adapted and prepared for their individual needs.

To us it seems a good omen that our alternative school, in which we place great hope for the future, operates and functions in a schoolhouse designed by a layman, built by a simple Ecuadorean carpenter, and equipped with handmade furniture and much "homemade" material. For many visitors who love solid and permanent surroundings, our improvisations may be disquieting or disturbing. The little book by C. N. Parkinson bearing the title *Parkinson's Law* has always given us back our sense of humor and our cheerfulness, even in dark moments of doubt. It argues with great humor that a company or an institution is doomed to a gradual death already at the very moment that it moves into a permanent building. According to Parkinson, all such enterprises that are alive and capable of growth are normally to be found in improvised or provisional quarters. Thus, seen from this viewpoint, we have no reason to hurry with the construction of a respectable schoolhouse!

Kitchen work is as popular with boys as with girls of all ages.

CHAPTER EIGHT

A Monday at Our *Primaria*

It is a cool Monday morning. The small group of primary-school
children, who arrive half an hour before the others in the first
bus coming from the east side of the Tumbaco valley, enter the
schoolroom with demonstrative shivers and chattering teeth. It is
easy to see that they have gone to bed a bit too late on the weekend.
Maybe, in all the goings-on at home, they have not gotten all that
they needed. They find me at a table near the printing press, preparing the weekly control sheets where the children enter their daily
activities. On the pretext of wanting to get warm, the children sit
down as close as possible to me. Each one gets a little hug. One gets
on my lap and announces her intention to remain there for the rest
of the morning. "You all look like you've come from the North
Pole!" I say, to open the conversation. The children say that I am
indeed right and declare that today they cannot do anything except
warm themselves up close to me. And so we sit there for a short
while. The children watch me putting data on the sheets. One asks
if he can help me with this; another child wants to write in the
names of the children. It does not take long at all until we are all
working together on these sheets. In the meantime the children have
warmed up enough to tell me about their respective weekends.

"My grandma visited us, and my mother really acted strange

the whole day," reports one of them. Another tells me about a family excursion to a hacienda, a third about going to the soccer field. In a very few minutes, the children are awake and lively. They move away from me and begin to make plans for the morning at school. Two of the children want to get ready something nice and warm to drink for the ones who will be arriving shortly from Quito and the other side of Tumbaco. They put a big pot of water to boil on the gas stove and go outside into the garden to pick herbs with which they want to prepare a tea. Then they put together three tables, lay a tablecloth, and start, with great ceremony, to set the table with cups, spoons, sugar, and napkins. "What do you think—will everybody be here today? Natalia had an earache on Friday—she won't be sick today, I hope?" The children count the cups intended for every classmate who is still missing. "Are we going to give Santiago tea, too? Last week he tripped me when we were playing soccer. We shouldn't give him any. . . . Well, okay, don't let's be like that—he'll be freezing this morning like everybody else."

In the course of these exchanges, Carmen suddenly has the idea that she could fill out the weather table for today. She asks her sister Alba if she would like to bring in the rain gauge from the garden. Alba comes back in, calling loudly, "Now we know why it's so awful—we had seventeen centimeters of rain!" Carmen and Alba pass around the rain gauge so that all can have an opportunity to be properly impressed by this news, and then, after some discussion of what day it really is, they write the correct date on the sheet hanging on the wall near the door for this purpose. Then they measure the humidity: 91 percent. "No wonder after such a lot of rain." And the temperature? Fifteen degrees centigrade. "That's enough to freeze to death!" They enter all this data. Carmen decides to continue work on her precipitation tables today, which she is producing for the whole year. For the moment, however, attention is drawn to an important event: the three other buses come up our driveway. The children leap out the door and run to the gate to greet their friends. They take the hands of the arriving children and pull them into the schoolhouse, inviting them proudly to partake of herbal teas.

Together with the children from Quito has also come Vinicio, our second teacher at the primary school. He has had the opportunity to "warm up" with the children during the bus ride, picking up their moods, letting them sit on his lap, tickling them, laughing with them. So we have no more need of great formalities to get the day started. Vinicio shakes my hand warmly. This is one of the few direct contacts that we will enjoy the entire morning. Each of us will be devoted to the children, in our own particular way as individuals and according to the given situation. We both have certain ideas for activities that could correspond to the needs of this or that child, this or that group. But we are in complete accord that the initiatives of the children have priority over our ideas. Each of us knows that the other will be completely involved with the children, just as on every morning. There is no position of rank between us, although Vinicio is twenty years younger and studies psychology in addition to his work at Pestalozzi. Once a week we spend an afternoon together, talk about our experiences with the children, exchange ideas or bring up doubts. But here and now we have eyes and ears only for the children and their needs.

Meanwhile, we have all been given a cup of tea. We sit or stand around, as though we were at a cocktail party. Small groups are formed. Over on one side the events of the past Sunday and the soccer scores are under discussion. Two of our boys are soccer fanatics and players as well, and are often teased a little about this by the others. The children wash their cups, one after the other, and put them away on the kitchen shelf, not always in exemplary order, it must be admitted. This little drink and the conversations with each other have helped us all to feel at home again in school. Individually or in small groups, the children go about organizing themselves for their respective activities.

Victor and Santiago, who spend every Sunday on the soccer field with their fathers, try to persuade a few of their classmates to join in a game of soccer. As none of them want to, they start a match against each other. A little group of boys and girls, for whom the television set is apparently the decisive factor on the weekends at home, agree on a game with wooden blocks that, together with a spaceship and various human figures of Lego and Mechano, set the scene for an entire TV film. From their gestures and intensive verbal exchanges, it can quickly be seen how important this means of expression is for them and that there is no place for adult intruders for the time being.

Three of the older girls are putting their heads together in the library. They have the tape recorder in front of them and are in the midst of a lively discussion. I accompany eight-year-old Denise to help her choose a book. The three girls give me a signal to indicate "Attention—recording in progress! Do not disturb!" We are as quiet as possible, hearing just enough to realize that it is a "scene in the family." Each of the girls takes over different roles in turn, making the appropriate changes in voice as well. Denise sits down next to them on a cushion and starts to read her book. Liz approaches the library. Denise points to the three with the tape recorder: don't make any noise, they're making a recording! Liz selects a book as carefully as possible and makes herself comfortable at a table. She unpacks her writing materials and begins to copy passages out of the book, in her good and very legible handwriting. Liz attended a public school for a year and seeks security in this activity, which does not demand too much initiative from her, at regular intervals. While she is involved in her work, I come to put an arm around her for a moment, letting her tell me about what she is writing. It is clearly obvious that she enjoys the attention and uses the opportunity to tell me about her mother, who sprained her arm the day before. Then she complains that she has no ideas and asks what she could do in arithmetic today. Since she came to us a few months ago, this has been her daily litany. She has never made use of any arithmetical material on her own. Again and again she asks us for instructions, even after she seemed to have understood the material on the previous day of school. Had I not known that Liz was locked in a small apartment alone during the day in the first years of her life while her mother went to work, that she was supposed to learn to do arithmetic in an abstract way, without an operational basis, and was hit by her teacher when she made errors in calculation, then I could have lost my patience with her more than once. So, like every day, I promise her that I will help her with arithmetic today. She is to call me as soon as she is ready to start. Liz bends over her writing again, and I squeeze her shoulder gently before I go off.

My glance falls on a group of six or seven boys and girls who are in the process of unpacking a basket filled with plastic bottles and cardboard boxes that I placed on a group of tables this morning, their remarks characterized by a number of specialist expressions. As soon as they notice me, Carolina runs to take my hand and pull me over: "Look, we want to build a town. What kind of glue can we use? Do you think we can liquefy the dried-up paint from last week, or shall we mix fresh paint?" I help them to bring over a few more tables so that they have enough space to work, explain to Pablo where he can find colored paper to glue on the houses and other useful items in the storage room, show Cristina how to wash out a stiff paintbrush, and soon go on my way again with the well-known words, "If you need me, just call me." Here is now another group with something to do, working along and able to realize its own ideas at this stage, as indeed it should.

Maybe my support is needed at the printing press? Alejandro and Natalia have thought out and drafted an advertisement, which they want to print. (In the back of my mind: the suspicion that their fathers buried themselves behind the Sunday newspaper yesterday. . . .) I ask them if they would like to read out what they have written. They look at one another questioningly. Finally they say yes, adding loftily that I could perhaps be of use to them with corrections, so that there are not so many mistakes in the advert. Reading it aloud, they double up with laughter. A few new ideas also come to them for the improvement of their text. I help them to look up the words in question. Finally the text has been formulated more or less as follows:

> Who wants to buy my house?
> Selling cheap:
> House with clay floor and crooked walls
> Windows with broken panes

Roof not watertight any more
Floor has holes
Worm-eaten furniture
Sofa with fleas
Garden with a lot of weeds
If desired, ghosts can also be supplied with house.
Price: a million sucres

They copy the advertisement on graph paper so it will be easier for them to plan and arrange the lines when doing the printing. Then they look around the room for someone who does not seem to be too busy. "Want to help us print?" Peter, who has apparently lost interest in the town-building project, presents himself. These three will be occupied with the setting of type and printing until it is time for the juice break. When the first proof sheet is done, they will call me again to assist with proofreading.

And again a look around the room to see if I am needed anywhere. Vinicio is sitting with a group of boys on a straw mat. Completely absorbed in a guessing game, they have eyes or ears for nothing else. They estimate lengths, depths, heights, diameters, distances between objects—in short, everything that comes in sight. After each child has given his estimate, measuring is done by means of a measuring stick. The boy whose estimate came closest gets a eucalyptus seed as a prize.

Out of the kitchen come sounds that make me look in that direction. Sarah and Tui, who speak only English to each other, are involved in an argument in Spanish with Edmundo and Patricio. From where I am, I try to understand where the problem lies. "We were here first. Why are you coming in here to bother us?" This comes from the girls in raised voices. "But we want to try out another recipe. Don't be so egoistic—you have to let us work here, too," say the boys in defense. "Oh, yeah—and then we can clean up after you! No, thanks—we know how you guys are!" "What do you know?" "Boys only want to cook and not clean up after themselves." Emotions are running high. I decide to move a little closer to the scene. Both parties immediately want me to take their side. I summarize their problems in words, without offering a solution. This moral support alone, as is almost always the case, is enough. After a lot of palaver, the children agree on what side of the kitchen each group can work, and both groups promise to each other that they will leave their side spotlessly clean afterward. Here, as well, I need not do anything else or get involved any further. The children will not only see to order on both sides of the kitchen, they will also compete against one another to "have the cleanest side." I am reminded of them only twice: the first time when Edmundo, who cannot read very well yet, does not quite understand his recipe and asks me for help, and then later when the girls bring me a sample of their finished product while I am demonstrating a new material for multiplication to Paulina.

The two youngest ones, Gabriela and Mariana, are still not able to decide on an activity for themselves. They go from group to group, watch here and there, do not touch anything. I try to see from their facial expressions and body language whether they are content in this half-passive activity, which has been going on for more than half an hour now, or perhaps might prefer a suggestion or initial idea from me. "Would you like me to show you something?" I ask Gabriela in as neutral a tone as possible. I know her personal story very well, and I know that she has problems with "authority," already at the age of barely seven. "No, I only want to watch" is the expected reply. I stroke her head as lightly as possible and say, "Yes, you don't want to do anything now—you just want to watch." Gabriela throws me a grateful look. A few minutes later, when I am already putting letters out of the Montessori alphabet together into words with Mariana, she wants to work with us. First they sort out the letters they already know, learn a new letter, form new words, and then have the idea of making a picture book with the new words. They illustrate each page of their book with colorful drawings and write the words below the pictures as best they can.

Calls for assistance are meanwhile coming from various corners. Carmen, who is drawing weather curves based on our daily entries, cannot recall how she calculated the monthly average the last time, using the Montessori material for division. It only takes me a few minutes to be sure that she is using the material correctly and can manage by herself.

Liz needs a little more attention until she feels secure with her material again and can cope with addition and subtraction of four-digit figures on her own. But she is only content if she can call me back after every step.

Alba and Tania are working with material to train logic and arguing about the correct distribution of standing, walking, and running men, women, boys, and girls in various colors. Here, too, by sitting down with them for a moment and formulating their problems verbally, I have provided them with enough help.

The three girls with the tape recorder have finished their drama after a lot of erasing and rerecording. Could they make a puppet theater presentation out of it and perform it for the little ones in kindergarten? We discuss the fact that they would have to be very well prepared for such a project. They decide to try to make a written transcript of the tape drama, then invite the others to take part in a competition to see who can produce the best hand puppets representing the characters of the drama.

The group of children busy with the construction of a town seems to have reached and passed the high point of its selected activity. I suggest that we carry the finished houses and cars over to the big display table. There the children notice that with sand, stones and small plants, they could make their model city much more interesting and attractive to look at. Equipped with wheelbarrow and shovel, two of them transport the necessary material over. One of the older children has another idea as well: with the help of a city map, the most important streets are to be determined and the model city made as similar as possible to the real Quito. So the main streets are laid out, the houses set up in rows. But there are no traffic lights or signs, no street names; an airport is missing. Following much consultation, ordering around, and running, all that is necessary has been located and brought to the building site. One child insists on turning the table so that its position corresponds correctly to the four directions. A compass must be consulted. Again it takes a long time until all opinions have been checked and brought into accord with each other. The crowning glory of the work is a ball-shaped object of sand and cotton balls on the south side of the city that can easily be recognized as Cotopaxi, the snow-capped and most visible volcano of Quito. With excited shouts the crater is filled with the contents of a box of matches. All the children are summoned, a few little ones even come over from the kindergarten to watch in amazement. Accompanied by cries of fear and enthusiasm, the volcano is ignited and explodes.

Those who were deep in concentration on their chosen activity before this event took place now return to it following this short interruption. For the others it was a good excuse to stop working, put their material away, and look at the clock. Goodness, it's long since time for the juice break! We had almost forgotten that we are hungry and thirsty!

The hungriest run into the "old house" and get the pitchers of juice and the cookies. The children make themselves comfortable at the picnic table, on the grass, or in the kitchen corner, unpack what they have brought to eat from home, perhaps making some trades of goods. Others, who have already had something to eat, start something new. They go to look at their plants in the garden, invite classmates to a game of checkers or Wari (an African game), visit a small sibling in kindergarten. Vinicio gives his fans a few new tips for the soccer game. They hold him in very high esteem, since he plays in the university league himself.

I excuse myself for a moment and go to get a cup of coffee and a piece of bread from the kitchen. Then I go and sit on the grass, only to have somebody on my lap right away, wanting a bite of my bread or a sip of my coffee. Emerson approaches with his book and wants to read aloud to me. Another boy urgently asks me to come over to his place of work; he has finally succeeded in positioning a grasshopper leg under the microscope and I must come to look at it. I promise to come as soon as I am free. A whole row of curious children and I stand in line for our turn at the microscope. Then we look for illustrated books about insects together. A few boys and girls want to draw them and write texts from the encyclopedia under the drawings. And so we suddenly have new interest groups forming. The enthusiasm of the children pulls me in many directions. In the course of two hours, I have come together several times with every child, either individually or in a group, have touched every child, listened to him or her, said something about the child's activity, answered questions, offered my advice, given encouragement, mentioned new possibilities; I have assisted when a child could not go on without help, demonstrated a new material, or helped to write down a result. Now it is time to remember who has not yet entered into serious and intensive work. "Who would like to try out a new writing game?" "Carolina, have you done any writing today? Do you want to do something on your own or over here with the others?" "Is it something good?" "They want to see who can find the most words that have to do with water in five minutes, clocked with a stopwatch." "Can we find words for sicknesses, too? My grandmother had to go to the hospital yesterday." I promise them that everyone can suggest a topic. Some children still have difficulty finding their own spontaneous written expression. They are grateful for initial ideas and suggestions: perhaps a subject for an essay (or even better: a choice of two), the free adaptation of a story or text, the beginning or the end of a story to which they must invent the rest, the description of a picture or description of objects that the children themselves put together, once in a while a dictation, a text that is to be put into the past or the future tense. Everything normally found in language classes is offered here. But it always remains exactly that: an offer, never a must, never compulsory. The happy undertone of learning something new, something interesting, should never be lost or—worse—destroyed. Often an undecided child, upon listening to our suggestions, finds something on its own: "No, none of that. But it's okay—now I know what I want to write. I want to write a letter to my friend and tell him about our last excursion."

We have all long since forgotten that it was a cold morning and none of us really felt like doing anything. Even in the voices of the children, one can hear the change after two hours of busy activity. The voices sound less shrill and tense, having instead a quieter and fuller quality to them. Some children are silent, absorbed in their work. The change in the atmosphere is also visible in the movements of the children. They move back and forth between the shelves and the tables with full trays of materials, get out of each other's way smoothly, organize themselves at a table or on a straw mat, make room for one another. A new harmony can be recognized in the way they walk, carry, and put in order, a joy in the mastery of the environment and a feeling of lightness of their own bodies. The children are now wholly "present" in the here and now. Their facial expressions are awake and relaxed. Their activities follow their own rhythm. After a period of concentrated work that requires sitting still, each child seeks its own form of movement: the gymnastic bars, the climbing net, with a ball or at the punching bag, with a hammer, saw, and piece of wood, in the garden, at the water table, or in the sand. The environment provides innumerable opportunities to work off blocked physical energy or obstructed emotion. The extent or amount is determined by every child on its own. We can be sure that the child has had enough "physical exercise" only when it returns to an activity of greater stillness or quietness of its own free will.

The children know that the morning at school is coming to an end. The younger ones, who have a flute lesson in the last thirty minutes of school today, come to ask how much time is still left before this lesson begins. It is a special day for them, a day that is different from the others. At the start of the school year, they made the voluntary decision to take part in the flute lessons, even writing a "contract" in their own hand: "I will take part in every flute lesson and practice fifteen minutes a day." They take this contract very seriously and remind me of the time for playing the flute long beforehand.

This is the most intensive half hour of the morning. Everyone would like to finish what he or she has not completed yet. At the beginning of the morning, the time stretched out endlessly in front of us, no hurry was necessary, and now time is getting short. "Do you think I can still do three arithmetic cards?" "Well, see how far you get in the rest of the time today. Just don't forget that you need time to clear up and put things away before the bus comes." This kind of dialogue repeats itself nearly every noon, since our school only functions in the morning. Most schools in Ecuador work half of the day (mornings or afternoons, and some even with an evening shift, since there are not enough facilities to house all the students of Ecuador). Only certain elite schools offer "babysitting services" past the official school hours. Sarah has discovered a new way to use the multiplication tables. She takes it as a personal insult that she is now expected to think about putting it all away, just when she was enjoying the work so much.

José has collected a whole series of objects on two tables, all of which he still wants to weigh today. First he estimates the weight of an object, puts his estimate down in a table, and then weighs the object with as much exactness as possible, using a pair of scales. It often takes a while until he has established the balance. The adding of the weights is still a slow process, and then he has to calculate the difference between estimated and actual weight. He has obviously taken on too much for this one morning. "Will I be able to remember tomorrow all the things I wanted to weigh today?" Thus he learns, in addition to weighing and calculating, something that will serve him for the rest of his life, whatever his work may be: how to plan his work and bring it into harmony with the time that is available.

Before I go over into the other schoolhouse, where the harpsichord also stands, to give my beginners their flute lesson, there is another little spate of tumult and commotion. The secretary brings out the copied sheets on which are listed the weekly homework exercises or tasks, on three levels of difficulty, one sheet for each child. From them the children can choose something for each day. These are ideas, suggestions—not forced labor. The children rush for the sheets as though they were chocolate bars. They begin to read down the list immediately and consult with each other: "What question do you like best?" "I know already which ones I'll do and which ones I don't like." "Can you explain to me what this is?" One child gives the sheet back to me and says, "This week I don't have any time. We're having company from Guayaquil and we want to go out with them in the car every day and show them things." For all children it goes without saying that the activities of their family are at least as important as those at school, if not more. Even if a child is absent now and again, because it can do something interesting with the family, this is also considered acceptable as a school excuse. "My son could accompany me on a business trip" or "My daughter wanted to go shopping with me yesterday" can be read on an excuse just as often as "Could not come to school because of a sore throat." Handing in homework is equally voluntary. All those who would like to have comments on their work from me put their notebooks on a particular shelf. Pictures, illustrations, and newspaper cuttings are hung on the bulletin board, handicrafts or objects of interest go on the display table, experiments or recipes are demonstrated to classmates during the week. Sometimes a child shows me his or her exercise book only after weeks have gone by, because the child wants to discuss a particular piece of work with me, and I see to my astonishment that this child has been working regularly, week after week, without feeling the need to include me in the research. Parents as well report that the children willingly discuss homework with them. But they know that it is entirely the business of the child whether the child does a lot of homework or a little, or none at all. If the child is interested in the work, the parents occasionally have the problem of getting the child to go to bed.

The distribution of these homework sheets is therefore a happy and ceremonial moment that gives Mondays a special touch and is eagerly awaited by the children. Thus the first school day of the week comes to a close in good spirits. The little flute players do their work with concentration up to the last minute and then run to the waiting buses. There are always a few children who are still wanting to finish their work at the very last moment. Others let the morning come to an end with play, reading, or a handicraft. Up to the final moment, there are no signs of tiredness or boredom. Quite the contrary: one can feel the need of the children to enjoy the time to the full and to "live life." This feeling continues on the ride home in the bus, even though the activities must be of a quieter nature, for safety reasons. Until they get out of the bus, the children are occupied with singing and making rhymes, conversations and games, learning German, French, or English, questions and answers, quizzing multiplication tables, or making plans for the following day.

CHAPTER NINE

Every Day Is Different

"How can there be a school with no timetable, no schedule?" is the horrified query of many a teacher who sees an open classroom for the first time. The structurization of our working hours is indeed minimal, yet sufficient to give each day a certain coloring or flavor, as it were, and the children certain points of reference for the run of events in the school week. The last hour of every primary school day is reserved for a particular activity, and this schedule remains the same for the whole year: on Mondays the flute lesson for beginners is given and on Thursdays the lesson for the advanced, on Tuesdays there is Orff music or movement, on Wednesdays English or French is offered, on Fridays it is storytelling. For some activities, the children sign up at the start of a school year and commit themselves for the entire year, pledging to come each time. Should they lose interest halfway through the year and stop, they may not return until the beginning of the new school year. They understand very well that the progress of the group would be endangered by irregular attendance. For other activities the children can make a decision from one time to the next. If they decide to take part in such a group activity, then they cannot leave the group before it finishes on that day. Once in a while it also happens that such groups do not take place because all are so deeply involved in other things that the minimum number of six participants is not reached. For all planned activities, participation is voluntary, and for those who do not want to take part, all the other alternatives at school are open, provided they do not disturb the working group. Whoever takes part in these groups does so on condition that he or she agrees to conform to group discipline—one runs the risk of being "thrown out" if one disturbs the others.

Other than these varying activities on the school premises, the children have the standing invitation to go swimming every Tuesday morning at a nearby thermal swimming pool and to go on an excursion every Thursday. The swimming pool, located at the foot of an extinct volcano in an idyllic valley, is constantly fed by fresh warm water. Around the time that we go, we are usually the only swimmers. Swimming lessons are given in accordance with the needs of each child. The youngest children are often afraid of water. So we let them sit on the edge of the pool for as long as they like, calmly watching the older ones swimming, diving, and going underwater. Some only dare to enter the water little by little and are stiff and frightened at first. By means of little water games as well as the freedom to experiment on their own in the water, as far as their courage will go, even the children most frightened of water gradually let go and relax, try out different primitive ways of swimming around, and finally request instruction. Long before they really can swim, they go out into deep water. Full of pride, they declare, "Nobody taught me how to swim. I learned it myself!" This confrontation with a new element, the gradual conquest of fear, the long period of experimentation in security, staying close to adults, who are there to help if needed and/or desired—without determining the rhythm of learning, however—all these elements are unconsciously carried over into the other areas of learning. Just as in the water, they lose their tension in other learning situations and believe themselves to be capable of more and more.

Another event that marks a point in the rhythm of the week is the weekly excursion, which takes place every Thursday without fail. Every other Thursday it is a hike, often connected with adventures in steep canyons, dark tunnels that we try to investigate with flashlights, streams that tear off our clothes and force us to undertake missions of rescue. On the Wednesday before, we plan what clothes and shoes must be part of the expedition and what containers are recommendable for bringing back home flora and fauna as well as geological objects. Such an excursion is often followed by a nature exhibition. The herbarium receives new objects of interest, plants and flowers are dried, drawings made, insects dissected and prepared for the microscope, textbooks consulted. Mothers receive gifts of rare plants, found in a damp nameless ravine. But the most wonderful souvenirs are the memories that the children have. While climbing or marching along, they tell each other the stories of their greatest experiences, over and over again. If there is a new child along who was not with us at that time, they paint the most colorful pictures possible of their various adventures: "Do you remember last year? Tania lost her shoe in Rio San Pedro. Santiago threw himself into the river with all his clothes on. Then we all jumped in after him. Finally we all went swimming in our clothes and had to go back to school only in underpants. And then came the best part: we sewed ourselves new clothes and made new socks and shoes. Rebeca had to give us all her old tablecloths and linens. We never had such a beautiful wardrobe. And you should have seen our mothers' faces when we got off the bus at noon!" On one of our recent expeditions, we had to slide down a ten-foot cliff on the seat of our pants, because erosion had more or less turned it into a sand dune, and this reminded them all of an earlier experience: "Don't any of you remember how we tried to climb up this cliff a year ago? Vinicio pulled us up with ropes, but we were laughing so hard that it took an hour to finally get us all up there."

Every excursion has its story. Even the nonathletes make great efforts to conquer obstacles. After all, everybody wants to get back home in one piece. When a child says, after a long climb, that it cannot go one step further, the others say benevolently, "So wait here. We'll be back in two weeks to get you." And how they rush at a little spring or waterfall to refresh their faces and hands after a climb! The simple pleasures and refreshments of life are discovered anew, even by the most spoiled of children. If a new pupil comes, one who is not so enthusiastic about physical exertion or is even a bit overweight, the others comfort their new classmate: "We used to be like you before, too. You'll get used to the excursions and lose some of your fat." It is very rare that a child makes use of the opportunity to remain at school. In most cases these are children who want to prove to themselves that everything here really is voluntary and that their autonomy is in fact guaranteed. When they hear the reports of the others about the adventures that were survived, they make their own personal decision not to miss the next excursion.

On the Thursdays in between these hiking expeditions, we take the children to visit places where we can get to know the work of adults, or the life of children under other conditions, or sites and artifacts of our culture. Such excursions must be especially well prepared by us, so that the children will be granted admission to places of work and given explanations suitable for children. We find it important that the children are not just hurried through a factory or a museum but that they also have as much chance as possible to poke their noses into everything, may touch, try out, and ask as much as possible, have conversations with workers and supervisory staff, enjoy an unforgettable experience appropriate for children— not just take a list of new facts back to school. So we speak, for instance, to the owner of a factory first; sometimes it is possible to find ways and means to let the children try out a process of work. Often we can take home byproducts (for us they are not "waste"!) of production, which are utilized for many projects and inventions at school.

At the Museum for Pre-Incan History, the children are permitted to touch various objects with the greatest of care, and the guide sits on the floor with them to exchange thoughts about history. At an orchestra rehearsal, the children may sit near the musicians and watch them play from close up. After the rehearsal the musicians even allow us to try out a few instruments. At the zoo the children help with feeding as well as with the stuffing of dead animals. The zoo includes a small museum in which all dead animals are exhibited. In a small laboratory works the nicest of taxidermists, a man who is himself not any bigger than a ten-year-old child, and the children have been good friends with him for years now. On a visit to the fire brigade, they trade a consignment of hand-painted pictures for a ride in a fire truck.

During informational visits to stores, the children overwhelm shop owners with questions about prices, country of origin of products, sales records. They write everything down in their notebooks, compare the prices in Quito with those in Tumbaco, and buy rations for the school. At various restaurants they compare methods of work, origin of raw ingredients, menus and prices, and note down the number of customers over different periods of time. From this data they produce curves, bringing them to the restaurant owners at the next opportunity. At an educational institution for the handicapped, they learn various work procedures, try to communicate with the deaf, and invite a group to visit our school.

The most impressive proof of the inexhaustible curiosity and desire for knowledge of children who do not feel themselves under any pressure was given on the occasion of a visit to the chemistry laboratory of the Central University of Ecuador. With the father of one of our Pestalozzi children, we had agreed to give the children only a small taste of chemistry, so to speak, and planned an introduction to the subject that was not to last longer than an hour. Three hours later we took the children out of the building, only with difficulty. They had participated in experiments for an hour, blown glass, looked under the microscope together with the lab technicians, and allowed the technicians to take blood. Their notebooks were full of the most wonderful-sounding scientific names, with which they organized reading exercises in the bus. In the midst of all of this, they had forgotten hunger and thirst. Their one worry was about when they would be invited to the university again. This excursion was followed by a long period of chemistry experiments, not only at school but at their homes as well.

Although we respect the principles of "storing up" and thus do not expect from the children an immediate expression or analysis of their experiences on excursions, these experiences do give constant incentive for reporting, painting, modeling, writing, and calculating.

A respectable number of essays on our contacts with the world—more than a few of them dictated to a teacher at the typewriter, as the youngest children cannot write well enough to give their thoughts a permanent form of expression—serve us as reading material that is very well liked. Especially impressive experiences are given written form in a handmade and self-illustrated book, and these also go into our library. Other expressions are printed and distributed to all. But all of this functions only if and when the children feel no pressure put upon them by adults.

If significant human contacts are made during an excursion, the excursion day is often followed up by busy activity in handicrafts, baking, writing, or painting and drawing. Letters of thanks as well as gifts give the feelings that have developed their worthy and deserving expression. Or, to give another example, a visit to an orphanage gives rise to the wish to donate clothes and toys to these poorer children.

After each excursion we try to decide whether the impressions are lively, authentic, and valid or too complicated and overwhelming for the children. Thus we ourselves learn from these events as much as the children do, enabling us to draw conclusions for later opportunities. All of this demands a great deal of planning, even though the planning is not seen at a glance in the form of timetable and school bell and so remains invisible to the children for the most part. Every center of interest, or corner, as we have called them earlier in this book, is carefully devised and planned, equipped with attractive and interesting materials scaled to different levels and corresponding to the experience and development of the children. Structured as well as unstructured materials must be present in large numbers and amounts. Each center has material for operative, figurative, and connotative learning. In this environment it is necessary not only for the adults to feel absolutely sure in the use of the material; they must also learn to assess the stage of development and the mental structures of a child. Only in this way can an adult give the learning child the best possible assistance in trying out and exploring the concrete materials. In this harmony of external stimuli and internal structures, which is expressed in tangible, intelligent

actions, we find the key to many doors that connect otherwise isolated fields of knowledge: on the one hand, the subject areas of
psychology and pedagogy, so often taught on a completely theoretical basis at faculties of education; on the other, the "subject matter"
that is to be taught to children according to the curriculum. In the
usual practice, these two areas are difficult to bring together, unless
the basic conditions of the child's organism are respected, an organism that has its own laws of nature: above all the need for concrete
activity, in contrast to a verbal transfer of facts and figures of
knowledge, and, connected to such activity, the freedom to move
and to speak about one's own experiences spontaneously with one's
friends and classmates.

What makes it possible, therefore, for a teacher at an active
school to plan his or her teaching is not what can be "recited on
demand" again, but exact observation of the spontaneous actions of
the children with tangible materials and other children. Day by day
we modify the environment using our observations of the previous
day. We move hidden materials to a new place to facilitate (renewed)
discovery; we bring in all sorts of new things and observe what
happens with them. We notice children who, through new and
graphic materials, achieve new forms of expression and a coordinated use of their hands. Others become lively through new elements of natural science and make unexpected progress in reading
as a result of this interest. And others need new parallel arithmetical
materials in order to become more secure in a particular calculating
operation before they can go on to more difficult material. This
constant changing of the environment, which does not disturb its
basic order and principle, however, provides ever new incentives for
refreshing new activity, thus preventing the children from becoming
bored.

In our planning we must learn to distinguish from case to case
which methods best initiate the activity of the children. The active
classroom allows us the greatest flexibility. We can, for example, add
new objects to the environment without a word and wait to see
what the children do with them. If they show interest, we can go a
step further and, after observing the first spontaneous activity, show

some of the children new possibilities for use. Another method frequently used in practice is for us to get actively and enthusiastically involved with a new material ourselves. The children usually come up in curiosity and ask what we are doing. Some enthusiastically watch a demonstration of the new technique immediately, while others remain unmoved and explain, giving great weight to their words, that they have no time now but will perhaps come back later.

Every once in a while we have conducted the experiment of suggesting a general topic for one week, inviting the children to put their minds to the topic in the greatest possible variety of ways. Let us take, for example, the subject of water: the children can paint pictures of it, build ships, make experiments with it, measure, weigh and calculate it, write or read about it, learn geography, go down to the river and play with it. However, it has almost always been the case that when the children decided on activities for themselves within the framework of a topic set by us, they have lost interest in it already by the following day. If we for our part have tried to insist on our given idea, their activity has soon showed a clear lessening of intensity and concentration. So we came to the conclusion that at least children under the age of ten are still too young even for such a "loose" type of planning around a topic and that it is better to accept and fall in with their own spontaneous interests from day to day.

More often than not, the children come to school already with plans of their own and kindle the interest of a group of friends with their ideas. On another day it may be "coincidences" that set off an avalanche of activities one after another, with us jumping to keep up and out of breath for a long time. Recently, for instance, a military helicopter circled over our school premises, making a good deal of noise. It flew off, then returned again. This went on for more than half an hour. All of us, of course, were outside, excitedly taking turns with the only pair of binoculars. The comments of the children became more and more imaginative, going to the very limits of fantasy. And when the helicopter finally landed on the property next to us, there was no holding us. We all climbed over the thorny stone wall, overgrown with agave plants, and reached the helicopter just as it was lifting off again. It seemed to us that we had practically been able to touch the wheels. We all had the feeling of being in direct contact with the big wide world.

This event gave us something to talk about for a long time. It was an occasion for making drawings and sketches, writing detective stories (one was published, thanks to our school printing press), doing research in books on helicopters and how they work, comparing the speeds of various means of transportation—and an eight-year-old boy began to read his first "big" book on this day, *Around the World in Eighty Days* by Jules Verne.

Another "coincidence" that set in motion a chain reaction of spontaneous interests was the birth of a baby llama, an experience of deep awe and admiration on the part of everyone. Every child began to talk about his or her own birth. Later we found the placenta in the grass, and there was no end to the pointing, shaking of heads, questions, and—last but not least—consultation of biology textbooks.

The events are not always as overwhelming as this one. Yet even inconspicuous or seemingly insignificant experiences lead the children into action in unexpected ways: a bird flying into the classroom and unable to find its way out, a spider that has spun a web overnight from one post to the next, or the neighbor's cat getting into a spat with our cats. Every so often there is a flood on our school grounds after a cloudburst or when too much irrigation water has flowed into our reservoir. Then boats are built, seafaring receives great attention, new plantations are laid out, canals for drainage and artistically designed bridges are constructed, jumping exercises and new kinds of water experiments are carried out.

These are the interruptions of everyday routine that are feared in "normal" school operations because they distract the attention of pupils from the programmed course of classes and instruction, but they are welcomed as enrichment in the active school. They bring life into the place, giving us new subject matter, new incentive for group conversations and for getting new materials, not to forget reading, writing, and arithmetic as well.

Very welcome, too, are small festivities and celebrations of something or other. We take them as an occasion for making numerous preparations, enjoying them with a great sense of purpose—one might even say business—and much pleasure. To prepare such special events, we hold big meetings. For instance, if a class from another school is coming for a visit, the children plan what they will cook for the meal to be eaten together with the others, what kinds of activities would be good, or how to act if the others do not respect our house rules. Should it be a cultural event at school, a theater performance, a film or a photo exhibition, to which parents are also invited, then the older children seize the opportunity to organize a bazaar and earn money for our big annual excursion. Cookies are baked, weighed, put into bags, and priced; handmade books of recipes, songs, or original poems are printed, bound, and decorated; windmills and small toys are built for the youngest ones ("If the little ones want a toy, then the parents can't say no," was the astute comment of a seven-year-old boy with a well-developed feeling for the business side of life). On such occasions there is a lot of work to be done. Costs are calculated and profit margins estimated. During sales hours, high spirits prevail. And when the proceeds are being counted, the excitement is great. The children spare no effort to put money into the school cash box. If the necessity arises, they shine shoes for relatives, wash cars, or carry baskets. A spoiled little girl who does not especially like to work offered to beg on the street during a general school meeting, but this idea was turned down as "undignified." So she turned to writing poems and painting, unexpectedly discovering her up-to-then hidden talents.

A very special celebration was prepared as a farewell party for Emilia, a little girl who was invited to visit relatives in Alaska before the end of the school year. Her farewell present was a book to which every child had contributed one illustrated page with good advice. The children cooked a marvelous farewell dinner and decorated the room for the festivities. While we were all sitting together at two long tables after having finished eating the wonderful meal, the children asked endless questions about Alaska, about the trip up there, and everything else directly or indirectly connected with this.

The party ended with a geography lesson, for which books and illustrations were brought over, to the great interest of all. Before the school year came to an end, most of the children wrote the most original of letters imaginable to Emilia about our experiences at school and during our excursions. The postage for these packets of letters was financed out of the school cash box mentioned above. The answers from Alaska were read aloud, to the great pleasure of everybody, and then placed in our Freinet file as important reading matter on the subject of Alaska.

It often happens that the interest of one single child influences the entire group for a time. Maria was undergoing treatment by an eye doctor. During the period of time that the treatment was in progress, she transformed the schoolroom into an eye clinic and became the center of attention herself for hours on end. In the library she hung up a sign on which was printed "Eye Clinic" and a sight chart. In front of them, Maria set up a desk with a typewriter and stamp and pad of receipts, together with other office supplies. It did not take long for her to have more patients than she could handle. She ordered all of them around with great authority, allowed no error to pass her scrutiny, and wrote out numerous prescriptions for glasses. An industry flourished: the production of glasses made out of cardboard and transparent paper in a variety of colors, depending on the eye disease. Play money was produced and circulated. A waiting room was arranged in the library. The waiting children used the time to read magazines and books. Those who had undergone eye treatment at the hands of Maria could then go on to activities of their own choice, wearing interesting and decorative pairs of glasses and undisturbed by the busy activity still going on at the eye clinic.

A few days later a practice for general medicine was opened on the other side of the library. Two school desks pushed together and covered with white paper served as an examining table. Stethoscope, blood pressure cuff, bandages, microscope, beakers, magnifying glass, eyedropper, and a variety of mysterious medicines appeared to take their places beside pads for writing prescriptions and reference books on the human body. A great number of children were again examined, treated, and sent to the pharmacy, which had opened soon after this practice and also had a section for homeopathic medicine, with herbs from the garden. All these activities did in fact take up a large part of the schoolroom and brought a lot of bustle with them, yet they by no means prevented "normal school operations" on the other side of the room, where other concentrated work was being done.

From time to time the school print shop turns into a daily newspaper office. Subscriptions are sold, news is collected and prepared for publication, teachers and pupils must be interviewed. Feelings and excitement reach a new high when the first proof is ready and again when the first issue is distributed. This spirit of enterprise often awakens when least expected. Not only primary school but also kindergarten becomes an institute of research. Children are measured, statistics on color of eyes, favorite foods, illnesses, and methods of healing are all put down in writing. The number of happy or sad, quiet or noisy children is determined for the different play areas of kindergarten.

No two days are alike. Never is there the same combination or course of activities. The moods as well are subject to change and must be taken seriously. Although the vitality of children and their readiness to be cheerful and happy are most often greater than those of adults, there are still "gray days" on which we must be prepared to give all kinds of help, to calm down and to comfort, if the day is to run its course in harmony. I remember one morning: A whole group of children of varying ages disappeared early from the classroom, taking some sort of handicraft and going outside to the small playhouse, as we call it, which serves as a place for little private conversations, play having to do with "family matters," listening to music, or reading aloud. On this particular morning it was full of children, whereas the classroom seemed so empty. Suddenly a girl who was crying appeared out of the playhouse and sought sanctuary on my lap. I was not able to find out the reason for her tears. After she had calmed down somewhat, I approached the playhouse and saw to my horror that another ten children were inside crying as though their hearts were breaking. I crawled inside and found a place to sit on the floor and asked whether I could help them in any way. The children fell silent and looked at each other in embarrassment. Had anyone had a fight? No, no one. Did they have any pains or anything like that? No, nothing hurt. At last they communicated to me, politely but unmistakably, that I had no right to disturb them. They just wanted to cry. It was nobody's fault, nobody had started anything, and could I go now so that they could continue crying undisturbed? So I left, completely at a loss and abashed. Here I could not make my influence felt, not even in a form of "creating a good atmosphere." This crying in concert went on for another quarter of an hour; then the children came out and went to their various activities with red and swollen eyes. I did not dare to ask any further questions, limiting myself to giving assistance in "external" activities. By the end of the morning, balance had been restored. We had no explanation whatsoever for this occurrence and entered it into our school diary as a kind of natural phenomenon. But what would have happened in this situation if we had forced the children "to stop all this nonsense" and go back to their work right away?

The active classroom makes use of a number of unseen helpful techniques to initiate the activity of children, to arouse their curiosity, to foster concentration and stamina, to unite the conscious and the unconscious, and it does not shy away from unprecedented or unexpected situations. A small wooden box with a slot and marked "Questions" gives us the occasion for an activity that is both planned and unplanned at the same time. Sometimes this box is ignored for weeks, and then suddenly an epidemic breaks out: questions, questions, and more questions. The children write and write, filling the box up to the top. Then they march around the school grounds with drums and cowbells, calling everyone to a general meeting. We sit in a large circle. The question box is passed from one person to the next. Each one of us may read a question out loud; the smallest children, who cannot read very well yet, are assisted by the older ones. There are purely personal questions such as, "Why does Florencia wear her hair long?" An answer to this type of question is voluntary, according to our house rules. But most of the questions are of a "scientific" or "scholarly" nature, frequently the kind that cause embarrassment to us adults because we either cannot remember exactly what we heard so many years ago or because we do not know how to explain what we know to the children. Most of these questions are living proof of the fact that children are universalists by nature, interested not in easily explainable details but in global knowledge. In his book *Psychologie et Pedagogie*, Piaget writes about this phenomenon:

> Pestalozzi . . . returned to the commonly held assumptions of the child which always carries the complete adult within itself, back to the idea of mental pre-formation again. Thus the Pestalozzi institutes exhibit, in addition to astounding characteristics of the current active school, so many antiquated elements. For example, Pestalozzi was convinced of the necessity to go from the simple to the complex, in all subject matters: today, everyone knows how relative the term "simple" is, and that the child begins with the whole and the non-distinct. Generally speaking, Pestalozzi was possessed by a certain systematic formalism, which is revealed in his timetables, in his classification of teaching materials, in his exercises of intelligence training, in his mania for demonstration; the abuse ensuing from this leaning is sufficient to show how little, in regard to such details, he took into consideration the actual development of the mind.[1]

The first time that we were sitting in such a circle and the question "Why is there air?" was fished out of the box, I found myself in a great dilemma and secretly wished myself somewhere else. Everything that I knew about the logic of children and their use of the word *why* at this age spoke against a causal answer to this question. If I was to believe the studies on the development of mental structures as well as my own experience, any verbal explanation, no matter how simple, would put me on thin ice. Fortunately, the chil-

---

1. Piaget, *Psychologie et Pedagogie*.

dren rescued me from my own doubts. With an open mouth, I heard them giving each other exactly the explanations that corresponded to their respective logic, thus setting off a "discussion," which was really no discussion at all because it served as the expression of each child, without the participants in any way considering the ideas of the others in a logical manner or even really listening to them. This egocentric form of discussion, often described by Piaget, is typical of the way children deal with each other when they know that there is no pressure from an adult authority. But was it not my role as a teacher to expand their knowledge, clarify their terminology, and raise their level of consciousness? I sat there in the circle and tried to feel what my task or role in this situation really was. And there was no doubt about it: It was an exceptional opportunity for me to listen, first and foremost, just to listen, and that completely and entirely. If I did not miss this chance by "messing it up" through my own behavior, I could gain the greatest benefit out of my present situation and come closer to understanding the thinking of the children entrusted to me. At that moment I wished I had turned on the tape recorder. The answers came thick and fast, and the children had to keep order among themselves to give each the chance to speak. "We need air to breathe." "Animals want to breathe, too." "Without air it would be too hot." "Air dries the wash." "The air moves the leaves." "God made the air." "At home we have a book that says why there is air." "Sometimes it smells good, then I breathe deep. Sometimes it stinks—then I don't like to breathe." "Planes need air to fly."

This is a small selection of the spontaneous answers. I asked the children if they wanted an answer from me as well. They did not hesitate a moment. "No, thanks. We've already answered the question." The next child took the box. I did not even have the time to worry about my doubtful role. Before the next question for discussion came up, I promised myself that in the next few days I would read up on various experiments with air and get the necessary materials ready.

"Why are there people?" Again great excitement and the necessity to call the speakers to order. "Without us the school would be empty." "God makes people." "So that people cultivate the earth." "Because somebody has to think." "People build houses." "Cars, too." "Factories, too." "People feed the chickens." "There are people in order to enjoy life." I spoke up once again. This time I only reinforced what the children had already said and promised to put out a few books for them later. This statement was tolerated and the box passed on to the next child. "Why are there parents?" The answer "So that we're happy!" came seven times. Once: "So that they give us food and clothes." Only a nine-year-old girl had the idea that "we wouldn't be here without parents."

Among all these "why" questions, there was only one that the children could not handle. I was officially asked for assistance in regard to the question, "Why do they speak English in the United States?" First I made sure, in an admittedly laborious manner, that they really wanted to hear something from me. When all were in agreement on this point, I told them, with the help of many anecdotes and illustrated books, the story of the *Mayflower*, the pioneers, the battles with the Indians, the liberation movements. The children listened with great fascination. They wanted to hear this or that in English from their English-speaking classmates, and got books out of the library dealing with the United States.

Up to now I have spoken above all of how activities are begun by the children themselves, and perhaps the impression has been given that adults in the open school never take the initiative and do not dare to take over direct guidance or leadership. That, however, would be a false picture. It must be clear, though, that any such direct suggestion or initiative on the part of adults is a sensible and logical follow-up to direct observation of the child in concrete situations. Only through the art of being able to perceive the spontaneous activity of a child is the teacher in a position to assess the interests and the stage of development of children. Sometimes we call together a small group of children in order to do "typical school" reading exercises. But the reading material and the method correspond to the needs and interests of the children. Or I speak directly to an individual child: "When you're finished with writing, I'd like to show you some new material for arithmetic that I've designed for you." Or to a group of boys: "Have you seen the new cards for experiments with fire?"

Children who cannot stand such direct invitations, or even instructions at times, show that they still have a problem with "authority." This is quite understandable when they have just come from another school; we handle such children with the greatest of care and caution. However, if the child has been with us for quite a while and still reacts negatively to direct guidance, it is to be suspected that the problem has to do with the home.

The active school does not work with *one* method—it creates and uses many different learning and life situations. Every situation and every child demands an adjustment. Every day must be felt anew. Every day a child should feel wholly alive. The child should be allowed to experience the present completely and not be hurried or harried by the necessities of an unknown future. In his essay "La psicología del cascabel," José Ortega y Gasset writes these sentences:

> Normally it is our belief that the best way to bring forth the perfect human being lies in adapting the child to the ideal we have of the mature person. In previous articles, the necessity of using the inverse method has been pointed to. Maturity and culture are by no means the creation of the adult or the scholar, but rather of the child, of primitive man. Let us cultivate perfect children, by forgetting as far as we are able, that they shall be men and women someday. Let us educate children as children, not according to the ideal of the model adult, but by standards of childhood. The best human being is never the one who has been less of a child, but the one who finds, upon turning thirty years of age, the most wonderful treasure of childhood.[2]

---

2. Ortega y Gasset, "La psicología del cascabel," in *El Espectador*, vol. III, 423.

Children concentrate on their self-chosen tasks for hours in a row. Here they are preparing mud to build their own "house," Indian style, in the outer areas of the school.

CHAPTER TEN

The Threefold Simple Curriculum

The issue of curriculum, of a schedule of subject matter, causes as much confusion and doubt among the fans as among the opponents of the open school, as does the question of discipline and freedom. If we speak to an adult about the freedom of a child to follow its interests and experience the joy of learning, this adult seldom fails to bring up the following objections: "And what if a child always wants to do only one and the same thing? What do you do if a child never wants to learn arithmetic or reading or writing? Don't you think that every child has to master a certain amount of subject matter in order to survive in our civilization?" Or there is fear: "How are these children supposed to pass an entrance exam for a secondary school, for more advanced education, if they do only what they like?" Our colleagues from other schools and the authorities of the Ministry of Education worry about how the official curriculum, which is valid for the entire country, can be reconciled, or even coexist, with an active school. In a country such as Ecuador, which, under one government, attempts to unite various racial and ethnic groups, going as far as to include the strong desire to incorporate remote settlements of peoples that are far from any passable road into the rest of the nation, it seems to be very important indeed to synchronize the curriculum for all children and thus effect a feeling of unity. Whether in Quito or Guayaquil, in the most remote village at an altitude of nine thousand feet or more up in the Andes, in a hidden jungle village deep in the Amazon region, or on the Pacific coast, there is a certain security, of course, in the fact that all children gain their knowledge from the same school-books and the same reading charts and wall maps, all printed in the capital of Quito; that in the course of every month, depending on the class, they exhibit the same knowledge in all subjects and can recite the same deeds of the heroes of the battle for liberation!

From childhood on, we become accustomed to the fact—that is to say, we are trained into this habit!—that after a period of forty-five or fifty minutes the school bell rings and the arithmetic books are closed, and then we open our history books five minutes later, and so on and so on, until we reach the end of our timetable. Per-haps we have often entertained doubts about whether there really is a certain amount of knowledge that should be learned in a certain numbers of years, whether there should be a learning objective, a certain end to this learning, which is to be reached at the close of a school year or upon leaving school on completion of formal school-ing if we divide up this prescribed knowledge evenly among the days, weeks, months, and years. And this is how it seemed to be. If certain classes did not take place or even whole school days were canceled for some reason, it was the task of the teacher in most cases to pull together or shorten the subject matter in such a way that the end could be reached at last and schoolbooks put away with a clear conscience when the school year was over. If there were gaps in the solid wall of expected knowledge, because of illness or lack of atten-tion on the part of the pupil, a private tutor was hired or cramming had to be done during school vacations.

To us as students it often seemed as though teachers were pleased and proud if they got through their extensive subject matter in as short a time as possible. We pupils shared this pride. I remem-ber very well how we bragged to our schoolmates in the parallel class during the break that we had gotten further in some subject or other than they had. We were an A class and learned faster than a B or a C class!

Most adults are in agreement that they remember very little of what they learned in school. Yet they consider it important to have their certificates and diplomas from various levels of education in safekeeping. People who have been forced by circumstances to adapt to completely new situations and values in life are often directly affected by this: what one learned at school becomes questionable or, at best, relative. Subject matter ingested without query or critique at an earlier time in life loses its absolutism, and the "best way to solve a problem" becomes a problem itself. Many of our personal friends from other countries who were living in Ecuador suffered for years from culture shock. At the start, some of them spent a great deal of time complaining about "these stupid Ecuadoreans." Yet after a number of years abroad, they no longer felt comfortable with their own compatriots back in their home country because these others had not "learned to adjust to other ways of life."

In his book *Future Shock*, Alvin Toffler describes how a similar shock will be faced in the future by all those who have grown up with the security of a fixed curriculum and unchanging values and ways of life. According to Toffler, this solid construction of reliable basic knowledge will be brought down by new research with its new findings so fast that what a schoolchild learns as valid knowledge today may be false and obsolete as early as tomorrow. "The illiterate of tomorrow will not be the person who cannot read, but the person who has not learned how to learn," warns Toffler. What is meant, however, by this "ability to learn," in his opinion?

Toffler is convinced that our schoolchildren of today will live as adults in a world different from the one we know in unimaginable ways. The knowledge and the methods of work that we teachers take as the basis of our authority may have brought us through up to now; however, we should get used to the idea that this same knowledge, these same techniques, could even become a hindrance for our children tomorrow. In one chapter Toffler turns his attention to how our educational system would have to be modified in order for it to be able to meet the challenges and needs of the future. He makes concrete suggestions that can help us rethink the school curriculum. Here are some of his basic demands for a reform of the currently prevailing system: a movable, flexible form of organization that operates case by case rather than generally or universally; decentralization; the penetration of schoolchildren into real areas of life and work in our present society; relaxation of rigid schedules and division into classes. Toffler suggests the creation of elastic curriculums, avoiding the necessity for all of us to work through the same subject matter, the same facts, the same areas of knowledge. In all of this, however, there is to be a general human context that offers guiding principles and points of reference as well as contact for further possibilities, which must not be lost. A systematic encouragement and furtherance of abilities that serve human relationships and social integration is to take the place of a homogenous, uniform, or standardized curriculum. The curriculum not only should be flexible and varied in form but also should deliberately take into account unknown factors of life and thus remain open to all sides, in all directions.

Preparation for an unknown future requires every young person to learn how to discard unusable ideas and replace them with new ones, rather than taking in established facts and figures that are of hardly any use in practical life any longer. The young person must learn to trust his or her inner "steering," or power of guidance and direction, as it were, which will make possible the right choice or choices, out of the manifold variety of new concepts and values, for the respective situation. From this firm footing, a secure base formed by personal judgment and integrated emotions, the individual, in a world full of constant change and unforeseen situations, is able to put information in order, back in order, or in new order; verify information; move from the concrete to the abstract and back again; and come at problems from many different sides.

Toffler predicts that in the future it will be more difficult than it has been up to the present to enter into and maintain valuable human relationships. The children of today should therefore already practice the cultivation of human relationships. By means of this developed ability, they will have an easier time as adults in their relations with other people who are truly suited to them. School hours should thus not be spent in "sitting next to one another" and "looking up front," which would represent a waste of opportunity. Constant direct contact of the children with each other and freedom to choose their work partners or playmates according to their own feelings are both absolutely necessary in order to practice readiness and openness for true human relationships in the future.

A further ability that is required of us to an ever increasing extent is the art of choosing, of making our own choices. How is this to be learned, to be done, when the number of offers of all kinds goes up all the time, without losing ourselves in a chaos of ideas, activities, and products available?

For Toffler there is no doubt that those persons who possess only knowledge acquired from outside to depend on and who have not developed any personal inner security will suffer a painful "future shock." We can but imagine the proportions, and that only to an insufficient extent, in the form of analogy, based on the milder disturbances that are already having considerable effect on the modern human being.

People who have only learned to follow a program applied to them from outside are likewise in danger of being "reprogrammed" as well from outside, if the pressure from a new society so requires. Without an active inner life and the consciousness of one's own humanity, even the most intelligent human being will be missing those specific human qualities, in the form of a personal inner reality, with which he or she can confront such forms of external programming if integrity of being is threatened. In Ecuador we can see in our official curriculums an especially painful gap in the association with inner worlds as well as the dynamic exchange between outside and inside—and these are what make our life worth living!

The active school puts a systematic cultivation of learning processes that are capable of renewal in the place of a generally binding and fixed curriculum. It wants to avoid giving children the illusion that education is something that one "finishes" in the course of various steps and levels, after which one has "done" it. The active school is wary of endangering the child's oneness with itself. If a young person becomes accustomed to splitting reality and postponing life until the bell rings or the state exam is passed, it will be harder and

harder, with every year that goes by, to regain a feeling of complete-
ness and wholeness. A curriculum that makes sense therefore begins
at the point where the child is, in the here and now. Such a curriculum considers the nature of the child and does not separate, in a
"senseless" way, the growing organism from its own senses: if you
sit still, don't try to look out the window, don't talk to your neighbor, keep your hands on the desk nicely, and listen to me, then you
can learn something sensible. Then the schoolbooks are opened and
the world is brought to the child from the viewpoint of a commission of educational experts. The teacher explains, writes on the
board, leads the discussion. The children listen and write down and
give the expected "right" answers, in their best possible efforts.

A curriculum that offers both sense and meaning preserves and
cherishes the unity of a child with its own self and world. Such a
curriculum is based on the singularities of the child's nature, all of
which compose the strengths of the young organism: the child's
urge for movement, its curiosity, its intensity of feeling, and its sen-
sual pleasure. Thus books, desks, and chairs are not banished, although at an active school they have much less significance than the
environment full of tangible objects and a variety of possibilities
for practical activity, an environment that is constantly changing,
continually seeing additions and modifications. When children are
truly occupied, involved in an activity, each one shows his or her
individual character: in the manner of movement, in the way of
talking, laughing, expressing pain, or making contact with others.
If we try to suppress the strong sides of a child, to convert it to our
adult perspectives as quickly as possible, to get it to become an analytical and reflective thinker, the child comes to lose its natural curiosity. The child's senses become dull, apathetic, "insensible"; its
inborn practical intelligence goes undercover, only to reappear later
in undesirable ways.

The previously mentioned book by David Elkind describes a
threefold curriculum that unfolds concentrically around every child.
The center always remains the child itself in his or her full reality of
life. Out of this center grows the harmony that pervades all learning
processes, together with the curriculum of the child's personal inter-

ests, its stages of development, and its gradual participation in a general culture.

The first of these concentric circles, in which the energy for all further processes is generated, has its focal point in the personal interest of the child. This interest stems first of all from the need to feel, to move, to love and be loved. It cannot be emphasized enough how important it is to keep in mind that a curriculum that does not take into consideration these basic needs of the child endangers the unity of the young organism and cuts off the learning process from

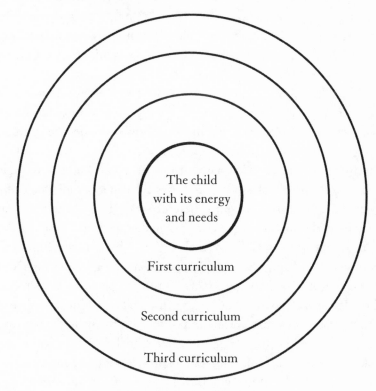

The child
with its energy
and needs

First curriculum

Second curriculum

Third curriculum

First curriculum: personal interests
Second curriculum: stages of development
Third curriculum: gradual participation
    in the general culture

The threefold simple curriculum

its original impulse, which must first of all serve the child's own laws of growth. As soon as we begin to bury this natural source of energy, we must rely on external motivations for learning: punishments and rewards, playing the children against one another, a promise of great successes that make the child "interested in" or "excited about" the future. Or, in the more positive cases, it can be the acrobatics of a teacher who can "fascinate" or "hold the attention of" the children in such a way that they learn with pleasure all that is offered by this teacher. But through these mechanisms the drive, the programming of the child is transferred outside, and the full experiencing of present reality—including the pain that a child can feel when in contact with itself—is replaced by promises of a future, which in turn, as we all know, is very difficult to trade in again for a real present.

What, then, are the objects of natural interest for children in their first years of school? Above all, real people: at first the child's own person and its own family, gradually extended to include strangers. Then come animals, plants, the natural elements, and all objects that can be handled without risk or danger. Finally there is contact with the life of adults, insofar as it has not become too complicated or unnatural. We must therefore take the child seriously in everything that it experiences or that makes an impression on the child outside of school. Every morning the children come and tell about what has happened to them, bring something interesting from their life at home, then convert, transform, or in some way utilize all of this in the form of painting, writing, playing, calculating, and the other activities that are made possible for them by the waiting materials placed at their disposal in our school. With the same unbroken interest, the children look for new incentives, for new opportunities to observe, to try out, to ask questions, and to imitate.

Slowly the circle of experience widens, and out of the small world of personal experiences develops the image of a multiform and multilevel reality. We are pleased about any and all original interests of a child and help it step-by-step to go on: How many new ways can you find of doing what you have seen others doing? What else can you see if you look more closely, more carefully?

How many differences can you discover? How many similarities? What happens if you do this or that in a different way for once?

Every operative, figurative, and connotative learning step of a child first has to do with its own personal interests. The child learns to write down experiences, to work out, estimate, or assess, to measure, to set up comparative curves, to read about the experiences of others in this field. The child speaks willingly and without reserve about its experiences and gradually notices that its own perspective is not always concurrent with the experience of others.

Stimulated through its personal interests, the child expands the circles of its experience, going through the curriculum of its stages of development according to its nature and the laws of growth and maturity. These stages are the same for all children, but their individual personal rhythm varies. Whether it is the intellectual or the social growth of the child, the stages of development influence all its thoughts and actions. Through its practical activity, each child works out anew the concepts of mass, weight, and volume, of space, time, causality, speed, movement, and geometry. This curriculum of development of the children is often very different from the prescribed school curriculum. The most common schoolbooks on the market bear witness to the fact that the inner development of children is hardly taken into account by educational planners.

For example, in a modern workbook for second-grade pupils, there is a list of various possible family relations given. The children are expected to rack their brains and find out, from the text next to this list, which person does what to another person if this person is the uncle of the other person, the father of a third person, and so forth. Have the authors of this schoolbook gone to the trouble of reading what Piaget has to say about the abilities of children to deal with the topic of such relations within the family? How are seven-year-olds supposed to be able to cope with such a text intelligently, without losing confidence in themselves, when it has been proven that—in accordance with their inner development "curriculum"—they feel comfortable with the concept of such relatives only shortly before the onset of puberty?

Here is another example from the same textbook for second-graders: the story of a dream and of a true event are presented on the same page, next to each other. The children are expected to determine which of the two stories could correspond to a dream and which to a true happening. And the child is supposed to analyze as well how these fine differences can be recognized. The next exercise is to produce a similar story about a given topic, once as a dream, once as a true story.

This task requires seven-year-old children to feel comfortable with and in control of reflective thinking. They are expected to be able to distinguish between dream and reality, first of all in their own experience, and then recognize them in a printed text (they have just learned to read as well). Again, the study of a child's stages of development shows that such reflective thinking is part of the natural capacities only from the start of puberty on; in younger children it appears only as intuition and as such should not be forced. A child of this age group could, however, become a champion in practical thinking if we only give it sufficient opportunity.

Not only language textbooks are designed in such a way that children must resort to guessing the wishes of adults (thus becoming textbooks of psychology rather than of language). For arithmetic as well, the most natural activity for the growing intellect of a child under the right conditions, most children need a sixth sense to deal with all the symbols that are difficult to bring into line with the everyday coming and going, giving and taking, measuring, carrying, and comparing—all of them, in fact, activities that are normally strictly forbidden during school hours.

The goal of the active school is to let each child learn in accordance with the rhythm of its development, through real activities in a real world, not one that has been flattened between the pages of a textbook. In a group in which the ages of children are different, it presents no difficulty to a teacher to reckon with the various stages of development represented by the children. The real-life situations unite children of differing maturity levels in a common activity. However, the level of learning can and must be different for each child. It is one of the most fascinating occupations of the active teacher to observe the children in their activity, listen to their conversations, and estimate their stage of development by means of their questions and answers. Through such observation, teachers are more and more often able to meet their schoolchildren on their own level and to feel close to them. Now, perhaps a reader will ask, "Is it not the work of the teacher to encourage adult thought in the children and to liberate them from their own illogical and childlike thinking?"

We can attempt to reply to this question in various ways. If we respect every child in the child's present stage, we allow him or her above all a large measure of personal security. At the same time, we allow the child to gather as much experience as possible on its present level, in order to continue on easily to the next level with a feeling of great enrichment. This is a natural and therefore slow process. Our task is to create the right conditions, not to speed up the process. In this connection we are reminded of a principle in Gestalt therapy: Don't push the river! If we as adults are capable of controlling our impatience so as not to disturb these inner processes, if we instead provide the necessary nourishment, the child learns to stand on its own two feet rather than be dependent on outside direction for the rest of its life.

From these initial concentric circles, which take their impulses from the personal interest of the child and its natural process of growth, comes about, in always new and wider circles, the third "curriculum," leading to a conquest of the world, to a dynamic connection with the experiences of other people, and to confrontation with a general culture. Slowly the child discovers that its own present experience is connected to the experiences of others in faraway places or in the past. Now it begins, little by little, to have thoughts about the future.

At this stage of new intensive interests, it is not only important *what* the child learns but also *how* it learns. The active teacher must never neglect to observe the children in their life situations and thus judge what new situations and/or exploratory impulses these small charges can accept at a given point of time. As long as the children are still quite young, an adult must take care not to interrupt the natural train of thought welling up from their experiences by an artificial division of subject matter. It is, after all, not the work of the children to learn "subject matter" but rather to discover common elements in analogous situations for the solving of problems, to find out conformities and regularities, and to check their application in new situations. This interlacing of subjects is of enormous importance if we do not want to destroy the feeling of oneness at a very early date. Once the basis for analytical thinking has been established, a division of disciplines into subjects to be learned may be of great use, in order to enable deeper involvement with various fields. Nevertheless, modern science points out that this sort of division must be followed by a renewed search for cross-links and connections again later, in order to make creative thinking on a higher level possible.

How does the active school manage to promote learning in children, as well as to foster their practical and intellectual abilities, without following an educational tradition accustomed to dividing everything that is to be learned into separate school subjects?

Let us look at the prepared environment once again in this connection, with all the various activities that can take place in it. Take, for instance, the "kitchen" interest center and all that can happen in this corner: A few children are hungry or have the desire to eat something that they themselves have cooked, to do something of a practical nature, or to demonstrate that they can prepare a meal all by themselves, without their mothers. Some may first go out into the garden to see if something good is ready to be harvested. They touch the plants, talk to a classmate about how long it takes for a beet or a head of cabbage to reach a certain size. When did we plant these beets? Could it be that they didn't get enough water? Let's just have a look at our water curve to see how much rain we've had so far this month. The next step: The children invent a new recipe for the available ingredients or look for one in the recipe box or a cookbook. They read, check to see if everything needed is in the kitchen. If necessary, all that is needed for tomorrow has to be put down on the shopping list. Now they measure out or weigh ingredients, calculate half or double the recipe. Peeling and chopping, frying—whatever the recipe calls for—all of this offers plenty of opportunity for practicing skills, for running back and forth, for stimulating conversation in the kitchen. The cooking time is estimated or looked up. In the meantime, all the equipment that was used must be washed and dried, the table cleared as well, so that other interested parties can also have their turn to work in the kitchen. Waste is sorted into different baskets, according to the categories of organic or nonorganic. When organic waste is taken out to the compost heap, it is a good opportunity to discuss various types of fertilizers with their advantages and disadvantages. (The children know the arguments in favor of organic agricultural methods and never pollute nature by leaving behind nonorganic waste during their walks and hikes.)

If cake or bread is going to be baked, the solar oven is checked for the correct temperature and its reflectors are adjusted according to the position of the sun in the sky; at the same time, the children estimate the hour. While their creations are cooking or baking, many children write down the recipe for their mothers—more and more families seem to be taking their meals "a la Pestalozzi," prompted (or obliged) by the children. Or the children think about what they could do in the time remaining. Then they invite various other children to their little feast. Plates are taken out, the table is set, the guests try a little bit of what is on the menu beforehand, just to make sure that it is to their taste before they sit down. During the eating there is a lot of conversation with laughter and further plans, and finally all the dishes are washed.

Here is another practical example of how a teacher can consciously foster learning and investigating on the part of children without distracting them from their self-chosen activity. Two children are deeply involved in keeping the water at the water table constantly in movement, with all kinds of implements and utensils. They stir it, splash in it, hit the surface, spray it high up, accompanying their games with various noises and announcements. I am helping a boy to clean the impression roller of our school printing press and decide to remain near the "water players" for a while. In a "by the way" tone of voice, I ask them, "Can you also make the water move if you don't touch it?" Astonished, they look at me. Then one of the children laughs out loud and blows against the surface of the water with full lung power. Soon there are more children attracted by this new concept of water operations, and they start a competition to see who can blow the hardest. While doing so, they talk about winds—the east and west winds, their vacations at the coast, where the waves were so high that they were afraid to go into the water. New ideas come up: a pair of bellows, a bicycle pump. The waves get higher and higher. A few minutes later a water pump comes into the act, soon after that hoses of different diameters as well, containers that are then connected up with straws. A water-course is set up and directed over various obstacles. "Ships" are let into the water, their travel times from point A to point B are clocked with the stopwatch. Around this now extensive water project, various small groups of children have taken up position, discussing and commenting on each new step. I ask two older girls, who are standing nearby but not actively participating, the following new question: "Can you move the water without using parts of the body or objects, without an incline, without any wind?" The girls try this and that, but every time, they have to correct themselves: "That's not right. Downhill isn't allowed." "You just blew through the straw." They are as far away as ever from the solution when one of their girlfriends calls, "Come and eat! The soup's boiling." One girl's mouth falls open: "Come on, I'll show you something!" She pulls her classmate into the kitchen and over to the pot of soup, which is bubbling away: "Look, it's moving, but not from stirring or blowing or going downhill."

And so it goes. I innocently ask a few children what makes the ocean move. The assumptions in regard to this point are of the wildest nature. We seek help in books about the ocean that explain the tides. Again come vacation memories. "Once the ocean was way far out and we could go looking for shells and starfishes. When the tide is out, cars drive along the hard beach." (Thus the children have found out that at such times, beaches represent the best roads in Ecuador.) "Once we saw a car that couldn't get to the exit in time before the tide came in and got swallowed up by the water." The older children read about the influence of the moon and make models of the position of sun, moon, and earth, together with their movements. They play with magnets and try them out on various objects. We play a game of association: who can write down the most words having to do with water in five minutes?

The next day we take lots of objects with us to the swimming pool and sink them. We clock the time it takes each one to reach the bottom. The children jump and dive and retrieve the objects from the water numerous times, drop them in again at deeper places, try out new diving techniques.

On Wednesday morning, the children find a big tray on which stand vessels and receptacles of all kinds, with very different diameters, plus measuring tapes on the tables next to the entrance of our school building. To those who ask with curiosity what they can do with all of this apparatus, I demonstrate how they can pour a cup of water into the various containers, then measure the water level and the diameter, putting this data down in a table. For the younger ones it is a difficult project, and they may manage to make up to five entries. The older children are better at it, and they learn how to produce a curve showing the relationship between water levels and diameters in an easy-to-read form.

On Thursday we make an excursion to a nearby river. The children throw stones into the water, practice throwing as far as they can, wade in the water, fish out tadpoles and algae. They send boats down the river with the current, discuss rivers in general and this or that question in particular, want to know where exactly—in what province of Ecuador!—the little boats will reach the ocean. Back at school, we get the maps out of the cupboard, follow with a finger the run of rivers, read the names of the provinces. Some children get a case of travel fever. With help from automobile maps, they calculate distances—using tangible materials for this—as well as gasoline prices and estimated hours for the journey. Others trace the rivers of the country on prepared map sheets and write in their names, paint or draw the oceans of the world, or produce a large picture of oceans and rivers, for which they also make use of the fish typical of Ecuador. Shells and dried seaweed are made into a collage. New variations of the topic of water are worked on for as long as the children's attention holds out.

In this whole process, the small forms of help, questions, and impulses that we adults contribute to rekindle the children's interest and allow them to find new possibilities and aids must be carefully measured out in doses. Children should never get the feeling that their interest is being "exploited" for the goals or aims of the teacher—whatever they may be and certainly in any case incomprehensible for the children. Any children who do not take part in these group activities have the cornucopia of all other opportunities at their disposal. Their interests are taken just as seriously as those of the children working and playing in groups.

And so, in direct relation to how we fully experience every day together with the children, the curriculum grows organically, so to speak, from the authentic needs and interests of the children and of the adults. The emphasis or focus of learning remains in the child and must not be transferred to teachers or textbooks. We always keep in mind that the children's own activity and their experiences come before any information that can be given by the teacher. Instead of constantly longing for the signal that it is time to go home, active children always live with the feeling that they can never get to everything that they want to do at school.

How can we be sure, though, that the children gain a satisfactory level of "general" or "comprehensive" knowledge with this method of schooling? When does one teach them how to bring together all these unplanned experiences into one logical whole? How do they learn to make efforts and to overcome obstacles?

Perhaps it is difficult for us to really accept the fact that we cannot explain logical connections to children of this age. Under the right circumstances of life, the brain, with increasing maturity, takes over little by little the function of processing all these experiences a child has had under positive conditions so that they are understood and can be applied again in new situations. For this process the active school gives us a wide field for observation. After all, as we see each and every day, children often expend far more stamina and energy on their self-chosen activities than we could expect of them in the case of actions dictated from outside. If they are allowed to choose, children will, of course, avoid occupying themselves with "lifeless" ideas that they cannot connect up with their experience and their feeling. For instance, the topic of history for smaller children could start with their own person. The children bring photos to school that show them at different ages. They make an exhibition and write their age at that time plus any other interesting and/or suitable data underneath these chronologically arranged photos. A child's birth stands for year zero, and on the negative side of the time line appear pictures and texts about family members who were already living then. This kind of family history later leads to more general chronologies that symbolize the history of our earth or our great civilizations.

To sharpen this primitive sense of history, we put the children into contact with all sorts of old things and old people. We invite a talkative grandmother to school or go to visit her at home. Old people are glad to tell about their childhoods and proudly show old objects. The children ask questions and try to understand what was different from today in the olden times. Maybe our hosts have old books that show life as it was a hundred years ago. At home the children do similar research in their own families. Then they investigate the street on which they live. Are there old houses? When were they built? What is the difference between the way they were built and the houses of nowadays? In this way the children never lose the threads of their own life, while learning interesting and worthwhile things about the past.

Using a simple camera, they photograph all that seems particularly interesting to them at school and on our walks. In the darkroom of one of the fathers, who lives near the school, they are permitted, in small groups going in one after another, to develop their own photographs. The best photos are hung in our "exhibition"; the others go into the archives, in which date and hour, exposure time, and all other external circumstances that are of interest for later viewers of the photo are carefully noted.

Many contrasts and new impressions await the children on their excursions. Instead of looking at pictures of goods in a beautifully illustrated textbook to learn arithmetic, we go to the stores. We ask the owners to let us touch the goods, make notes of prices, and ask questions about manufacturing or country of origin. By doing this the children learn not only how to calculate but also how to deal with different types of people, how to ask questions, to practice courtesy. During these—admittedly long-winded—experiences, they store up a variety of sensory impressions. This way of letting children live and grow quietly also has other unexpected results. One of our friends, a professor of psychology in Norway who has himself written books about Piaget, complained recently in a letter to us, "I am getting tired of seeing culturally advantaged children occupied with classification and serialization, at schools which are allegedly based on Montessori and Piaget." In the course of his travels to many different countries around the world during the last few years, in his capacity as president of a social foundation, he has come into contact with so much misery and underdevelopment that he is now posing the question, "Would it not be better to enable children to have an education in which they can learn not only logical thinking but sympathy for others as well?"

But how can we put "pity" or "empathy" into the curriculum of our schools? Our experience with the Pestalozzi children, who exhibit great social differences among them, teaches us that it is possible to promote both intellectual development and understanding for others at one and the same time. If we allow the children freedom in the handling of tangible objects, because we want to favor their intellectual growth, the children take over our values and consciously place the main emphasis on mastering the material world. The same freedom applied to experimentation with human relationships of all kinds, often difficult for us educators to recognize as "schoolwork," is necessary in order to foster social understanding in children. Last but not least, children will feel from us teachers very clearly whether we give them freedom of action because we want to sharpen their wits or because we deeply respect their real needs. It is our respect for their full humanity that not only wants to "promote" the children, so that they become logically thinking adults as a result of our scientific methods, but also accepts them today in their childlike being, an act that is perceived by the children themselves as love. The same attitude, which allows us to learn to fulfill the authentic needs of children, and through which they in turn maintain or reestablish contact with their own feelings, is taken over by the children. To the same extent that they themselves feel loved and respected, they gain the ability to pass on this respect and this love to others, and to feel and fulfill the needs of others.

During the last school year, a number of groups of children from other schools came to visit us. One was a third-grade class from an elite school in Quito. The day before had been taken up with planning on the part of the Pestalozzi children: they would cook a big meal for lunch for the visitors, show them their favorite games and books. The visitors got out of their bus in orderly rows, wearing their prescribed uniforms, put their school satchels in a corner, picked up the scent of freedom in their noses, and began to run wildly around the entire school premises. Their hosts tried to invite them to eat and to play. By concentrated and united effort, they were able to get the visitors to the lunch tables, decorated with great care. The guests had hardly finished their lunch—in a great hurry and finding fault with the food—when they rushed away from the table with nary a thank-you and were uncontrollable for the rest of the morning. Our children were greatly disappointed at this behavior and wanted to know why the others were "so strange." When they heard that these children have to sit still in school most of the time, they showed understanding for them, washed thirty additional plates, and went about their own activities from then on.

On another occasion we had a visit from thirty Indio children. Their need for physical activity is not great, as many of them walk for kilometers to get to school every day. These children were starved for concrete materials, and there was a corresponding run on them. Our children divided up the work responsibilities. One group showed the visitors their favorite recipes. The schoolroom was soon full of delicious aromas that had a very enticing effect on all present. Other children demonstrated their favorite games to the visitors and introduced them to the use of the school printing press.

In both these cases we had deliberately avoided giving the children instructions on their proper or expected behavior, assigning roles, or describing the idiosyncrasies of the visiting children beforehand. In each case the children adjusted spontaneously to the given situation. We left it to them to draw their own conclusions from their disappointment with the children from Quito and their positive experience with the Indio children. We do not believe that sympathy and humanity can be taught or cultivated. The only method of practicing it is . . . to practice it, "actively" and together with the children.

Over a period of some weeks, our children maintained intensive contact with an orphanage. They invited the children there to our school and went to visit them several times as well. Before each visit, many of their projects were concerned with the strong desire to do something to pleasure the orphan children. They baked cookies and sold them at a 50 percent profit to their relatives and family friends. They collected second-hand clothing and toys, had fun putting prices on these things and calculating the whole value. We observed the children closely when they presented their gifts, trying to detect any touch of condescension. We found none. The visits to the orphanage were highlights for them. They enjoyed cultivating friendships there as well as playing with the games and pet animals of the orphaned children. They felt honored to be permitted to help these children bake bread. With delight they helped to make a fire in the big wood oven, kneaded the dough, and asked for a little loaf for themselves "to take home so that the others get something from our wonderful morning, too." A few of our children who do not have a harmonious family life at home became thoughtful during their visits to the orphans' home: "Maybe the children aren't really so poor? I think they have it good here—they always have somebody to play with, and they don't have to see their parents fighting all the time."

Where are we to set the limits of the curriculum if school and life are not separated? Once we had an experience that was by no means planned in advance and is certainly not described in any textbook for elementary-school pupils. On a cool morning in Quito—it was still too early in the day for our planned visit to the Museo del Blanco Central, the "Gold Museum," named for its many artifacts of gold—we paid a visit to our "relatives" at the zoo. This zoo, the only one in Quito, is attached to a military school, which also includes a riding school. Our children were just heading for the exit when they were magically pulled to one side, as it were, by a unprecedented happening. An elderly horse, apparently of no more use to the riding school, lay on the ground with all four legs tied together. A soldier was just pointing his rifle at its skull. My urgent impulse was to get the children away as quickly as possible. I looked into their faces. Twenty-five pairs of eyes were glued to the scene of horse and soldier, in the greatest of concentration. Twenty-five children's hearts quaked in terrible expectation at this moment that had suddenly placed them on the line between life and death. The next moment reverberated with the sound of the shot. A great fountain of blood shot up in the air from the head of the horse. It quivered and shook and died. Several soldiers with big knives immediately approached and cut up the cadaver, throwing the meat to the lions and tigers. It was impossible to move the children away from this spectacle. Those who had been shaking the most were now the most curious. What did it look like there inside the horse? Did it have the same entrails as humans? (A few of them had recently become interested in anatomy.) We postponed our visit to the museum and stayed at the zoo until the last piece of horsemeat had been consumed by the lions and the tigers. On the ride back to school, the children were oddly quiet and reflective. Here and there a song was started, as usual in the bus, but the enthusiasm for singing was less strong than on other days.

At school the children capture the impressions they have gained in the outside world in handmade books, printed articles, or pictures. In the Freinet file, we keep material about our excursions to the world of adults for later use. Short reports, dictated by the children or sometimes written directly by us, go into the collection bearing the title "Our Life." They are taken out again and again to be utilized as firsthand reading material. Another file with "discoveries" shows the steps taken by the children in their experiments, but the solutions are left open. An arithmetic file holds the real situations that gave us opportunities for work with figures at home and in school, for all interested parties. Newspaper and magazine clippings dealing with all kinds of fields are pasted onto white sheets of paper and commented upon. With the help of a simple index, they are put into various folders. Thus, in the course of time, a considerable amount of information is collected about a great variety of areas, which offers the younger children welcome reading material and the older ones background material for presentations.

As we have seen, the school environment is adjusted to the changing interests of the children and the growing curriculum. Learning processes follow a natural rhythm for the most part: first, interest as a result of internal or external stimuli, then long periods of active experimentation, with a widening of the self-chosen activity to include other fields of knowledge—reading, writing, and arithmetic—in connection with these fields and topics of interest, which result from the dynamic relation of children, adults, and the concrete world. Yet children seldom follow this "ideal pattern" in a straight line. The majority of them devote considerable time and energy to free play, which brings together constructive as well as representational elements, that is to say, elements stemming from the inner problematics of children. Such games of free play flourish and bloom best where no opinion from an adult is to be heard. In *Play, Dreams, and Imitation in Early Childhood*, Piaget states that this symbolic play, which in its earliest forms fulfills important functions in the formation of a child's intelligence, has a new and significant role in the concrete operational stage of development (that is, between the seventh and twelfth years of life, after which it gradually disappears):

> Finally, a third and more important reason explains the diminution not only of symbolic play but also of play in general. It is the extent to which the child attempts to adjust to reality rather than to assimilate which determines how far the distorting symbol is transformed into an imitative

image, and how far imitation itself is incorporated into intelligent or effective adaptation.[1]

This rather dry explanation from Piaget suddenly came to mind
and took on new significance when I saw it in the context of Mike
Samuels's book *Seeing with the Mind's Eye*. This book deals with
our "images" and "visualizations," which are the natural form of
thought for small children, suppressed for the most part by adults
in favor of conceptual thought. They have their origin in early experiences in which we still had a feeling of being one with the world
and in which we let the world into us primarily through our senses.
Samuels describes how adults, too, can give these inner images the
attention they deserve so that they receive new strength and intensity, thus having as well as creating meaning for us. If it were possible to live with these images and cultivate them even after leaving
the realms of childhood, they could serve our personal integration,
preserving our inner life and providing a meaningful relation to
external reality. The ability to look inside ourselves strengthens our
personality while connecting us to the rest of humanity at the same
time. It makes possible creative thinking, gives healing powers, and
helps in the planning for practical life.

This thinking in images stands opposed to thinking in concepts
or terms, systematically encouraged in the traditional school system.
According to Piaget, it is during the years of school that these inner
images could gain the greatest degree of harmony with external
reality. Yet it is during these years that school discipline forbids the
practice of a large number of activities that have such harmony as
their effect, and that could strengthen the child from within and
teach it to live in harmony between its inner and outer worlds. If
the child follows these images that it has, they become fantasies and
daydreams far from the reality it finds at school, where the child
deals with concepts and terms that are all without a content of emotion and all capable of replacement at any time—yet that represent
for the most part the highest good of education for adults. Cut off

---

1. Piaget, *Plays, Dreams, and Imitation in Early Childhood*, 145.

from his natural need to interact with an interesting outer world and thus deprived of creating images related to concrete reality, the child tends to doze off into fantasies and daydreams, at the same time stocking up on a great deal of concepts and information void of real meaning—all this while his parents are convinced he is "getting a good education."

The active school does not deny the importance of concepts, which fulfill valuable functions in the life of adults. But it allows the child time to acquire such concepts in accordance with its process of maturing. This goal should be reached without endangering the ability of visualization. If children learn in concrete situations, with harmonious movements and the full use of their senses, their inner life is strengthened and empowered, brought into harmony with external reality. However, if we utilize "depictions" or "portrayals," illustrations or an entire system of audiovisual technology instead of real life, there is the danger that these internal images, which should form a three-dimensional reality that speaks to all five senses during the concrete operational stage, will become unreliable, unable to provide enough strength and intensity for our inner life, as Joseph Chilton Pearce shows so impressively in his books.

In Ecuador audiovisual methods have become the latest fad in kindergartens and elementary schools. They seem to me to be an effective means of making children passive and easily manipulated, managed, controlled from the outside. With the onset of the stage of formal operations (around the age of fourteen), such media are certainly helpful, in order to bring young people into touch with much information. In terms of the active elementary school, however: the deeper the understanding we are able to gain of the active school's implications, the more important the role of contact with a living world becomes.

CHAPTER ELEVEN

Reading and Writing as
Self-Expression and Self-Expansion

There are very few visitors to our school who are not impressed by all the new possibilities and fresh perspectives of an open education, by the basic principles of respect as well as a method that goes along with the nature of a child rather than fighting this nature. Most admire the materials placed at the disposal of the children and take pleasure in the atmosphere prevailing among children and adults. At last, however, many of them express their worry in the form of something like this: "We were told that here the children don't learn to read and write. We are in agreement that this is not part of the kindergarten curriculum. But we have heard that the children in the primary school are not forced into learning these things, either. What do you do if the children refuse to learn to read, year after year? And what if they still can't do it at the age of twelve?"

At the root of these worries lies the conviction that the teaching of reading and writing—and arithmetic, too, of course, but this subject will be discussed in the next chapter—is the most important task of the school. Second, it is believed that this art should be learned by all children in the same rhythm and that the age for it is likewise an established norm. And third, this cannot be accomplished without systematic and repeated exercises, through which children experience "how life is," namely "a serious matter"—as opposed to "fun" and "play"—in the nick of time. In this process it is possible for the adult to differentiate between the gifted and the less gifted from the very beginning. Thus, in the general opinion, it can be seen early on in life who will be suited for higher forms of education. In other words, all of us have more or less the same picture in our mind's eye in connection with the term *school*: orderly rows of desks and chairs—perhaps grouped together more loosely in modern schools—at which children bend eagerly over their notebooks, busy with writing and reading several hours a day. Now and again they throw questioning glances at the board or the teacher who is dictating (in Ecuador, much time is spent on dictation, even up to the higher classes), or they turn the pages of a textbook. Thousands of words, sentences, and pages must be written by a schoolchild before the child can at last take his or her place in civilized society. No one asks whether the child will devote a lot of time and energy to writing in later life. Many adults, in their professional and personal lives, read and write only a fraction of what they produced or assimilated as schoolchildren.

Is this systematic filling up of copybooks and workbooks truly the best way to introduce children to the world of the written word? For some time now, thoughtful educators have been giving support to the idea of making this tiring and monotonous work easier for children. But a wave of reform is followed, time after time, by the counterreaction of "back to the basics" when classes of freely educated children without solid knowledge of spelling and grammar stand at the gates of higher education.

In *Compulsory Mis-Education*, Paul Goodman speculates that every more-or-less intelligent person in our civilization of today, which exhibits the written word in public everywhere, would have to almost inevitably gain the ability to decipher written texts sooner or later, even without a formal introduction to the arcane secrets of letters and characters. In his little book *Methode naturelle de lecture* ("Natural methods for learning to read"), Celestin Freinet describes with great sympathetic understanding the beginnings and the progress of a child who, following the need to be a part of and in harmony with its environment, spontaneously learns to read and write, almost all by itself and little by little. For this it uses, in an innocent manner, the same mechanisms by means of which it has learned to speak and to walk, namely its need for movement, for imitation, for self-expression, and for the development of more and greater possibilities for human exchange. Just as in the case of these arts, which every small child learns without "method," progress is made possible by constant attempts, comparison, and correction. The child continually looks for new models, and asks for help if necessary. With much delight, a one-year-old child "paints" on the table, making use of its porridge or juice. Mud, paints, everything that leaves traces when it is smeared—all of these elicit the desire to "write" from small children. What good fortune for the child if adults allow it to do so, also providing on a continual basis new possibilities for this initial spontaneous expression that gives the child so much pleasure! If the child could count on the support of its environment up to school age for these attempts to paint and to write, without losing its courage for trying out new things as a result of praise or scolding, impatient correcting and constant direction, then our schoolchildren would show the same interested desire and complete devotion in regard to the art of writing as the little "piggies" who fearlessly paint around with any material and on any surface that we do not expressly forbid to them.

About the second or third year of life, a child begins to write its first letters and words in this most natural way. From the age of five on, it shows interest in all things written and often copies words and sentences with great perseverance. The child wants to write real letters and happily dictates to others long texts that were too much to copy. All of this is a spontaneous expression of the child's growing organism, which naturally assimilates the elements of its environment in accordance with the inner structures of its age, always striving for new differentiations in movement, feeling, and sensory perception, at least up until the eighth year of life. Adults, however, judge this first love for the written word in a way that is valid for them—therefore egocentric—because of their unfamiliarity with the inner standards and criteria of a child. The adult gives this first form of writing on the part of the child an "intellectual" value, thus trying to lead the small child according to the sense of adults. Many children who experience the full attention and recognition of their parents only when they act "intellectual" find, through early reading and writing and an adjustment to adult logic, an infallible way to experience the love so necessary for their growth.

If we allow the child its own rhythm of learning, we often get a surprise: around the sixth year of life, at which age children normally start school and are supposed to learn to read and write in earnest and by means of method, the children of the free system, in many cases, show a decrease of interest and perseverance in writing. Instead of painting letters with great patience, something that corresponded to a real need before, they now show an urge around this time to experiment on a new level and an interest in working with what can be counted and measured. This is easily understood if we are aware of the fact that a six-year-old child is just at the point of transition into the concrete operational stage of its development— and that his previous interest in letters had been part of his sensory-motor-emotional stage, rather than the expression of an intellectual inclination. Just like the child who is learning to walk and thus concentrating all its energies on this new task, apparently not making progress in other areas, the six-year-old temporarily loses interest in practicing actions in the realm of fine motor control and goes over to discovery of new connections, through which it arrives at a greater understanding of the world.

But no two children are alike in their development. Particularly during these periods of transition from one stage to the next, the open system has the great advantage of offering constant stimulus and impetus for language learning, without, however, giving lessons "in uniformity." In the second half of the seventh year, in those who have enjoyed a vacation from it, a new and intensive interest awakens in the art of writing. The children learn overnight, so to speak, what others have acquired in a long and continual process. To take our own son as an example: one week he could not write on his own, without a model or pattern to copy; in the next he was writing long essays and letters with which no one was permitted to help him. But however this process goes on, corresponding to the character of each child, the most important thing is to avoid a situation in which the child becomes a failure early on, only because the child has been taught at the wrong moment and under difficult conditions.

Before I try to describe various ways and means by which children can be helped to learn reading and writing on an individual basis, I wish to point out two basic differences between the traditional elementary school and the active school. In our society of today, in which children have less and less opportunity to be active in the full sense of the word—whether it is in nondangerous forms of play or participation in the life and work of the community where they live—the active school sees its work as follows: not only to teach the children knowledge and skills but also to provide them with a milieu in which they can be active and responsible in their own childlike way, without constantly causing offense, without disturbing or running into danger. Of course, this is especially important for city children. They live in limited space and usually cannot explore their neighborhood without risk and meet their peers. Their parents work in jobs or professions that are frequently incomprehensible to children. Many move so often that a feeling for community is lost entirely. On the other hand, it is important for rural children to be offered an experience of school that does not cut them off or alienate them from their accustomed life. School should be a confirmation, a verification, an endorsement of their real-life experience and show them how to reach a gradual abstraction and symbolization of their tangible experiences without having to give up their cultural values. Only in this way are we able to prevent them from feeling inferior to the inhabitants of towns and cities, with their spotlessly clean collars and marvelously matched colors of ties, or from renouncing their own origins and moving to urban areas themselves. Thus the active school becomes a place that helps to process life experiences and enables children to make up missing experience if necessary.

In this sense the active school invites everyone, teachers and pupils, not only to use a prescribed and straight route for the acquirement of skills and knowledge but to discover many different paths. This method may seem a waste of time as well as superfluous to those who want to get through as much subject matter as possible in a short time. It has, however, double advantages: on the one hand it promotes the natural creative predispositions of a child, and on the other it foments the child's curiosity and urge to discover, rekindling these inclinations again and again, instead of tiring and boring the child with the repetition of all that the teacher knows better anyway.

Both aspects are to be found reflected in how the active school handles the problem of language education. We see the school first of all as the place in which children are permitted to live every day to the full. In this milieu the spoken and written word is accorded a place of honor. It is not meant to be an object of exercise and cramming but, rather, an important element of a language-conscious culture, enjoying respect and even a form of celebration. All the hundreds of spontaneous activities of the children, which bring them so much satisfaction, reach a level of greater consciousness through language. Yet there is never a doubt that reality—tangible actions, personal interests, and feelings—is in first place, that language must stand in the correct relation to reality, that speech without action is not highly esteemed. If a child only stands around, giving long speeches to the others but not lifting a finger, one need not wait long for comments such as this: "Why do you talk so much without doing anything?! Get a knife and help us peel the potatoes. We can talk while we're doing that, too." The concrete action guarantees the right relationship between any form of verbal expression and reality, particularly at this age. So we respect spontaneous speech above all, which naturally accompanies every activity of the small as well as the older child, also serving to keep the activity going. We are always surprised by the great amount of egocentric talk that takes place, but it turns into real one-to-one conversation or a discussion through free social intercourse among peers. Free oral expression does not signify "forbidden whispering" accompanied by feelings of guilt. And it does not mean the question-and-answer game led by adults that calls for knowing the right answer or remaining silent when in doubt, in order not to make a fool of oneself.

What sense does it then make for children to express themselves in written form if they do not even feel free in verbal conversation? If the written form of expression of children is to be full of life rather than a cliché of regurgitated facts heard or read by them, we must not suffocate the liveliness of oral expression. This happens, though, when we accord the teacher, who has the most practice in speaking, the greatest right to speak in the classroom as well.

In the previous chapter it was discussed how different areas of subject matter to be learned merge into one another and that lessons in different subjects do not need to have lines of demarcation between them as represented by ringing bells and the closing of certain books and the opening of others. If we wish to come to reading and writing with the children, we need, other than a few technical aids, valid experiences above anything else: things that tremendously interest us, human contacts that give us warmth as well as require it of us. In these we find meaning in our doing and experience a personal participation that serves as a motive power for the complicated act of writing and helps us to overcome obstacles. This is an important principle for adults, thus how much more so for children, who must truly rely on the harmony with their feelings for a healthy process of growing!

Out of the manifold opportunities at an active school to connect concrete reality with its symbolization, namely the written word, some examples may be useful in this context. At the start it is the teacher who sees to it that the written word is present everywhere, leaping out from the various interest centers at everyone who looks. Later the children take over. Large symbols, signs, and announcements are produced, modified, or replaced by new ones, according to need. For instance, at the water table: PLEASE PUT ON APRON. Or: WHO CAN FILL A BOTTLE WITHOUT ITS RUNNING OVER? At the sand table: HERE WE PLAY WITH SAND and PLEASE DON'T THROW SAND IN ANYBODY'S EYES. In the kitchen: WHOEVER COOKS HAS TO CLEAN UP, TOO. At the printing press: ATTENTION: HERE ONLY LIES ARE PRINTED. At the terrarium: PLEASE WATER PLANTS. At the nature table: THESE

STONES WERE BROUGHT FROM RIO SAN PEDRO. At the animal cages: CAREFUL WHEN OPENING DOORS—THE DOG LIKES TO EAT RABBITS.

Everywhere they look, the children see such signs, printed in bright colors with magic markers, not to be overlooked. It does not take long for the children to start hanging up similar signs and decorations. Some interest centers are especially suitable for written information and activity cards. In the kitchen it is, of course, the recipe box with simple cooking and baking instructions. The experiment corner has its own box with suggestions from which the children are always getting new ideas for projects or things to do—the same is true of the weighing and measuring center. WHICH IS HEAVIER: A CUP OF WATER OR THE MAGNET? HOW LONG WOULD ALL THE TABLES BE IF WE PUT THEM TOGETHER? WITH HOW MANY MARBLES CAN YOU BALANCE A CUP OF RICE? MAKE YOUR ESTIMATE FIRST. The possibilities for such actions are unlimited, of course.

Each center has a sign bearing its name, ARITHMETIC CENTER, for instance. Next to it we put up lists of all objects stored on the shelves. Each object bears a label with the same name: wonderful material for comparison for beginning readers! Rules of play are clearly written on the numerous games of all kinds. Various suggestions are also given everywhere one can make something: in the sewing corner, the carpentry shop, the mechanics' workbench, the arts and handicrafts corner. We make regular shopping lists for the kitchen that hang in full view until the shopping is done. Then there are lists of names of children who have organized themselves into various work groups. On the sides of our shelves, which are covered with cork, hang pictures with the descriptions corresponding to them, interesting press clippings, publications from the school printing press, announcements about excursions, news that must be exchanged among various children, letters that have come from the world outside.

Long before a child is ready to use didactic material or read a book, he or she sees the written word at every turn, at every glance. The library and the reading corner naturally occupy a particular position in this connection. The reading corner is a cozy and comfortable place, with soft cushions, fiber mats, and a low table on which lie daily newspapers, magazines, soccer news periodicals, comics, and booklets of riddles. The bookshelves serve as room dividers as well, giving this space to sit and read a personal and homey atmosphere. Books for every taste and all reading levels, grouped according to language, are offered: fairytales, true stories, adventure, information, dictionaries and textbooks in all subjects, encyclopedias, and handmade books in three languages. This reading corner is seldom empty. Other than reading, it also allows rest and recuperation if energy is running low or someone is coming down with the flu, a place to listen to music or to a story read aloud, leaf through books still too hard to read, and last but not least, meet one's friends. When a child wants to read something aloud to an adult, he or she calls one of us into this nice corner. There we sit, crowded up against each other, often with our knees drawn up and our arms around them, or arm in arm, listening and reading aloud by turns. With the beginners we read sentence by sentence in turn. Later these portions become paragraphs or pages. The excitement of the story is maintained and/or heightened with this method, there are no signs of weariness, and without being conscious of it, the children gradually fall into our rhythm of reading, emphasis, and pronunciation, thus becoming able to read fluently and expressively, without pressure.

Large shelves hold a variety of didactic materials, most of them coming from the Montessori system for reading, writing, and grammar. Here as well our three languages are represented. The German- and English-speaking children do learn to read and write Spanish sooner or later, with no great strain or effort, but it seems important to us that each child learns to read and write in his or her mother tongue at the start. The introductory material is already available in the kindergarten. But some six- or seven-year-olds still benefit from the sandpaper letters (a basic learning aid of the Montessori method), which they tend to use when they are not sure of the way a letter is written. This movable alphabet lends itself to fun games of combination and serves as preparation for work with our school printing press. The well-equipped language shelf has boxes full of small objects for the first attempts at reading and writing, word and sentence cards with illustrations, commando cards, syllable blocks, essay topics, words and sentences to be put into the order called for by various categories, grammatical material of all levels of difficulty up to and including sentence analysis.

Next to this shelf is located our school printing press. We use it, following the example of Freinet, as an instrument for learning to read and write, and beyond that, for a number of other purposes as well. The more secure the children become with writing, the more the printing press serves to help them expand their expression and at the same time improve their spelling. They learn to "polish" an essay, a poem, or their announcements until these forms of written expression are truly "ready for publication." At an age when their curiosity about many things leads to a lessening of their interest in beautiful writing and division of pages, the printing press always brings them back to the necessity of presenting the written word in attractive form. Typesetting of letters and printing, drying, sorting, fastening together, and distributing the result give the children new contact with concrete things, opportunity for cooperation with friends, responsibility, and the necessity to organize their work.

Freinet's books as well as those by Hans Jörg give abundant and illuminating information about the various possibilities of a school printing press that are open to children. Our experience with this excellent device can add the footnote that its importance in the active school is a bit different than at a traditional school. Besides the printing press, we also have a great variety of other materials at our disposal that provide the children with just as much freedom of movement, cooperation, and creative activity. So it is no surprise that in this situation, the printing press is not craved as much as in those schools that offer much less opportunity to stand up, walk around, touch, and try out or have spontaneous talk with friends. Sometimes two or three weeks go by with no attention paid to the printing press—all the energies of the children are concentrated upon new discoveries. But from all this activity and liveliness, the printing press profits in the end, as soon as the children feel the desire to set down their experiences in writing and to publish them in some form. We believe it is important to allow the children this coming and going, and we are all the more pleased to see the fresh and often very original texts that spontaneously come about in this fashion. A few samples from our archives, translated from the Spanish originals, may bear witness to the love for writing shown by our children.

A seven-year-old boy writes:

> *Don't Go Away!*
> Please, don't go away.
> I will be here alone.
> I'm sad because you're going away.
> Without you I can't fall asleep.
> Stay with me, for I'm afraid of the dark.
> Please, don't go away!

An eight-year-old boy lets out his feelings:

> *Angst*
> The whole city has gooseflesh.
> At midnight the ghost gets out of the coffin.
> We pull the blanket over our noses.
> The ghost wants to scare us.
> It changes into a bat
> and looks for a new victim.
> With sharp teeth it bites a neck.
> I close the window and
> bury my face in the pillow.

Vinicio, our young teacher, had played wild games with the children at the swimming pool. When they arrived back at school, they preserved the experience for eternity in the following form, with the aid of the school printing press:

> *Complaints against Vinicio*
> Just you wait till we get you!
> We'll pay you back a thousand times

for what you did to us.
Hear our accusations:
Vinicio threw my shoe into the water.
Vinicio pushed me into the water,
just when I was nice and warm in the sun.
Vinicio drowned me.
Vinicio stole my towel.
Vinicio took the place by the window in the
    bus away from me.
Vinicio, what will become of you?

Here is an echo from the school kitchen:

All the Things We Eat
Veronica eats everything you give her.
Carolina eats only pancakes.
Alba eats French fries all day.
Tania eats strawberry jam.
Florencia makes *choquilla* from margarine, cocoa,
    and sugar,
but nobody wants to eat it—
except her.
Carmen eats vegetarian meat.
When we're all together, we eat
potato soup with fresh cheese, beaten egg,
    and lots of
parsley from the garden.

Here is an excerpt from a report about an excursion:

The Tunnel
We took along flashlights.
Thank goodness we had on sturdy shoes,
for the way down was full of rubble.
The fastest of us came to the tunnel first.
We turned on the flashlights

and walked on the tracks through the tunnel.
Good that no more trains go through,
otherwise we would be really dead.
In a niche we found the bones of Atahualpa.
In another one we found a hidden prehistoric
   lance.
We turned off the flashlights and
scared the last ones.
There were a lot of screeches!

And so it goes—in our archives are poem after poem, essay after essay. As long as they are still new, we let them hang on our bulletin board for a while, so that the children read them again and again. Every child puts a copy of whatever comes off the printing press into its ring notebook. By doing this we gradually come into possession of a reading book that reflects our own life and is full of memories for everyone. The children show off their works proudly at home and know the texts almost by heart from having read them aloud so much. On the last day of school, when children everywhere normally have their heads full of nothing but their school vacation, three of the children printed these lines and distributed them among their friends:

Last Day of School
We are together for only a few hours more.
A few hours to play with each other.
A few hours to cook something good
and eat it with each other.
A few hours to learn something new.
A few hours to tell about our adventures.
Why does school vacation come so fast?
I think we will miss each other very much.

In a German language textbook for second-graders, I encountered a two-page spread entitled "Reflection on Language." Based on two similar stories, the children are supposed to think about the different use of language in these stories. Let us recall how high the percentage of egocentricity is in the language at this age, and how low the level of reflective ability is, and we will have no difficulty whatsoever imagining to what degree such an exercise must have direction from the teacher. The children sit there, leaning over their books in great concentration. The teacher asks a number of pointed questions, skillfully leading the children to the point where they agree with the reflections of this teacher within an appropriate period of time.

In the same language book, we find a work unit designed to lead the second-grade schoolchildren into a critical analysis of opinions. On a beautifully designed page of the unit, we see a good twenty completely or partially contradictory opinions. It is a wild and colorful collection of statements about sports, health, characteristics of people, about the Negroes and the Chinese, about problems of the generations, about teachers, pupils, red-haired and black-haired people, furniture, and traffic. Out of all these opinions, one group of pupils is supposed to select the opinions they consider to be right, the other group all the opinions it sees as false. Sentences chosen by both groups are to be discussed first. The point of the game is for the children to attempt to convince one another of their own group's standpoint with its collection of "right" or "wrong" opinions, using examples and giving reasons. In this exercise the pedagogue hopes to teach the class something about prejudices, logical argumentation, and good examples. At the same time, it is suggested that the examples given be used to find adjectives as well.

Can we really educate children who are just beginning the concrete operational stage of their development, who therefore—according to Piaget—should be developing their structures of logical thinking through the use of concrete objects and situations in the next five to six years, into higher or greater abilities of thought by means of speaking and discussion exercises? Do the demands of teachers and textbooks really correspond to the spontaneous interests and the logic of the children for whom they are meant? We know from our "theoretical" knowledge of the development of a child that children can deal with causality, finality, and inversions or reversals only now and again during the concrete operational stage, that children suffer confusion if a problem has more than two or three elements and lies, in addition, outside their own realm of personal experience. In practice we may see that intelligent, clever children often adjust to our adult ideas in astounding ways. However, we also know the price they pay for it: a certain emotional insecurity and a certain rebellion, which comes out into the open during puberty, at the latest. And a multitude of children do not succeed in this adjustment and then live with the conviction that the fault lies with them.

The active school does without any practicing of logical debates in language lessons—unless they come from the children, spontaneously—and places the main emphasis on actions that, in accordance with nature, lead to clear effects or consequences. The ability to reflect is to grow out of the many tangible situations, little by little. As a result of the pressure exerted by real-life situations, the child gradually sees itself compelled to leave its egocentric way of thinking behind. The child begins to perceive different points of view and to live not only according to its own desires and needs: if I leave the table dirty, then I have no right to complain about the disorder of the others. If I say a stupid thing about another child, it will not be long before someone makes a negative remark about me. Even the very youngest soon learn that a bottle runs over if you fill it too full and that there can be unpleasant consequences if you do not pay attention and run into another child when carrying a tray full of things. Life shows its negative sides very quickly in a situation in which the powers of the children have a reciprocal effect on each other all the time. Illusions are destroyed faster and the necessity for reflection comes very clearly to the fore. Instead of "reflecting on language," the children learn to think about life.

Language education therefore takes place in the ready and tangible situation of our reality. The first books produced by first-graders themselves are picture books that reflect their world and their personal experiences. They dictate a suitable text to a teacher or an older child and then go over it again themselves with colored pencils. The library has quite a respectable section of first reading books such as these: "We Go to the Swimming Pool," "Our Sandbox," "Excursion to Rio Chiche," "Our Animals," "Carolina's Birthday Party," "What Adults Are Like." It is an entire series of reading books, composed and illustrated by the children themselves.

The older children put out a chronology called "Pestalozzi News." It is written by the children, or the children with the help or participation of teachers, and reports on the most interesting events of the week as seen by the children. "The rice burned. It took a long time to get the pot clean again." "A giant spider had spun her web from one pillar to the other. We got the big ladder and looked at it with a magnifying glass. Then we looked all over our grounds until we found a suitable husband for her. But the other spider didn't want to stay up there." "Today was Ladna's birthday. Her mother sent a big chocolate cake. We cut it very carefully into thirty pieces so that nobody got too much or too little cake. But we still had three pieces left over at the end and had to cut them into thirty minipieces. We had a very nice party. Each one of us gave Ladna a picture as a souvenir of her eighth birthday." These news sheets are hung in the library, making it look a bit like an old-fashioned Viennese café.

The whole atmosphere of the active school is suited to giving even the most timorous child confidence and trust. How can a child open up, give its feelings and thoughts forms of expression, if it still has no basic trust, either in itself or others? When the child then writes his or her very first little texts, we do not mark the mistakes. We adults naturally believe that a child will never learn to write correctly, that the child will become accustomed to the wrong spelling and never get rid of it if we do not eliminate the errors from the very beginning. We underestimate human intelligence and the inborn drive to pit oneself against reality, as far as one's own powers allow. "Fluency comes before exactness"—this principle is also true of the process of learning to write. When a child gives me its free essay to read, I ask whether he or she would like me to help with the correction of mistakes. If the answer is no, that is the end of it. If it is yes, I make a little card for every misspelled word, on which appears the correct spelling. For the children it is like playing detective to set correctly and incorrectly spelled words against each other and then to make their comparisons.

The correction of errors is a natural prerequisite before we give our works to the school printing press. The language shelf is also equipped with homemade copybooks and cards with the help of which the children can improve their inexact spelling in the course of time. On days when the children have "no better ideas," they like to write something that helps with their orthography and look for examples from books. Again and again we hear the question, resounding from all over the schoolroom, "How do you spell . . . ?" Whoever knows the answer offers it freely to the one in need. Sometimes we adults pretend that we do not know the right answer and look in the dictionary together with the children.

The children do not always have original ideas for "free essays," and the often-heard encouraging "Write what comes into your head" does not always lead to an inspired text. A connection to other subjects, including arithmetic, often leads more directly to articulate expression than "language for the sake of language." Supplies of helpful materials, constantly modified, replaced, or recycled, facilitate the finding of ideas for children. For instance, we put the first names of all children on individual cards, the family names on cards of a different color. Then suggestions for work are made. Which first name belongs to which family name? What does the child whose name it is look like—please write a description including height, color of hair, color of eyes, and so on. Ask various children what the names of their parents are, when they were born, what their favorite game is—and write it all down. These small reports and writing games are only one step away from statistics, curves, and similar operations, which actually have little to do with "language."

We have a variety of cards on which children discover similarities and opposites, then put them into order in lists—this leads to an orderly notebook and logical division into sections, as does the Montessori material for grammar. Sometimes the children simply have the desire to "copy" something: a story, poems and songs, unusual names of animals from the encyclopedia, countries with exotic names. Such things, and similar exercises, which are in fact copying, do require a higher level of concentration, however, and it is achieved because the exercises are voluntary.

The stopwatch is a popular partner for many of our writing and thinking games. Who can write the most words in five minutes? The most words that have to do with food, with traffic, with water, with school? With things that one can smell? Hear? Enlarging and reducing sentences, finding adjectives, putting the verbs of a dictation into the past or the future, doing this during the dictation itself, completing stories already begun or writing a beginning for an already existing end, taking essay topics with closed eyes from a box, describing pictures, writing poems, making rhymes: all of these are ideas also practiced in traditional language lessons, yet there is a different taste to them at an active school. Here the children can say no: "I don't feel like it today. I'd rather make a new cookbook for my mother's birthday." And the cookbook is produced with great love, while ten other children play a game of association with the same enthusiasm. Older children mix with younger ones. Some write thirty words in five minutes, some only six. And the big ones praise the little ones: "You can write really fast already!" Games like Scrabble and word lotto also attract children of different age groups. Thus competitive games become "family affairs" in which winning is not as important as the pleasure involved in doing something together.

For reading we follow the same path and have the same goals: what I do with pleasure today will be a cherished habit tomorrow. Alba, who could not sit still even for five minutes, learned to read from action cards. After every word read, she jumped up to execute the action corresponding to the card. If she was left to read a little book of five pages during this stage, she exhibited a nervous twitch and looked out the window with longing.

There is a big basket with a changing collection of folded papers, held together by paper clips. The children arm themselves with "fishing rods," that is to say, a stick with a magnet on the end of a thread. They fish out a paper and think over whether they want to do what is written on their slip: "Feed the rabbit." "Build a sand castle." "Record sounds using the tape recorder." If they like the idea, they translate it into activity.

Children make unexpected progress in life when they come across texts that really catch and hold their interest. A little soccer fanatic read nothing but things about soccer for a whole year before he widened his horizons. Thanks to his real interest, he had developed an excellent reading technique.

Maria came to us as a ten-year-old. Her mother had taken part in one of our courses for adults and was then in a position to detect signs of a school neurosis in her daughter, although her grades gave no grounds for criticism. One of the signs was that Maria took no pleasure in reading. Quite the contrary: as soon as she was sitting in front of an open book, she began to perspire profusely and her voice, normally assured, began to tremble. When I once made the suggestion to her that she find the longest words in a given story, not yet having any idea of her particular problem, she promptly got a nosebleed. I tried to calm her fears of reading for months. We sat close to each other while reading, I put my arm around her shoulders, and we took turns reading aloud, because she mixed up everything after only a few words and understood nothing of the meaning of what we were trying to read. The books that she brought over for reading were of the uninteresting sort: schoolbooks with boring texts, geological descriptions of kinds of stones, and similar things. It was impossible for me to get her to try out a funny or exciting book. She seemed completely convinced that reading had to be awful. After such a terrible reading session about "basic food-stuffs," I asked her if she had really found it interesting. She looked at me in astonishment and answered in the negative. "Then why do you want to read it?" She suddenly had to laugh. But the spell was finally broken when I acquired a book on sexual education for adolescents and hid it among the other books without saying a word. It was Maria who first discovered the book, as I had hoped, having noticed that she was a prudish girl who did not dare to show her curiosity about such things. She went to the farthest corner of the library with this very well illustrated book with its excellent explanations. Half an hour later she had finished it. Then she called all her girlfriends and read passages to them. It was like a conspiracy: giggling and "oh"s and "ah"s, loud discussions and admonitions to be quiet. Then Maria suddenly saw me at a distance and came running: "Imagine, I read a whole book. But is that reading now?" She still could not believe that one could discover a whole new world by reading and take pleasure in doing it! From that day on she went on a daily search for interesting books in the library and borrowed things to read at home on a regular basis. And then her mother began to complain, "Maria doesn't want to go to sleep at night anymore. She reads under the covers with a flashlight."

Writing and receiving letters is one of the most effective means to awaken and to maintain a spontaneous interest in reading and writing. For a long time now we have been searching for a suitable correspondence group here in Ecuador, a group of children who could correspond regularly with our children, as a group and on an individual basis. However, in the schools here such correspondence would be seen as a pure waste of time, because the teachers already have their hands full trying to get their curriculum into the heads of their pupils. At home these children have no desire to do any more writing, since they have already been plagued with it the entire morning at school. So we are now looking for such correspondence groups in other countries, in order to exchange not only letters, photos, and drawings but interesting material about our countries as well, to enable living studies of geography and sociology.

An active school full of illiterates? I believe the danger to be very small, even if our children do not learn to read and write before the age of seven or even eight, because they first have more important problems to solve. After all, language is meant to be an expression of their life. How does it help the children if they can read and write wonderfully but their real-life experience has little to do with this?

In this chapter I have been able only to sketch the way we approach language education here in Tumbaco at our school. In addition to the books of Montessori and Freinet, which are worth serious study despite their "advanced age," I would like to recommend most warmly two authors who offer many fruitful ideas on this topic: one is Herbert Kohl and the other is John Holt. In the latter's book *What Do I Do Monday?* the interested reader can find a veritable treasure trove of usable suggestions, which can be adjusted to one's own circumstances, for living practice in language teaching. We are in complete agreement with these authors that there is no one true method in this field. We must give the children the opportunity to develop their own style of life and, with it, the development of their language.

A teacher trainee from an Indian tribe in the south of Ecuador was especially interested in the children's spontaneous work in the primary school garden.

CHAPTER TWELVE

Arithmetic for Fun and Pleasure

As I began to note down my most important thoughts and main ideas for this chapter, I felt a well-known uneasiness in the pit of my stomach. This discomfort is a "friend of old," so to speak, an unmistakable signal that I am about to touch upon things that once caused me pain. Now, taking the time to respond to this feeling, I recall things from the past: memories and images, scenes I was once a part of. Here are some of these recollections, long forgotten yet still with me.

I am sitting in Munich at the breakfast table. I cannot get down my roll with marmalade. The coffee has an unpleasant aroma for me at this moment. I leaf through a notebook of formulas nervously, not really knowing what I am looking for. Today we have to take a math test.

At the sound of the bell I am standing with my classmates in our classroom. We are in a state of nervous agitation and promise one another to cross our fingers for each other. The teacher enters. We go to our seats in torment. While the fearsome test papers bearing the fateful mathematical problems that are to be solved—in three different versions, so as to ensure that one cannot copy from one's neighbor—are being distributed, my stomach reacts with terrible cramps. My breakfast is still lying in my stomach like a stone.

A few precious minutes are lost as the signs and figures on the paper dance in front of my eyes; I cannot judge whether the test is easy or hard. Then I pull myself together and try to decide which question I should do first. Here my mind goes blank—I have no memory of the time that follows. My recollection begins again two hours later, as I put my test paper on the edge of my desk, in accordance with instructions. The teacher goes down the rows with a look on his face that reminds me of an executioner and collects the papers in exact order (maybe someone has been able to copy—this way he can discover the crime more easily). When he reaches out to take my paper, I feel the stomach cramps start again.

A week later the teacher comes into the room with the feared folder in his hand. We all stiffen and go numb inside. Our external reaction is to throw significant glances at each other. A few courageous ones pretend complete unconcern. Everyone knows what is coming now: a ten-minute sermon about "such people who have managed to make it to this grade, although nobody can understand why or how," then continuing with "people who really are not so stupid, but blew it in this test," finally coming to those "who really have no reason to hope, but were lucky this time." The lecture goes on and on, and then comes the worst of all: "When you get your paper back, the only thing that interests you is the mark. So before you all get them back, we are going to go through the most important steps and write them on the board, so that you see the right answers and do not have to ask me unnecessary questions later." To every correct answer that appears on the blackboard, my stomach answers with cramps. I am unable to remember, no matter how hard I try, what answer I had gotten a week ago; I could swear that it was all wrong. Toward the end of the class hour, the tests are given back in the exact order of the marks, from high to low. The relieved sighs of those receiving their papers first are audible (comment from the teacher: "Don't let it go to your head—the school year is by no means over!"), whereas the last ones are stewing in their own juice. Comment to those at the bottom: "Exactly what I expected!"

How did I manage to stay more or less in the middle in math

for the duration of all my school years, and then get an A in my senior year? I remember that years later, when I was well out of the reach of my math teacher, I was still waking up at night with nightmares of having to do my math finals again and not being able to remember the calculations or formulas. For twenty-five years these memories have been carefully registered in my whole body. When I arrived in Ecuador I discovered for the first time that dealing with numbers could be an enjoyable game. From the Chinese, who live on the coast here and are the most successful shop and restaurant owners, Mauricio learned how to use an abacus. On some evenings in the jungle, we made it a pleasurable pastime, attempting to achieve greater and greater speed. Later we utilized this art of calculation in practice as well, and even tried to compete with electronic calculators. Since then I have lost my fear of figures a bit and enjoy beginning at the beginning with the Pestalozzi children. With them I discover the joy of combining, sorting, putting in order, forming patterns, drawing limits, measuring, weighing, and comparing, as well as finding forms, treasures, and symbols. We count and calculate, make friends with figures as though they were members of the family.

All these operations are completely natural for children. They are among their favorite things to do long before we think of talking about "arithmetic." Every movement of the body in time and space, every game with tangible things, every participation in the life of the family, in short, every relation to human beings, animals, or objects is, in reality, arithmetic and early mathematics for a child. But at the moment that we well-meaning adults take over the leadership, there is the danger that the natural flow of the child's thoughts and actions will be interrupted, that the child has to adjust to our abstract way of thinking, jumping over a number of its natural stages of development like an acrobat, in order to follow our explanations, fulfill our expectations, and prove to us its intelligence. Such acrobatics cause fear in many children, and as adults they still feel as though they are walking a tightrope when dealing with mathematical operations, a tightrope that can suddenly sag and give way beneath them. Others enjoy this feeling of height, which seems to take them far above a hard reality and provides a feeling of being superior, of ascendancy.

Teaching arithmetic in such a way that it leads children into abstract thinking before they are ready for it can be a critical factor in the process of alienation of an individual from reality. Thinking and feeling, thought and emotion, are still one when a child enters school and can remain unified for the rest of his or her life if they are not subjected to an artificial separation. Concepts that could be derived step-by-step from meaningful connections and life experience are robbed of their value and made all too open for manipulation if the process is shortened in too much of a hurry. These artificially learned concepts obey only the laws of expediency and lack the grounding of a "gravity" of their own that sees to internal and external balance.

Through Piaget's studies we know that the ability of abstraction in a child appears much later than we would normally imagine. The natural adaptability of children to given circumstances and the ability to compensate for a lack of true understanding by means of clever imitation, guessing, or learning by rote have often hidden this fact from us. In dealing with abstract numbers and their relation to each other, however, many children cannot fall back on the tried-and-true knacks and tricks that serve them so well in other subjects. Therefore it is no wonder that many children of normal intelligence get the feeling early on in their lives that they just have no talent for arithmetic.

At Pestalozzi I know of no child—except in cases of recent entries to our school from one of the traditional sort—who is afraid of arithmetic. The active school simply takes for granted that every normal healthy child has more than enough ability when it comes to dealing with numbers but that the child needs a very long period of working with tangible materials before being ready to move from the concrete to the abstract, as the natural result of the child's organic maturity and its experience with tangible things. Worried parents are always asking us, "But how are we to know when and if the children will ever be able to do math without concrete material?" In practice there can be no doubt about it: when a child gets too lazy to get all the material down from the shelf and go to all the trouble of spreading it out on the table, preferring instead, of its own free will, to do arithmetic in its head or on paper, then the time has come to help him or her with this. But as long as a child has obvious pleasure in moving things around, arranging, touching, and looking at the materials, enjoying the discovery of similarities and differences as well as the beauty of the patterns in his or her use of more and more parallel materials, it would be a great shame to put a stop to these valuable experiences and prematurely limit the child to pencil and paper. How flat and monotonous the pages of textbooks and workbooks are compared with the mountains of material to be found at an active school!

Although we avoid leading our schoolchildren toward abstraction too early, that does not mean we do without arithmetic. On the contrary, in all they do and everywhere they look, the children find themselves motivated to become involved with numbers and all the operations associated with arithmetic. This goes on in the sector of practical life, in the playful interaction of their energetic organism in the midst of an environment that favors movement, and through frequent use of our fully equipped arithmetic laboratory. These three areas are never separate from one another; they are each other's natural complements.

An American handbook for teachers maintains that the following basic terms and concepts must be "taught" before the seventh year of life so that later instruction in arithmetic can be successful: sizes and shapes (large/small, high/low, straight/crooked, and so on), lengths and distances, contents, quantity and amount, comparisons, determination of place, time, and speed, money, sensory description, and the use of numbers from one to ten. In our view, the best way to learn these concepts is through the child's own activity, aided by the free flow of descriptive words. At the water table and in the sandpile, during concentrated play with containers and implements of all kinds; in the kitchen during the processes of weighing, measuring, counting, and comparing, pouring and stirring, fetching and bringing, setting the table and serving food; in the garden when measuring beds, making furrows, putting in seeds, replanting and watering, writing down the date and waiting for the harvest; in the carpentry workshop when measuring and paying attention to angles; at the printing press when counting letters and spaces as well as the printed sheets, cutting paper, preparing ink, organizing the work process; in all manual activities that bring with them the operations of cutting, dividing surface area, drawing straight lines, folding, decorating, mixing, kneading, and shaping: in all these activities, which children learn to do so naturally and which make them happy, well-balanced people, we find all the practical basics of arithmetic, in addition to a great variety of sensory impressions and energetic movements. In each of these activities, only a small step forward, a little impetus, and a bit of help are all that is necessary to move on to "real" arithmetic; in the midst of the children's respective favorite thing to do, they can be brought into contact in a most enjoyable way with set theory, with addition and subtraction, with multiplication, division, calculation of surface area and contents, with percentages and other operations that for many students turn into nightmares.

Let us assume we are cooking for four. Then some children come in from outside and we ask helpfully, "Can't you double the recipe?" Calculation starts immediately and continues until all ingredients have finally been doubled.

Before we go shopping for the school kitchen, we make an estimate of how much money will probably be needed, using the shopping list as a basis. One child goes to get a slightly higher amount of money from the office and must sign a receipt for it. After this a small group goes into the village to do the shopping. Everyone checks the prices to find out whether there have been any increases and watches to see that the shop owner makes no mistake when adding up all the items. Purchases are divided up as evenly as possible among the children, so that no one of them has more weight to carry. Back at school everything is weighed again, prices are likewise rechecked, to make sure that all is correct. Finally the prices are added up a second time. Some think they can do this faster with paper and pencil but make mistakes. Others are a bit slower with the abacus and may or may not get the same results as their friends.

How big is the difference, how much is the error? How does it correspond to the change we brought back? The final sum is entered into the household record book. Then accounts are settled with the secretary in the office: the original signed receipt is exchanged for the cash register receipt and the change is returned.

At the end of the month, accounts are done again. Have we kept to our estimated budget? Monthly outlays are compared with those of earlier months. One speaks of how high the cost of living is getting, how expensive everything is, inflation and other problems of our times. The children slowly develop a sense of whether the funds remaining at the middle of the month correspond more or less to half of the budget—can they splurge a bit or must they curtail their spending? They talk of expensive and cheap food. At the store they ask for the "cheaper cheese" like experienced housewives and negotiate extras "thrown into the bargain" when buying tomatoes or onions. At the end of the last school year, they drafted a petition to the directorate of the school to push through an increase in the kitchen budget that read as follows: "Dear Director Mauricio, Foodstuffs are getting more and more expensive. Prices went up by 10 percent this month. Soon we won't be able to bake any more cakes. Don't you think that's bad? If so, then give us a little more money for the kitchen!"

When the children want to have a party and the budget does not allow any more money for this purpose, they agree that each one will bring something from home. There is a lot of consultation, many suggestions, equally many counterproposals, debating. The problem is a real one and the results can be felt by all. Concepts such as gram, pound, all sorts of amounts, liters or gallons, become familiar to all children.

These beginnings in the field of practical arithmetic are possible for all children and open to all. The younger ones prick up their ears when they hear the older ones talking. Everyone would like to write legible figures soon, so he or she can help with the entries in the housekeeping book. Dealing with numbers is present everywhere one looks or goes, as a natural function of human intelligence. Yet the normal flow of life is never interrupted. Among the weekly homework topics are to be found suggestions for practical calculations. The smaller children count windows, doors, pieces of furniture or clothing, plates, cups, and other household utensils, electrical outlets in the house, electric bulbs. They trace the hands and feet of family members, ask the age of relatives and family friends, measure the contents of cooking pots and the bathtub by liter, search for the longest, shortest, highest, and lowest object. The possibilities are unlimited. With a little imagination, children's houses are transformed into laboratories offering inexhaustible opportunities for mathematics.

The older children calculate using purchases from the shopping; they calculate age differences, measure people, distances, and objects using norms of measurement. They convert currencies, get information about prices in stores and travel agencies, count pedestrians and cars in a given period of time, make curves for various categories; they calculate surface area and space, averages and percentages. Everything that is used at home and thus part of experience can become a mathematical problem to be solved. Helpful parents occasionally send us a series of homemade arithmetic card files that show the "living arithmetic" of the family and can be put to use by classmates as well. Many similar examples of practical arithmetic can be found in the enjoyable little book by Celestin Freinet entitled, in the French original, *L'enseignement du calcul*. Those who work with "active children" can easily add on to these initial ideas.

Arithmetic is, of course, present everywhere in all the movements that children make: races, high jump or broad jump, swimming, ball games, tests of strength, whatever we call sport—all of it can be the most exciting form of arithmetic instruction if we let the children measure off the fields, if we equip them with measuring tapes, stopwatches, paper and pencil. The most extensive list of such ideas for arithmetic that are connected to a child's urge for movement that I have ever found is in John Holt's book *What Do I Do Monday?*. There children of all ages can learn to deal with lengths and heights, speeds, periods of time, performance curves, heartbeat, respiration, weights, conversion of units of length and time, estimates and comparisons—at all levels of difficulty—

without sitting at a desk for more than ten minutes at a time. I urgently recommend the perusal of this book to every teacher who has always been convinced that arithmetic cannot be taught without being still and sitting still!

For the quiet children or those who are out of breath, there is no lack of games that can be played without expending a great deal of physical strength. Shuffleboards with high and low numbers offer practice in the skill of aimed throwing as well as adding plus and minus points. They can be constructed in varying degrees of difficulty in order to practice both large and small numbers. Equally popular are games of chance and board games; otherwise considered pastimes for the weekends, they give elementary-school children growing security with numbers, adding up throws of dice, gaining an overview of situations, and planning ahead. If we have a guilty conscience when children exhibit too much fun in their play, we can give support to the arithmetic corner in the form of arithmetic lotto and dominoes for number combinations and set theory. Since these things are almost never available in stores here in Ecuador, we are accustomed to constructing new games ourselves. This way of doing things may also be recommended in situations in which the purchase of such games for experimental open classrooms would be too expensive. It is important not only to provide a few of these games but also to keep the interest of the children awake and fresh by means of constant variations. Pick-up sticks can be made by children, often in a much more original form than the ones you can buy. We have also constructed an inexpensive chess game together with the children. The African game called Wari is especially popular here at Pestalozzi. Wari is a strategy game for two players with twelve holes set in two parallel rows of six holes each, plus two bigger ones on both ends where each player keeps his or her stock of won seeds. The game consists in moving the forty-eight seeds (or pebbles, or little balls) according to very specific rules, with the purpose of stealing as many as possible from the adversary. In the beginning we played outside, making the necessary fourteen cavities with an old spoon in the sand or the earth. Later we made a ceramic form of the game, and now we have two Wari games made of wood for frequent use at school. To anyone who wants to find out something about the maturity of pupils and their ability to learn from experience, I can warmly recommend watching children of different ages at a game of Wari.

The play center is also equipped with geometric puzzles of various levels of difficulty, thinking blocks, labyrinths, and other such games, all of which invite the children to put on their thinking caps and solve problems. In addition, there are construction games and building blocks in a large variety of sizes and shapes, cars, if possible an electric train (too expensive in Ecuador, unfortunately). I invite those who draw back in horror from the idea of seeing schoolchildren playing with such "childish rubbish" during precious class hours to challenge themselves to find out how many mathematical contexts and connections coming from play with building blocks, construction games, cars, and electric trains they can find in the course of fifteen minutes. I am convinced that this self-challenge will lead to more respect for the play of children and prompt us to be of help to them so that they are able to make new connections and develop higher forms of thinking from their free activity.

This brings us to the third area of our active arithmetic lesson: the arithmetic laboratory, which we could not do without, in my opinion, despite the freedom allowed for practical life as well as movement and games. Without its help we would reach, in all our efforts to let children experience arithmetic as a living function, the limits of the concrete all too soon and be obliged to take recourse to paper and pencil, arithmetic books, and abstract explanations. Besides a great deal of natural unstructured materials, the laboratory contains a complete assortment of structured materials that help the child to build the bridge, very gradually, from the concrete to the abstract.

At the start we let the children measure with steps, length of hand or foot, fingers, elbows. But a bit later on they need measuring tapes and sticks that represent the norm as well as a great selection of interesting instruments to measure openings, cracks and grooves, widths and heights. Thus equipped they measure everything that can be found in their milieu. When they handle the usual instruments for geometry later, their use of them is permeated by the recollection of all their other measuring experiences in concrete situations. For weighing operations, marbles, seeds of all sorts, sand, and water are first used. Later we progress to standardized weights, and the simple homemade scales become household or letter scales, bathroom scales or a spring balance. Playing with sand or water, the children are content with receptacles of any size, representing no standard norm. Little by little they come to need standardized containers and measuring instruments of all kinds in order to carry out exact arithmetical operations. To work out concepts of time, which are formed only after concepts of place, we utilize a number of aids that illustrate the passing of time to children in the midst of their activity: drips, hourglasses of various sizes, clocks easily set by hand, metronomes, stopwatches, stethoscope—all of them are at hand.

The arithmetic laboratory contains many baskets and boxes with basic materials that can be counted, measured, and weighed: seeds of all sorts; stones of all shapes, sizes, and colors; shells, roots, sticks, leaves, feathers, corks, bottle tops, rice, corn, beans, tea, coffee, salt, sugar, sand, marbles, nails, paper clips. It is an endless list that can enjoy endless forms of variation and combination. Every new arithmetical concept can be processed in manifold ways, then extended and consolidated by means of new variations. To strengthen the ability to generalize and to apply this ability to new situations, every child needs much more experience with "the same thing, just a little bit different" than an adult would assume. Before we go on to new levels of difficulty, we should make it possible for the child to have experiences of a new quality on the same level.

Yet even the richest selection of unstructured material has its limits. Sooner or later we are faced with the necessity of providing the child with the opportunity for concrete experience with exact correlations, with the help of structured material. The Montessori material for arithmetic is of inestimable value in bringing order to many concepts that still remain vague after the use of unstructured materials. Without its help we would constantly find ourselves in the old role of explaining concepts. The Montessori material has all the qualities of tangible materials: attractive appearance and sensory impressions of all kinds. It leads the child from the qualitative and quantitative concept of numbers up through all the necessary levels of arithmetic: from simple addition to the division of decimals, the finding of square roots, and the independent derivation of the formula for cubic content. The teacher can simply leave the material in the hands of the child until the child has exhausted its own possibilities for play. The teacher recommends, "See what you can do with this. When you can't think of anything new, you can call me. Then I'll show you some things I have tried out." When I watch the children during their creative play with these materials, I often recognize new possibilities of use that enrich arithmetic learning.

Some Montessori teachers feel more secure if they show children the "right" way to use the material from the very beginning, the advantage of this being that the children learn the arithmetical steps "in the shortest way" and do not lose so much time. However, for the development of mathematical thinking, the shortest way is the least fruitful. In order to solve mathematical problems, we need only learn how to push the buttons of a machine nowadays. Therefore it is not such a stupid question when some children ask us why we have to learn arithmetic at all any longer. In the creative use of structured material, like the Montessori material, for instance, the playing child approaches discovery of mathematical thinking. Via many detours the child discovers connections, possibilities of shortcuts, reversal. It is truly a journey of discovery: not lacking in danger of losing the way, yet offering the prospect of discovering unknown territory and overcoming unexpected difficulties. What children write down in the course of their discoveries is often laborious, but it reflects the excitement and joy they feel in their doing. Here as well, positive experiences in concrete situations long precede their transformation into symbols.

Such constantly varying experiences with the concrete material, always open to modification and variation, are so much richer in value than working through a textbook that asks for underlining, drawing circles, copying exercises and doing them. Let us take as an example the material with which a child familiarizes itself with the decimal system: individual beads for the units, chains of ten, squares of a hundred, cubes for thousands, all put together out of beads.

The child can carry out all four arithmetical operations with this material. If the child gets 8,537 as an answer, for example, this figure can be experienced in all three dimensions. The child builds the tower constructed of eight cubes with great care, so that the tower does not fall down on the child's head, letting his or her eyes wander up and down this construction with pleasure. Next to the tower lie the five squares. From their height it is easy to see how much lower they are than the very high tower. Often only an admiring gesture is enough to draw the child's attention to this. A carefully worded question from the teacher at the right moment . . . and this child finds its way on to the next higher arithmetical operation, spontaneously and without urging or pressure.

Here is an example of how children automatically find shortcuts, all by themselves. The way of doing arithmetic described here was "discovered" by an eight-year-old girl before my very eyes. She then went on to recommend it, full of pride and joy, to her girlfriends. Maria Gabriela put out a great number of colored multiplication chains in quadrilateral form (the rows being distinguished by means of the different colors). It was a colorful design of chains of different lengths and colors. When her pattern was complete, she was to find the total number of beads by counting them. But she kept losing count, making errors. Then she came to a quick decision. She put all the chains of the same color together and got, for example, 5×7, 3×2, 5×4, and so on. She could already do some multiplications in her head, others had to be checked by counting. When she proudly showed me her "invention," it was but a small step to show her the generally known method of notation for this operation: $(5 \times 7) + (3 \times 2) + (5 \times 4)$, and so on. From that point on she tried both methods. Sometimes she laid out the chains and then wrote down the contractions; sometimes she invented a "tapeworm"—a chain of multiplications and additions—on her paper and then put out the chains to correspond to it.

A material for beginners often holds great possibilities of discovery for advanced arithmeticians. A square piece of cloth that is divided into sixty-four squares like a chessboard by bands sewed on it offers young children the opportunity to do addition of small sums in a crosswise direction. The child soon discovers the increasing values from one row to the next and sees with pleasure how the chains of the same color run diagonally across the cloth. While it is content with this "game" at the time, an older child is puzzled, if not to say intrigued, by the various diagonals of the same colors going across the cloth. Do they mean anything? If the curiosity of the child is aroused, pointing out new connections is great fun for both teacher and pupil.

Montessori material is very expensive to purchase, of course, and for many it cannot be afforded. Here in Ecuador, where an unfavorable exchange rate plus shipping costs and import duties would make buying it an impossibility, we must make most of it ourselves. Out of beads that the Indios wear around their necks in rich array, we produce the most attractive of materials. Native woods provide the raw material for most of the pieces made by hand in the carpentry workshop. The geometric material is not left alone for a single day. Who would regret the work that went into its manufacture?

Is it not frightening for a teacher if children of the same age cannot learn multiplication tables by heart at the same time? How can we be sure that a slow child will ever learn them? Our problem child Alba made the slowest progress that I have ever seen in a child. Her need for practical work with a lot of movement seemed inexhaustible. She never tired of using the didactic material over and over again, putting the little balls into the holes of the prepared boards. After a long time she discovered the multiplication chains, first the rows of two. Stimulated by this success, she went on to the chains for threes. She held the container with the chains in her hand, full of awe and respect. "If I want to, I can count the chains. But today I don't want to. Today I want to do them in my head." She walked to and fro in the classroom, wrinkling her forehead, and counted in her head for the first time: "Is it five?" She came over to me. I shook my head. "Don't you want to take out the chains?" She was steadfast in her refusal. "I can do it without them." This went on for an hour. She wandered around the classroom like a scientist on the track of an unbelievable discovery. She counted and counted in her head, holding the box in her hand like a treasure. She was determined to do without the aid of its contents. After this hour of hard work, she had conquered the threes up to thirty. "Nobody taught me. I found it out by myself." This conquest goes hand in hand with a feeling of happiness that has influence on all areas of her life. Her mother reports, "Alba is no longer the horror of our family. She seldom looks for arguments, doesn't find fault with what I cook, and doesn't constantly beg for money to buy sweets." Does undesirable behavior on the part of our children have something to do with the way they learn to read or write or do all the other things that are so useful for them?

For the quicker children, the transition from concrete to abstract occurs less dramatically and is often hardly visible to the teacher. Instead of gearing the entire class to the fastest children and pushing it on, we adults would be better advised to observe the slow transitions carefully and thoroughly, drawing new and much more enlightening conclusions from them. It could be the slower arithmeticians who do us great service rather than driving us to despair in group instruction.

CHAPTER THIRTEEN

Exploring the World

*For any human being caught up in the intricacies of ordinary ev-
eryday life, early education must provide the eye that sees, the mind
that comprehends, and the spirit which leaps to respond. Art teaches
and develops them all. That is the real justification of the important
place it has in education here today.*

—SYBIL MARSHALL

If we apply Sybil Marshall's thoughts to the active school, they
take on new significance as well as an additional meaning. We
can apply them not only to the important and often neglected subject of art in schools but also to the "art of life" in its overall and
global sense. At open schools all over the world, educators are in
agreement that the elementary school is not here to stockpile knowledge in the heads of children but to stimulate and encourage insight,
to give a "first taste of learning," thus promoting the process of
learning as a lifelong activity. Looking at it from this perspective,
we will find it easier to get away from the old model of "subject
teaching." Instead of carefully and rigidly separating natural science, geography, history, physics, chemistry, music, physical education, and art from one another, we help children to open their
minds, hearts, and senses and to "explore and conquer the world"
step by step. The more respected a child feels, the more coura-

geously it is able to initiate and consummate this process of opening up to the world—both the outer and its own inner world. It is easy to see that art, music, and physical education make sense only in contact with tangible materials and in concrete circumstances. Even in traditional schools, sketching pads and paint boxes are augmented by a variety of interesting materials. Here in Ecuador these possibilities are recognized only slowly and with hesitation, and classes in the arts still remain boring and sterile in most cases. Although the general population in this country has a natural attraction to music and rhythm, the enjoyment of music, as soon as it is taught as a school subject, is quelled almost systematically. One of our friends, who conducts a small orchestra and plays three instruments himself, maintains that he "understands nothing about music," only because he could not get the correct reading of notes into his head while still at school. Music classes are limited to monotonous rehearsal of patriotic songs, or religious ones at Catholic schools of one order or another, plus a hopeless drumming of basic music theory into children's heads—the latter could be learned in not more than three class hours by any child having access to musical instruments. However, from the experience of other countries, we know that meaningful and practical music classes provide real pleasure for both teachers and pupils and can become some of the most pleasant memories of one's school years.

In physical education the necessity of practice as well as direct interplay and teamwork with the real and tangible environment has never been doubted. Who would get the idea of substituting a lecture or a presentation with slides for a physical education class hour? We do, however, see physical education teachers who do not make a great deal of effort themselves, preferring to remain stationary and equipped with a whistle and wearing a spotless gym suit while barking orders at the children, who get their usual and obligatory sore muscles once a week. At least, however, the children learn to swim in real water; they do gymnastics on apparatus; play with balls and gain valuable experience with time and space; learn coordination, interplay, something about gravity, signs of weariness, speed, and so on—things that can give them information about themselves and the world they live in.

In a traditional school in Ecuador, where children are supposed to sit still and learn by listening, reading, and writing, these "subjects" are often the only chance the students have to get out a bit and the only source of movement in their entire school schedule. Some children who spend the morning in a state of sleepiness and disinterest wake up momentarily in these classes and show their lively side. It is the use of concrete materials that gives the children a reason to get up off their chairs, walk around, go and get something, take it back again. A little chat with one's neighbor does not bring immediate punishment of some sort. Skill or strength—both enjoy high esteem. More life comes into the children, and their bodies get what they need, making direct contact with the environment.

In the active school these "movement subjects" are not distinguished in a strict sense from the "real school subjects." Art and handicrafts, practical types of work, music, dance, and sports are valuable forms of expression for the active life of a healthy organism. They are great aids in building up self-confidence, achieving a feeling for balance, and fostering skill and harmony with one's environment. Moreover, they can become the starting point for innumerable kinds of "research," through which children and teachers can enter all fields of formal knowledge. If, for instance, a child plays with water for hours, the structures of comprehension necessary to understand physics, geography, and many other related areas of knowledge and experience are formed in the child. When these inner organic contacts are present, both the prerequisites and the readiness for formal learning are given. If they are not there, one has to fall back on methods of cramming sooner or later. In the previous chapter I mentioned John Holt's suggestions in regard to sports activities that, through the use of measuring tapes and sticks, stopwatches and other such equipment, lead to all operations of arithmetic and the art of setting up and keeping statistics. The most interesting aspect of this kind of teaching is the fact that the body of the child and its life processes are the focus. Instead of suppressing the urge to move that children have or evaluating it only in the form of competition, it becomes the starting point for exact observations, comparisons, measurements, and calculations. Here is one example: The length of a track for a race is measured first of all. Then the children take their pulse and write it down before the race begins. Afterward they repeat this operation and compare the results. They rest, let's say for five minutes, take their pulse rate again, run down the track once more, make their comparisons a second time. All results are written down and estimates are made. How long does the body need after such a race to function "normally" again? What is the correlation between the increased pulse rate and speed? What happens when the runner has to carry weights? A large number of questions come up, they are put in relation to reality, which in turn generates new questions; techniques of measurement, calculation, and notation are practiced. And all of this is done without ignoring for one moment the natural need of children for movement.

Or take handicrafts as an example. The children build boats out of different materials, in different shapes and sizes. We give them the freedom to go about doing this as they see fit, even though we could easily foresee that some of their creations are beautifully decorated but not very seaworthy. We keep this wisdom to ourselves. Rather than confronting the children with our greater experience, we make it possible for them to go down to a nearby stream on a little excursion. With a lot of excited shouts and many bets, the various boats are put in the flowing water to set sail on their first voyages. "Why does your boat stay on the surface and mine capsizes?" Again it is reality and not the authoritarian judgment of adults that compels the child to ask questions, reflect on a problem, and make corrections. "This time I want to build my boat different, so it doesn't lose the race again." This may be the right moment at which to offer illustrated books with models of ships, to measure them, then convert the measurements to the desired scale, organize trial runs in the school water tank, and discuss the findings. A few children go on from here to the history of seafaring. They devote themselves to reading about the great sea journeys of exploration; they study maps, learn geography, become interested in ocean currents or whatever has to do with oceangoing ships. The active school gives priority to the concrete activity of the child, but it does not stop at that—it also shows ways that a child can gain knowledge secondhand. Yet the most important thing is that knowledge is not "put upon" the child from outside but follows from the natural curiosity of children. Therefore it does not matter whether it is a question of the child's own or others' experience: the point is that the impulse stems from an active search for comprehension.

How can we achieve it—that children explore and conquer the world without losing themselves in the process? We believe there is no other way than always to proceed from the personal and concrete experiences of the child. Each child comes from home with its own experiences, and we have no right to cut the child off from its reality at home after it comes through the door to school. The environment of the school must be formed in such an interesting way that the senses work on as high a level of consciousness as possible. The individual prerequisites of children are, however, so different that the respective decisions made out of free will, stating, "This is what I want to do today," will of necessity be equally varied. Recently we were sitting in the primary-school room, silent after the end of the school day, deep in conversation with a married couple who had moved close to our Pestalozzi school for the sake of their three children, when the oldest of these, their ten-year-old son, came wandering in. We could literally see how his attention increased a number of degrees after entering the schoolroom. He seemed to prick up his ears, his eyes opened wider, and his hands moved as though they wanted to grasp something. Slowly and thoughtfully he went around from one interest center to another. Finally his eyes fell upon the printing press. He pulled up a chair and, without saying a word, began to put in place the letters a child had left in a small box that morning because there had not been sufficient time left to return them to the press.

This awakening of the senses in a stimulating environment is what causes every child to make the connection to its own early experiences. This process in turn leads to new activity, to the solution of practical problems, to the posing of questions. If this process of internal and external activation is able to take place anew each and every day, we give the organism of the child opportunity to fulfill old needs, to avoid new blocks, and thus to open up new channels through which an understanding of outer and inner experiences can flow without hindrance or obstruction.

In the favorable atmosphere friendly to children of an active school that is well equipped with a wealth of stimulating materials, a similar process occurs in all situations: for every new material that the children find waiting for them, they need a period of time for a free "trying things out" that often seems unbearably long to us adults. When we first set up our little scientific laboratory, the children kept finding new variations of mixing fluids in test tubes, shaking them, heating them, letting them settle to the bottom, suctioning them up with eyedroppers, filtering them, and—as the grand finale—showing each other their "experiments," complete with explanations. A large work surface had been covered with a plastic tablecloth, just to be sure. The children had to clean up everything after all their experimenting but were otherwise left to themselves with their operations. Only once in a while did one come to us to show off his or her wonderful work. In general the joy in trying out things and the concentration were so great that the children completely forgot everything else around them. Weeks of such undirected activity went by; we had to continue bringing more and other basic materials. Then at last the time seemed ripe to offer ideas and new proposals. After the first hunger for free activity had been satisfied, movements were calmer and facial expressions were more thoughtful, and the children seemed inclined to allow themselves to be guided into new directions by questions and suggestions. In this second stage they called us more and more frequently, showed results, asked for advice, and appeared willing to become involved in conversation and write down findings. Even later on, their interest had grown so much that they had discussions without concrete activity and obtained new information from books.

If we follow this process attentively and truly allow the full time for the things that a child needs to try out freely and approach playfully, two remarkable facts become apparent: on the one hand, children come up with many more variations and questions than we ever would have touched on during directed classes, and on the other, they go through phases that seem to have nothing to do with "pure science" but quite definitely with emotion. An example from the annals of our school may throw some light on this point.

From conversations with Alicia's mother, I knew that the relationship between the two of them had been tense for quite some time. The mother is an "artist type" with long gray hair, dressed in an unfashionable way for society here. Her circle of friends is a bit out of the ordinary, she avoids normal social life, and she has as well certain difficulties in giving her daughter human warmth and maternal love and affection. She feels herself often bothered by her daughter when she wants to paint, forgets that Alicia needs other children to play with and that the natural beauty of the lovely valley to which she has retreated to make a home for herself and her daughter is not enough for the child. Alicia compares her mother with other mothers and has been living for some time now with the fear that her mother may even be a "witch." This story had come to my ears during a talk with Alicia's mother, who had come in to request advice for positive coexistence with her daughter.

Alicia was experimenting in the laboratory. She had just gotten to the stage of counting drops, holding the test tube up to the light, mixing, shaking, and writing down her results. The typical pedagogical observer could easily have gotten the idea that all conditions were now right for the introduction of the next phase, namely guided instruction. But suddenly her facial expression changed unexpectedly. Her voice, which had accompanied her activities, became a singsong. Her movements became rapid. She mixed all sorts of strange things. I heard her asking another child, "Do you want to play witch with me?" More and more children were attracted by the game. It got to be a real attack of witch fever, and I began to fear for the safety of the fragile instruments of the lab. On my advice the children took themselves outdoors and got into faster and more furious play with unbreakable props. They mixed sand, water, and paints, chopped leaves, squeezed the juice out of various plants. In the end there was no receptacle to be seen that was not filled with "poisonous" liquids, no stick that had not been bewitched. The game became so intensive that the entire class was pulled into play. Witches' dances were performed, songs having been invented for this purpose. It was only with great difficulty that I was able to get the children to clean up their indescribable mess when it was time to go home. For two more days the game was revived by individual groups of children, then it disappeared, came back again in the tame forms represented by puppet theater and printing press, and was never seen again. Chemistry became "scientific" once again, and Alicia's mother reported with relief that her daughter showed more trust in her, bothered her less when she was working at the easel, and often came to sit close to her and paint on her own.

How often do we catch ourselves wanting—and trying to get—children to see the world from our own adult perspective as quickly as possible! And yet we cannot remind ourselves often enough that our impatience only leads to a prolongation of the state of childish egocentricity as well as limitation or postponement of the child's ability to open up fearlessly to new impressions. It is the ability of the young child to let in experiences and sensory impressions in a free flow, without separating them from each other or putting them in logical relation, that allows the child to store up a rich treasure trove of living experience. This treasure is processed gradually, later providing the raw material for formal thought. We know from Piaget's study on judgment and thought processes in children that most children feel insecure with logical connections up to the onset of puberty. For a long time it may be a riddle to them whether a person from Geneva can be Swiss at the same time, or whether all Swiss are also from Geneva.

Representatives of the active school consciously include this in their "program." They allow children new experiences on each day of school, with new materials and in new combinations and contexts. The senses are meant to be awakened and sharpened, descriptive words to be practiced, and intelligent actions encouraged. All the things brought into the classroom for the purpose of stimulation and animation may be touched and used, not just looked at in awe. Excursions gradually extend the area of the child's experience and build the bridge to the area of experience of the adult. After the ninth or tenth year of life, the desire grows in the child to touch upon and become involved in topics or areas that are beyond its personal experience in terms of time and space. Let us take as an example a small child who, in accordance with its early predispositions, handles rhythmic instruments and learns to accompany its first songs. Later the child will perhaps show interest in learning a simple instrument of melody. With growing skill, suitable material, and a little help, the child makes its first primitive instruments. Later follow experiments with transcription of tones as well as their amplification and deadening. From here it is but a short distance to an interest in the hearing process, which is nourished by illustrations from books, drawings of the child's own, measurements, and comparisons. If a child has been able to experience fully its level of maturity and its spontaneous interests in accordance with these stages of development, then an understanding of the history of musical instruments, an enjoyment of good music, and a feeling for the significance of modern sound technology will not present any difficulty for the child.

By means of this method, which takes as its starting point the personal experience of the child and is borne by respect for the internal processes of the child, we are at last able to make clear the basic differences of the outside world to be explored. In his *Guide for the Perplexed*, Ernst Shumacher divides the areas of knowledge that deal with the outside world into two main categories: the "descriptive" sciences, such as natural science, and the "instructional sciences," through which we learn to examine how systems work and their possibilities of application. Chemistry and physics are the foremost representatives of the latter category; formal logic and mathematics aid in the successful exploration of these areas. The decisive question of a researcher in the investigation of this category is, "What must I do in order to achieve certain results?" A playful, not always careful handling of things and substances enables a child to explore this world of unfeeling objects and reactions and thus to develop logic through this continual, repeated, yet always changing activity.

In contrast to this, personal association with living things, planting, giving care, observing, experiencing birth and growth, aging and death, imparts respect for a world with feeling that follows its own laws. Just as the child is able to feel itself and knows itself to be respected, it recognizes and feels the needs of other living things. To the same extent that the child knows itself to be protected from manipulation and false or bad treatment, it learns to treat other forms of life with esteem and to protect them if necessary.

At the end of the last school year, we drew up for the first time a five-page "certificate" or "report card" for our children, in which the attempt was made to describe, that is to say, put down in written form, the various activities and the progress of each child. This information was meant to give parents an idea of the child's work at school and to do justice to the demands of the Ministry of Education, without using the usual system of marks. The faculty of teachers of a public school in Quito gave every activity listed in this certificate the number of the grade in which this subject matter is usually done. The following remarks received surprising comments:

Treats animals with care. *Impossible—all children are inconsiderate!*
Takes care of plants and premises. *Children can only destroy!*

If schoolchildren are to learn to explore the world in the right way, we can do nothing but let them experience—in direct contact with the real world—the qualitative difference between the more or less lifeless things that can be manipulated and living nature in all its innumerable manifestations. No moral sermons about environmental protection, no slides or artistically illustrated books, can manage to give a child the feeling for living things. We believe that children who have experienced respect for their authentic needs and desires will protect all living things in this world. Exploring the world—does it not mean learning to love and to respect life? Only when children do not lose the feeling for their own life can they appreciate the value of life in other living beings and learn to take on responsibility for their surroundings in this world.

CHAPTER FOURTEEN

Freedom and Responsibility

At our Centro Experimental Pestalozzi, we see many visitors pass through our gate: parents searching for a suitable school for their children, the parents of our Pesta children spending their "regular morning" with us or showing relatives and friends of theirs the school, curious teachers from other schools, instructors and students from both the universities in Quito, sometimes visitors from abroad as well. They touch something here, something there, admire the variety of the materials, perhaps cannot resist trying out an experiment themselves or beginning a game. They may shake their heads in disbelief at the idea that one can figure out square roots using a handful of colored plugs (a declared hobby of one of our children is to demonstrate to unbelieving visitors the extraction of square roots from five-digit figures). They recall the classroom of their own childhood and marvel at "how times change," how a schoolroom can look like an atelier or workshop. If they have studied psychology, they are full of praise for all the tangible material that promotes the development of intelligence, a fact for which there is substantiated proof.

Yet it is a rare adult who does not register his or her doubts and fears, in one form or another, in regard to the freedom of the children. If we hear the word *freedom* in connection with *school*, our

227

imagination immediately produces horrifying images: children who, at the sound of the bell, throw open doors and represent a danger to the corridors and stairs of the school with their shouting and pushing, children who beat each other up and give insolent answers to teachers, who break windows and destroy school property, scribble in books with indelible ink, tear the legs off unfortunate flies, do not allow their hair to be cut, and schlepp their feet like old washerwomen.

Others have a milder form of this fear of freedom: Won't the children get used to doing just what they like best all the time and avoid difficulties of any kind? How are they all supposed to get a balanced education? How are they going to get accustomed to the discipline necessary in our society at a later date? Confronted with the necessities of life, will they suffer a shock that razes all the advantages of the active education? A teacher from a good old traditional school expressed her worry in the following words: "You cannot teach multiplication tables if it isn't quiet in the class!"

Our convictions are in fact influenced by the way our brain functions. In his book *The Mechanism of Mind*, Edward de Bono describes in an astonishing way how dependent we are, when analyzing something, on the mechanism of our mind that prefers extreme contrasts in order to come to a decision or judgment as quickly as possible through the effect of such oppositions. As he argues, such a fast judgment is of great advantage when it comes to self-preservation. Partial views, tones of gray, and fine detail are sacrificed in favor of a yes or a no decision. However, to come to a deeper understanding, it is necessary to drop this attitude or position of self-defense, to relax and take one's time, in order to look at something from various angles or viewpoints, to "get a feeling" for it, and to speak de Bono's magic word *po*, which he writes about in *Po: Beyond Yes and No*. With this word we can—as he advises—initiate a process that makes possible unexpected and novel solutions. It means something like "let go, open up," "the solution that you need is surprising and does not come out of the direction you have been thinking in up to now."

If we apply this principle to the problem of freedom in the

schools, the first thing we notice is that there can be more than just two contrary ways of approaching the issue of discipline. Perhaps we have been accustomed to dealing with the terms *authoritarian* and *antiauthoritarian* up to now. Authority means that we believe in order at school and use our authority to produce it. We want to see results and we presume that an adult can best determine the "what, how, and how much" of work to be done through which such results can be achieved, by means of pressure if need be. The main weight of this argument lies in the demands that surroundings and the prevailing social structure make of the individual, indeed force upon him or her without consideration of inner realities.

An antiauthoritarian education may be preferred if the overwhelming power or predominance of these outside demands causes us concern, if we wish to give an individual as many rights as possible, even if the exercising of these rights should lead to all sorts of stress for the environment.

In real life, however, there are countless situations in which neither the authoritarian nor the antiauthoritarian principle makes sense. Actually, all life would long since have disappeared from our planet were it not constantly maintained by a natural law that, always and in all things, tends to a balance between outer and inner, high and low, heavy and light—indeed, balances everything that tends too much to one side without consideration of the other.

Let us take as our example for this a situation in which a group of adults rents a vacation house. Every single one of them has the desire to relax and have a good time. None of them wishes to take on responsibility or tell another what to do. All hope for a harmonious and enjoyable vacation. It is easy to see how, even in such an apparently unstructured situation, spoken or unspoken rules will influence this period of living together as well as the actions of each individual from the first moment on, how bits of responsibility and roles are distributed, here and there forms of freedom are limited. Even when no one person feels himself or herself to be the authority and no one would tolerate authoritarian behavior on the part of another, leadership is taken over and accepted for the time being. Let us say that one of the vacationers knows the place already from previous visits. The others will take his or her advice: which are the best restaurants, which hiking path is too strenuous for some yet just right for others. If one person is an experienced sailor, the others will be happy to take instructions or go for a sail as passengers. Another loves adventures with risk. Others with similar tendencies but less initiative will follow the lead of this person. Sometimes a member of the group will be interrupted in the middle of a favorite pastime by another member; should there be an emergency of some kind, all will forget their momentary pleasures and be prepared to make sacrifices.

Such "functional" discipline is applied consciously or unconsciously in all situations of life where—and when—a natural life has not been given up in favor of an artificial form. In ever changing gradations, shades, and guises, this is also the discipline of the active school. Let us look at an example from everyday practice that very well illustrates this form of functional discipline. Two boys are hammering away at a piece of wood. They are completely absorbed in their work and forget everything and everyone around them. Several other children have difficulties hearing each other, their communication is disturbed, and so they call out to the noisemakers, "Can't you guys go and hammer outside? We can't hear ourselves think!" "Okay, if you ask us to," reply the two carpenters, and they take their activity outside the front door.

Concrete activity of children with concrete materials brings a lot of movement along with it. There are always moments during the school day when children loaded with materials they are transporting from one place to another almost run into each other. They learn to go past one another, make more or less polite reference to their own clumsiness, and apologize. They ask each other, "Can you clear a little space for me at your table?" "Who can lend me a few thousand?" (This refers to the tangible materials for arithmetic!) "How much longer do you need these chains?" If a can full of beads is knocked over and the beads all roll on the floor, other children who happen to be close by bend down as well to help pick them up, as though it were the most natural thing in the world, provided they are not in a state of total absorption in their own activity.

It is the case with many of the structured materials that we own only one of them, or there are but a very few sets. It happens again and again that someone must wait until another is finished with the material that he or she wishes to work with. Children and adults see themselves faced with new situations time and again; they must decide whether their activity affects the freedom of another or whether they feel disturbed by another. They learn to judge how far they can tolerate such disturbances and where they must draw the line. Our house rules, which enable us to live and get along together and provide the necessary security and safety for each of us, are few but effective—they are respected by all. Those who refuse to follow them are corrected by their classmates, not always in a gentle or polite manner. The rules are so simple that "a child" can personally experience and comprehend why they are necessary. What is used must be put away again so that someone else can use it. The activity of an individual or a group must not bother others. People may not be injured or hurt in any way; materials may not be damaged maliciously or intentionally. Whoever takes part in a voluntary work or activity group accepts the discipline of this group.

Protected by this functional system of order, yet still free to go about their self-chosen activities, the children gradually gain an ability to concentrate and thus a self-discipline that is comparable only to the devotion, perseverance, and absorption shown by a creative person at work. They feel themselves so deeply at one with their activity that they spare no effort in this work and often forget to eat and drink. The activities of the other children around compel each individual to choose—out of the wide range of stimuli—either those that lie closest to his or her own interest and to follow them, ignoring all others, or to filter out from consciousness all impressions from outside and give attention only to this personal interest. According to studies on the function of the human brain, as discussed by Gordon Taylor in *The Natural History of the Mind*, human intelligence is fostered by exactly this ability to choose the stimuli corresponding to one's own organism. With this we can begin to doubt whether it is really worth all the effort to get a class quiet by means of all the stress and strain attendant on this, in order to have at last, following pleas, threats, and/or punishments, the wonderful silence in which all can then learn multiplication tables or concentrate on some piece of work. In the active school we see the highest forms of concentration every day in the midst of a truly excessive range of distractions.

What is this ideal of ours that has such sway over us that we only define learning as that which is done under the instruction of an authority, according to a fixed schedule, marching to the same drum, with often monotonous repetitions of the same kind of exercise? Do our schools try to utilize methods that awaken the authentic interest of children and thus in turn their gifts and talents in the most effective way, or is the greatest possible conformity of the children to the prevailing society the thing most important to them? In *The Third Wave*, an analysis of our sociological reality, Alvin Toffler describes how the conditions of our generally accepted economic system influence the methods and ideals of the educational system. In his chapter on the "unofficial curriculum" he writes:

> As work shifted out of the fields and the home, moreover, children had to be prepared for factory life. . . . If young people could be prefitted to the industrial system, it would vastly ease the problems of industrial discipline later on. The result was another central structure of all Second Wave societies: mass education. Built on the factory model, mass education taught basic reading, writing and arithmetic, a bit of history and other subjects. This was the "overt curriculum." But beneath it lay an invisible or "covert curriculum" that was far more basic. It consisted—and still does in most industrial nations—of three courses: one in punctuality, one in obedience, and one in rote, repetitive work. Factory labor demanded workers who showed up on time, especially as assembly-line hands. It demanded workers who would take orders from a management hierarchy without questioning. And it demanded men and women prepared to slave away

at machines or in offices, performing brutally repetitious operations.[1]

According to Toffler, generations of young people have meanwhile come out of this more and more strictly controlled school system and guaranteed the functioning of the industrial model of life. This educational style of the second, that is to say, industrial, wave has been taken over by the capitalist as well as the communist countries. The countries of the Third World, having reached the second wave only at a later date, are no exception in this regard. Quite the contrary: in fear of perhaps missing out, the schools in these countries exhibit even more drastic methods than are still considered acceptable in the more "progressive" nations.

If we follow Toffler's arguments a bit further, we find that we are already on the threshold of a new, third economic wave. Even for those who insist on absolute conformation of the individual to the needs of society under all circumstances, the question arises whether the educational ideals of the second wave will remain those of the third wave. For Toffler, in any case, there is no doubt about it: the third wave will no longer demand the same combination of punctuality, obedience, and willingness to do routine work but rather will favor certain abilities that distinguish us from the wonder machines of microelectronics, or are supposed to. For these skills we need the highest possible level of integration of all our mental structures, free access to our emotions, and a power of judgment and decision that is yet to be achieved by microelectronics despite all its refinements.

Decision and judgment: these are two concepts that lead us directly to the issue of freedom and responsibility. In order to make decisions, we need the opportunity to practice them unceasingly and in the most varied of situations. Although it is on a higher level of consciousness, such practicing is comparable to the use of our muscles. A small child learns how to walk not by listening to lectures or reading about the right sequence of movements and the laws of

---

1. Toffler, *The Third Wave*, 45.

balance, gravity, and speed but through untiring practice. The child falls down innumerable times and gets up again just as often. Once in a while the child needs help, but above all it needs freedom of movement and a varied environment in which it can overcome new difficulties without great danger and achieve a mastery of this discipline of walking. If a small child is just at a sensitive stage for learning to walk, it is untiring and persistent, sparing no effort whatsoever.

Even this everyday example can teach us how much the extent of freedom of movement determines the degree of responsibility. As long as we take the child by the hand, it leaves the responsibility as well as the leadership up to us. We see to it that the child does not step in a puddle, stumble over a stone, or get run over by a car. But if the child goes off on its own tour of exploration, it is much more attentive to obstacles. The child thinks a long time about whether it can dare to jump over a ditch, and examines every obstacle very carefully to decide whether it feels up to it. The child's consciousness in the act of walking is on a higher level, so to speak: it feels responsible and learns, in this responsibility, to correct its mistakes. If the child falls and hurts itself, then it learns to endure the consequences of its own actions. In contrast, a child that is led by the hand by an adult, to whom it transfers responsibility, also "walks," yet the quality of this walking is not the same. The level of consciousness in the act of walking is different, lower: the adult looks ahead for the child, corrects its direction. The inattention of the child is immediately compensated by an action of the adult. And if it does fall, the child does not feel fully responsible for this mishap. The child will be much less prepared to connect the pain with its own error and may even accuse the adult, "You didn't watch out."

There can be no doubt: if our children are to have the ability to come to decisions, make judgments, and take on responsibilities, they need countless opportunities to practice this "art" today. If school is to serve as preparation for a future in which, assuming we believe Toffler's analysis of the flood coming in as the third wave, demands on the individual will change together with a changed and changing society, we must change the "hidden curriculum" in schools today. What human qualities will be of importance in the third wave, replacing the combination of obedience, punctuality, and routine work? Toffler makes it clear and graphic for us: processes of production will be taken over by highly intelligent machines that are obedient, reliable, punctual, and without aversion to routine. Human beings, in contrast, will plan and direct the work of these machines by virtue of their creativity and imagination. They must be able to prevent problems in the production process as far as possible, organize complicated tasks of work, and foresee bottlenecks. Therefore they must possess a high degree of attention and ability to adapt to unforeseen situations if they are not to be the slaves of these intelligent machines, forced to hurry over at the most inappropriate times to avoid a catastrophe.

Moreover, we could imagine that the individual will have more free time and private life through this liberation from monotonous routine work. The family—or whatever we will then call a circle of people living together in a close relationship or relationships—will probably spend more time together than is the case today. Today it may be difficult to see whether a husband does not talk to his wife very much because he comes home from work already dead tired or because he does not really get along with her anymore. If we have a lot of time for each other, we must learn anew how to communicate, how to master our emotions and our human frailties. The new "hidden curriculum" should therefore give our children the opportunity to get to know their feelings in many unexpected situations and learn how to deal with them in a responsible way.

When we try to unify these elements, we must of necessity arrive at the assumption that the future will challenge well-integrated people, who differ from the intelligent data-processing machines in their creative powers, power of emotion, and a high degree of consciousness. Creative and analytical thinking, feeling, deciding, judging and assessing, responsible action at a high level of consciousness: all of these must be practiced in school today. The old teaching methods that limit consciousness and repress feeling, that place the most important responsibilities in the hands of an authority, should not be sufficient for us any longer. Even if we mean well by our children and are convinced that we know what is good for them, getting them to do our will (whether by good means or bad) does not constitute doing them a favor any longer, if indeed it ever did. It may hurt them and us as well (use of a muscle out of practice is known to produce a case of sore muscles), but we must learn to feel, to decide, to judge, and to be flexible in unforeseen situations, and we must learn all of this today.

In spite of our fear, we must deal with the issue of freedom in schools. Are we now perhaps looking at each other questioningly? When were we ever free? At school? At work? How much experience with freedom do we have that we can share with our children? Let us recall occasions during which we experienced ourselves as alive, in possession of our feelings, full of interest, as a "complete and whole human being." From such life situations—be they in the family, with friends, on vacation, in particularly interesting work—we must construct the model for the "school of the future": a school of being, which does not shut out knowledge by any means; only when I "am" can I really "know."

John Holt, who has advocated new forms of education for many years in the United States, writes the following in regard to this:

> Some might say here that the freedom one person gains another must lose. Not so. There is no one lump of freedom, just so much and no more, from which everyone must try to claw the biggest share he can get. The greater freedom I have and feel—and in large part I have it because I feel it—has not been won at someone else's expense. To some extent, and I hope more all the time, more freedom for me means more freedom for others—administrators, teachers, parents, and above all students and children. The less we are bound in by some tight and rigid notion of the way things have to be, the more free we all are to move and grow.[2]

---

2. Holt, *What Do I Do Monday?*, 62.

The problem of freedom has already been touched upon in chapter 6 of this book, which deals with the influence of Piaget on the field of pedagogy. With great emphasis, Piaget repeatedly points out that a human intelligence worthy of the name can be formed only through the freedom to act and to experiment, to make mistakes and to correct these mistakes. It is his considered and absolute conviction that only the association with peers leads to social responsibility, that authority reinforces egocentricity and postpones or even prevents the transformation of an individual into a "person."

In his book *The Undiscovered Self*, C. G. Jung paints an impressive picture of the modern human being. He discusses how we normally live in the belief that our small consciousness encompasses the whole of truth, yet in reality we are unconscious of our own hidden feelings, impulses, stirrings of emotion to an extreme degree, and are thus unable to estimate or comprehend their power. Because of ignorance of our own undiscovered self, our "shadow," we live in inexplicable and puzzling fear and tension. Normally we do not feel free to become conscious of our own shadow and then take over responsibility for ourselves as well, as the result of growing consciousness. So we like to pass on this responsibility to an authority that promises us security and leadership. The dark feeling that causes fear, stemming from the depths of our own unconscious, is projected onto our environment, our fellow human beings (who apparently never leave us in peace), an opponent, a political party or an enemy nation, an antagonistic race. If all these unconscious projections are manipulated by a power that has meanwhile taken over responsibility for us, it does not take long to arrive at a point of destruction of an entire world. Jung shows with this that reaching a higher degree of consciousness is not only indispensable for greater self-realization of an individual but essential for the preservation of humanity as well.

Another insight into the problem of freedom is given to us by Arthur Koestler in *Janus: A Summing Up*. In the chapter entitled "Free Will in a Hierarchic Context," he argues that free will depends on a greater wealth of available possibilities for action. The lower the position of a living thing on the evolutionary ladder, the smaller the number of choices it has in terms of free will. The higher up the ladder, the greater the selection and the greater the opportunity to exercise free will. All these gradations of free choice and free will that are represented in creation can also be found in every human being. Koestler illustrates this by using the example of a driver in a car on a well-known road with little traffic who sets his consciousness on "automatic pilot." He performs all operations in connection with driving automatically, thinking all the while of something else (the same way a child in school does, sitting in a boring class and doing what is expected, yet in reality far away and thinking about something entirely different). The task of steering his car has been placed by this driver on a lower level of consciousness, taken down, as it were, from a higher plane. At the moment the driver wants to overtake another car, however (or when the teacher approaches the pupil's desk), he gives up his half-conscious routine work and switches to a higher level of consciousness. If he sees himself confronted with a truly dangerous situation in traffic (or the teacher calls the pupil to the board), an even higher level is realized.

All our lives we perform actions on such differing levels of consciousness. The automatism of such routine actions frees us for new attention or careful notice on the higher level, but sinking too frequently to a lower level threatens to make us creatures of habit or automatons and can decrease our ability for full consciousness. This is critical for the duration of our life, but especially in the formative years of growth, in which most of our habits are formed. Use of our higher consciousness enables us to have a higher level of free will. If it is to develop to the full, it has to have practice in new and changing situations by means of making decisions. Behind this practice lies hard work, a fact seldom suspected by the outside world.

Freedom is not the same as a state of "no rules." Koestler takes chess as an example. Its rules are the same for a beginner as for a master player. However, the higher level of thought of the master chess player allows for a much greater number of possible moves. His freedom is therefore greater, although both follow the same rules of the game. The "house rules" of the active school can be compared to the rules of chess in this sense. They are binding for everyone, including the adults, and serve all of us at Pesta—we achieve new levels of consciousness through sensible and meaningful decisions and thus take over new responsibilities. In the words of Koestler:

> Habit is the denial of creativity and the negation of freedom: a self-imposed strait-jacket of which the wearer is unaware. . . . Another enemy of freedom is passion, or more specifically, an excess of the self-asserting emotions. When these are aroused, the control of behavior is taken over by those primitive levels in the hierarchy which are correlated to the "old brain." The loss of freedom resulting from this downward shift is reflected in the legal concept of "diminished responsibility" and in the subjective feeling of acting under a compulsion—expressed by colloquialisms such as: "I couldn't help it," "I lost my head," "I must have been out of my mind."[3]

Passions—are they not the sufferings and unsatisfied desires from one's childhood that are often successfully blocked, since connected with pain, yet always present?

In the open classroom, where a great deal comes out that is normally hidden from view or blocked off, we can observe many different kinds of "unfreedom." There are children who for some reason have gone without sufficient human warmth and physical contact. They cling to teachers and classmates like the proverbial leeches and can make only limited use of the large selection of material. In all that they do, they want an adult close by and call one every few minutes if that is what they must do. The many opportunities to learn through their own mistakes in an autonomous way are sacrificed all too often in favor of attempts to satisfy a deep underlying need.

---

3. Koestler, *Janus*, 240.

Many children who have formerly lacked the necessary freedom of movement come to us. They must then make up for lost time and fulfill this need in an impulsive manner. Some of them make the impression at the start that someone is hunting or pursuing them mercilessly. They do a lot of daily kilometers in their free play. Only little by little do they calm down enough to perceive the many possibilities for quiet activities. Others lack personal autonomy. They have been led by the nose, instructed, persuaded, pushed over here, and pulled over there. These children have to assure themselves at every opportunity that they will truly be granted independence here. They stay out of the way of adults as much as possible, as though these adults were a bit "fishy" or uncanny. As long as this mistrust is still in existence, they miss many opportunities to experience or to learn something interesting, of course. They answer no to all proposals, even stay at school when the others go swimming or on an excursion—until they comprehend that no one will force them into anything here. Only then do they begin to make real decisions.

We could go on with this list of many types of unsatisfied needs, following with their respective forms of unfreedom. In the active school they appear very clearly as inner limitations of the individual. They hinder a child's power to make decisions and its ability for harmony. How can we help children like these to gain a higher degree of freedom, reach a higher level of consciousness, and open up to their environment without fear? Jürg Jegge, in his two books entitled *Angst macht krumm* ("Fear Deforms") and *Dummheit ist lernbar* ("Stupidity Can Be Learned"), describes the "warping" effect of internal and external compulsion, using numerous examples. What contribution can we make to "straight and tall," intelligent, open, and aware children? For Arthur Janov there is no doubt that blocks must be done away with and old needs first of all fulfilled. In the active school we give children the opportunity to satisfy their unfulfilled needs or unsatisfied desires, as long as it does not adversely affect the well-being of the others or limit their freedom. It may cause us pain, for example, if a child misses its sensitive period for formation of fine motor control and thus may never write as elegantly as a child who practices beautiful handwriting just at the right stage of its development. We must let the child run, climb, and jump now, because this need stems from an early phase of development and would create tension for the entire personality of the child if it remained unsatisfied.

If we respect these inner conditions and allow them to find legitimate expression, our efforts to win the trust of the child can be crowned with success. This trust will determine whether we can help a child and how. In a later chapter I will talk about such therapeutic processes in which growing freedom and a growing consciousness of responsibility go hand in hand. These processes are always accompanied by inner relaxation, increasing sensitivity, and openness toward the outside world.

These thoughts on freedom and responsibility would not be complete for me without a mention of E. F. Schumacher and what he contributes to the discussion of this topic in his invaluable book titled *A Guide for the Perplexed*. He also speaks of the hierarchy of consciousness as it goes up through the four major worlds. He describes how each and every activity gradually shifts from outside to inside on the way up. A stone can be moved or changed in some way only from outside and has no inner part in this movement. Plants, however, already show a limited ability to adapt to external circumstances by means of internal changes. Animals extend the possibilities of activity through their growing consciousness and their free, systematic movement. They can express happiness and sadness, trust, fear, expectation, and disappointment, thus providing proof of their "inner life" and clear transformation from object to subject.

All these levels from the external to the internal are also represented in the human being: pushed around on many occasions like an object, compelled to adjust to various circumstances of life in order to survive like a plant, induced to act by drives and emotions, in most cases unconsciously, like an animal. Yet not all of a human being's actions are subject to such conditions of outside motivation. The human being carries within a new power that is lacking in the other three worlds and that we could call inner will. This will gives a person the power to move and to act, even when no motivating force from outside comes to bear. The human being possesses an "inner space," a seat of creative possibilities, that is established and enlarged by the forces of life, the consciousness of the outside world, and this person's own self. As Schumacher writes,

> Only when a man makes use of his power of self-awareness does he attain to the level of a person, to the level of freedom. At that moment he is living, not being lived. Numerous forces of necessity, accumulated in the past, are still determining his actions, but a small dent is being made, a tiny change of direction is being introduced. It may be virtually unnoticeable, but many moments of self-awareness can produce many such changes and even turn a given moment into the opposite of its previous direction.

And he continues:

> To ask whether the human being has freedom is like asking whether man is a millionaire. He can make it his aim to become rich; similarly, he can make it his aim to become free. In his "inner space" he can develop a center of strength so that the power of his freedom exceeds that of his necessity.[4]

And the enlargement of this "inner space"—is it not an extension or expansion through inner experiences that cannot be weighed, measured, or counted with prevailing scientific means but without which a human being is not truly a human being with real self-confidence and a consciousness of self? I do not believe that we should develop methods at school that are intended to cultivate this internal consciousness and the inner experiences of a child. Our task is certainly to help the child find its way in this world, in space and time. But this orientation necessarily takes on a different character when it takes place in consciousness of the inner life of children. At

---

4. Schumacher, *A Guide for the Perplexed*, 30.

a school that undertakes to serve being itself, we will be dealing with measurable experiences as well as those that cannot be measured or quantified. We must be prepared at any time for a child's own will to come out of this inner space, which we must learn to respect. The inner space will not serve only an inner introspection or contemplation, however, "entire of itself," so to speak, to use the words of John Donne; it will correspond to a field of strength that brings about activity in both directions, inside and out. For the activity that makes its way from inside to outside, we as educators must provide a corresponding outer room and learn not to stand in the way in it. In his well-known books *Small Is Beautiful* and *Good Work*, Schumacher gives many examples of how such creative activity does not limit itself to the inner life but can produce unexpected solutions for old problems in a new and more humane way.

Thus it should now be possible for us to have at least an inkling of the answers to the questions posed earlier. Valid answers, though, grow out of practice, a form of practice that makes proof possible. Every day we have the experience that children in their urge for knowledge are never one-sided—and they do not shy away from difficulty—if the motivation for their activity comes from inside. At their own time and in their own rhythm, they open up to all fields of knowledge. Likewise, they know no hate of certain subjects that they never felt up to or intelligent enough for because these subjects were presented to them in the wrong way or at the wrong time. Above all, they have built up, in their years of self-motivated learning, so much personal security that they will not be crushed by the demands of society or become undesired elements because of lack of discipline. In the appendix to his book *On Teaching*, Herbert Kohl publishes interesting research findings, gained over a period of years, from comparisons of extensive groups of traditional and alternative pupils. They provide clear proof that the advantages of alternative educational methods are to be recognized for many years to come, during university study and finally in family and professional life.

Self-directed art work is popular at all ages, and a valuable experience whether performed in solitude or in a group.

CHAPTER FIFTEEN

Children, Teachers, and Parents in the Active School

The open classroom is as much teacher-centered as it is child-centered. More precisely, it is a person-centered environment, which is open to the teacher's growth as a thinking, feeling, acting human being no less than the child's. As Charity James has written in Young Lives at Stake, *"Teachers' lives are at stake, too. They should be experiencing the same kinds of support, respect and optimism about themselves that we ask them to accord to young people."* —CHARLES SILBERMAN

L et us then take a closer look at the persons involved in the open classroom and their relationships. When doing so we notice to what a great degree parents should also belong to this sphere of relationship. In our particular situation as the only nondirective school in this country, this stands out especially clearly. In countries where this type of upbringing and education are at least somewhat widespread, where concrete results have long since become known, new parents may feel calmed by the moral support of other parents. Here in Ecuador we can hope for understanding based on previous knowledge only in the rarest of cases, perhaps in those who know alternative schools from having lived abroad. For the typical Ecuadorean parent of a family, such experiences in other countries offer only poor comfort, as the doubt always remains in regard to whether such a "modern" system can function only in developed nations.

Thus we have become more and more conscious, through the experiences of the last few years, of the necessity of close cooperation with the Pestalozzi parents. But before we can enter into a personal relationship, there is often a certain selection that takes place as a result of the conversations that we have prior to accepting a new child. Faced with the demand for "respect for the needs of children," many a loving parent has fled. Particularly critical is the basic attitude of parents when it comes to primary school. Those who have shown interest during the preschool period find it easier to understand the method of the primary school. But each new school year brings us a small number of children from other schools. With them we must be sure that their parents are not simply seeking an escape route from a negative situation but understand enough of the basic principles of the active school to arrive at a valid decision. The children from the parallel kindergarten, Pestalozzi II, are automatically entitled to a scholarship for the *primaria* of Pestalozzi II, but these parents, too, must go through the mill of preparatory discussions. These precautionary measures are followed by the signing of a contract. In this contract the school undertakes to provide all the elements of the active method, and the parents promise to take part in a course once a month and to visit the school once every trimester to observe the children in their activity.

A further security check for comprehension and sincerity on the part of parents naturally comes about through our practice of "preschool." Whereas children officially begin school in Ecuador at the age of six, we accept children for primary school only at the age of seven. Between the sixth and seventh year they may come into the classroom of the "big ones" if they are interested in doing so. Should they, however, prefer the kindergarten, they are just as welcome there. This arrangement is the result of our experience with our first year of operations in the primary school. It could be clearly seen that the six-year-olds, in most cases, had a great desire to go back to preschool as soon as the excitement of "finally being in school" had worn off. However, these children were obviously pressured at home to "get on with their work at school," meaning the presentation of notebooks full of work and similar visible results of a successful education as fast as possible. These children were therefore often caught up in the conflict between their own desire to spend more time in preschool and the wishes of their parents, who wanted them to behave like real, meaning good and diligent, schoolchildren. Yet just at this age it seems that the differences from child to child are particularly great. Some have more or less completed their preoperational stage of development and are visibly ready to enter their concrete operational period and do the work corresponding to it. Others have not yet achieved this inner degree of maturity and need more time to grow.

Particularly impressive are the signs that indicate a lack of readiness for school in children who could not truly deal with emotional difficulties during the first years of their lives. If these children are allowed the necessary freedom, they follow a natural drive, trying—in the course of this particular year—to restructure their emotional structures as far as possible before entering the next stage of development. These six-year-olds talk like babies for months, play with dolls, look for friends of younger ages, and land in the lap of an adult many, many times to cry themselves out. They can feel that such behavior will not be looked upon with approval by the older children, so they feel more comfortable with the younger or youngest ones. Thus it is more often social pressure than intellectual immaturity that keeps children like these at preschool.

Parents who place more value on social recognition than the well-being of their child, unconsciously in most cases, recoil at the idea of letting their child play at preschool one year longer when all the others are carrying around a heavy school satchel full of books and spending their afternoons doing homework.

Time and again we hear from our Pestalozzi parents how difficult life can be for them when they insist on an alternative school for their children. In a country such as Ecuador, family ties are much closer as well as more powerful than in the progressive countries. Young people who wish to go their own way are put under pressure from all sides. Therefore we see it as our duty to point out this danger, especially to interested parties asking about our primary school, and to provide as thorough an introduction as possible to the principles of an active education. The monthly meetings have a double aim: on the one hand, the study and discussion of important aspects of active education, and on the other, the encouragement of human warmth and relationships among the adults, who can give each other moral support in their convictions and who in fact become good friends in many cases.

At these study meetings we often hear many anecdotes about the life of the Pesta children at home. The perplexity and helplessness of these parents when they are obliged to deal with the criticism of numerous relatives gradually turns into pride in their "active" children, who more and more often prove themselves to be intelligent and enterprising persons able to master any and all situations in life. One mother said the following about her eight-year-old son: "Last Sunday everybody was in a bad mood. Not one of us wanted to make breakfast. We were arguing about who works more during the week and who deserves a quiet Sunday the most. In the middle of this argument, when the fur was flying, Santiago disappeared unnoticed into the kitchen, made toast, scrambled eggs, and coffee, set the table, and called us in for breakfast, beaming." (Santiago came to us as a "hyperactive" child—he had already been labeled an incorrigible case and unsuited to a school education by two other schools.)

These experiences, when one's own children solve problems, when they remain calm and collected in stress situations, and especially the astonishing fact that they are never bored, being used to finding interesting activities for themselves all the time, give our parents an enormous boost. They begin to compare their children with those of relatives and friends. And they begin to notice that their children need fewer "amusements" to be happy than other children do. They prefer simple rather than fancy and expensive clothes—after all, they need their clothes for "work"—do not suffer from chronic fears of tests and marks, do not complain about their teachers or "awful" classmates, and do not require the assistance of the family for their homework. Active children like to get up in the morning, are very seldom ill, and need no costly private tutors or psychologists. Most of them would rather be at school on Saturdays and Sundays, too, and for the majority, their school vacations seem too long as well.

Active children bring a breath of fresh air into the family every day. A growing number of parents find this new feeling for life infectious. They begin to discover new interests themselves. They often develop a taste for books that have to do with the development of their children or issues of human existence in general. Some parents become "active" themselves and offer to help with the manufacture of materials, preparation of excursions, or supervision at the swimming pool. Interest in the mornings that parents must spend at school in accordance with their contracts increases more and more. During their first visit parents initially feel insecure; they have no real idea of what and how they should observe, what questions they can note down for discussion at the next parents' meeting. The second visit already sees them enjoying direct participation. They observe not only their own child but the children of other families as well, families they have gotten to know a bit better. They are pleased when a child comes over to them: to read something aloud, to ask for help with a difficult exercise in arithmetic, a handicraft, or baking a cake.

Such changes in the lives of adults do not always take place without a crisis. Sometimes it is only one parent who feels an urge for change in the family or in his or her personal life. This can lead to tensions in the marriage, which in turn bring unexpected difficulties for the children involved. Thus it is necessary for us to develop a sure sense of the parents' crises great or small and create opportunity for help, if these parents are interested in our support. We experience with pleasure how parents, through their children, start to search for alternatives for themselves and achieve, here and there, a form of the proverbial new lease on life, sometimes experiencing a great deepening in their own lives. Yet we must beware of hoping for or expecting such changes. This has become perhaps the most difficult aspect of our work: providing for the children a humane and respectful environment each and every day, even if the change hoped for in the home environment does not take place, while at the same time being ready and willing to give aid and assistance when parents cannot deal with their own changes of stance or mind-set.

The greatest difficulty that the active system brings with it for us adults is the demand to let the children live the way they really are—today. It is astonishing how difficult it is, in fact, for us to make possible for them a rich experience of their childhood being without burdening them with our own past or our expectations for the future. Normally we live in a state of constant concern for our children, trying to motivate them for everything that seems important to us, continually overlooking, however, the importance of helping them *where they are*, namely, in the places where they are already motivated by their own interests. Because we ourselves first have to learn to unite theory and practice in one act, into one action, so to speak, we take fright—not once, but many times over—at the dynamics of the children who, thanks to the active system, are not forced to live in this tension. We notice that we take seriously the "inner space" of children only to the degree that we ourselves reckon with an inner space. And only to the degree that we are willing to stand on our own two feet, make decisions, and take over responsibilities are we then able not only to allow this process to children without fear but also to support it by means of our own experience.

The active system provides us with myriad opportunities not to see the children as a closed and conformed group but rather to see each one as a unique person. They are mixed in terms of age and intelligence; in the last school year, we put together all age groups from six to ten in one room. This practice of "family grouping," often applied in open schools, has various consequences, all of which we regard as positive. For an adult it becomes more difficult to treat the children as though they were "cut out of the same cloth," as though they could adhere to a uniform and consistent rhythm of learning or be interested in the same things day in and day out. The children themselves in this situation show much less tendency to try to top one another with their performance. They can easily see that the younger children know less but that this does not mean they are not as bright as the older ones, just as the older children are not smarter because they can do more. If we are accustomed to urging or "pushing" children by playing one against another, by praising one and scolding another, by offering rewards or threatening punishments, thus attempting to foster class unity, then such a lack of competition may seem a disadvantage. But at the active school there is no necessity to fit children to a homogeneous program of learning or make them adhere to a common standard. Each child has its own standard and its own goal. We take it as a given from the very start that every child is different. We expect various ages, various levels of maturity, different levels and kinds of intelligence, and reckon with factors of differing emotional conditions. Our attention is thereby distracted from a comparison of the children. We educate— and remind—ourselves to let every child be as it is and to measure the child's progress against itself.

In the place of pressure caused by grades and the necessity of adapting to the rhythm of an entire group of peers—conditions forced upon an individual child artificially, from outside—a form of natural dynamics results through the vertical grouping of children. It promotes organic growth: smaller or weaker children have as their models older or more intelligent children and are unconsciously activated by them to learn more, while older children, knowing themselves to be standards or patterns for younger ones, instinctively search for new methods and new subjects to explore in order to shake off the "copycats." Above all, however, the children's drive for never-ending activity does not come from constant outside motivation; its strength comes out of real interest, and this reflects a true interaction or reciprocal effect of outer and inner forces. In the active school, children overcome difficulties and obstacles over and over again—they do not take the path of least resistance, as many believe. And they do this not as a result of pressure from "above" but as a consequence of the fulfillment of authentic needs, which are reinforced by the manifold variety of natural differences among children and not—as in traditional schools—by the attempt of the teacher to collect all children at one level and lead them as a homogeneous mass to new subject matter.

Life shows us that the "slow" or "dumb" ones at school who successfully withstood the pressure to make them the same as the others do not always remain in their "back positions" later on. The classic case of Einstein, who was considered anything but gifted while at school, is probably not the only example of its kind. However, we must fear that far too many children who show little skill for adaptation at school lose their belief in themselves and give up any further development for the rest of their lives. It is equally true that the "best in the class," those who were always able to do everything right for their teachers, often make their way in life only if they find refuge in jobs and professions offering them various means of protection from unforeseen situations in life.

In the active school, the singularities of individual children are respected and preserved. "Pressure from inside" and the expansion of the "inner space" are accorded just as much right as external necessities. The need to be alone can be fulfilled here, just like the growing need for group work. Blocks from earlier years can be dissolved if we allow the children to give the necessary attention to old problems of an emotional or intellectual nature. New problems can be taken on when the child feels open and ready for it, and they are solved with greater ease. We avoid a school drill that blocks contact with a child's original feeling of and for life and works against the openness of the child toward both outside and inside.

Furthermore, we encourage not only these everyday or "normal" differences but much more blatant social or racial contrasts as well. And we see to our great joy that children who feel respected in terms of their most important personal needs also accept such differences. It seems equally important to us that children with obvious handicaps are permitted to mix with normal healthy children. Therefore we always accept a certain number of handicapped children who would otherwise have no opportunity to attend school together with normal peers. The excellent results we have had with this are to be ascribed to the large selection of concrete materials, the respect for individual needs, and the constant association with children of normal development. Within the dynamics of these differences, a life together at school in cooperation with each other provides great advantages for the handicapped children and considerable benefit to the nonhandicapped ones as well. Here they have the opportunity to practice the great virtues of human tact, tolerance, and active helpfulness every day. They do not succumb to the temptation of putting a label on their handicapped classmate and treating him or her accordingly. With great impartiality, showing no prejudice, they address themselves directly to what they have in common, with no surprise—or shock—at the differences, and build up a human relationship that is positive and helpful for all concerned.

For a year now we have had a fourteen-year-old boy here at school with us who towers above the other children but has obvious problems with fine motor control. Because of the lack of a special school for his particular handicap, he had spent seven years in a general school suffering all possible efforts to teach him reading and writing, yet never achieving more than a first-grade level in these disciplines. Only after he was given the opportunity to fulfill his real needs within the framework of the active system did a desire awaken in him to keep up with his seven-year-old friends in their schoolwork. The normal children knew that Gustavo had been very ill and "could only learn slowly." His companions of all different ages accepted him without any reservations, even invited him to attend all birthday parties and to participate in all games at school— not one of them had the idea to make fun of him in any way whatsoever.

And how about the teacher who works in the active system and whose life is "in the game" just as much as the children's? In the summer of 1982, as I was working on a concept for this book, making first drafts, one of our intensive summer courses of introduction to the active system was in progress. On its first day two bejeweled women, related to each other yet addressing one another as "Madame Dr. So-and-so," honored us with their presence. In addition to this already acquired title, they were desirous of obtaining a diploma in the area of an "introduction to the active educational system." At the end of the first day, however, they suddenly remembered that they had already booked and purchased airline tickets for a vacation trip taking them to Spain; thus they were regretfully unable to continue their participation in our seminar. In other words, they quite literally took flight from the danger of having to making the closer acquaintance of an alternative that also threatened to examine their own values. The rest of the twenty participants, among them three young teachers from traditional schools, were sincere in their search for new solutions yet could not foresee how deeply they themselves could be affected, as was to be seen later. Each of them went through a kind of crisis in the course of the seminar and needed the help of the group or a person of their confidence in order to deal with it. One of the young woman teachers told me in tears, "I can't listen to the presentations on child psychology anymore—I keep remembering all the many lessons that I've given with the cane in my hand."

The participants were much more touched by their individual use of the concrete materials and by listening to a tape recording of a session of play therapy than by our formal introductions to the field of child psychology. The recording documents how an eight-year-old boy "plays through" scenes of arguments between his parents, he himself caught in the middle, helplessly pulled back and forth between the two of them. One young woman had memories so strong that she had to leave the room in tears. The others admitted later that they had been able to keep their composure only with great difficulty. Arising from the sensitizing process, which had been considerably furthered by the daily handling of tangible materials, the contact with their own structures of feeling and moving was unexpectedly made. The result was a flood of old memories and a growing doubt of all that had been learned from outside yet often not brought into harmony. In such situations of crisis, a novice needs help from others who have had similar experiences and are still involved in a process of becoming more sensitive.

After the course was over, we took a week off, putting up our tents on a beach lined with palm trees on the northern coast of the country about a ten-hour drive from Tumbaco. This gave us a certain distance from the daily work at Pestalozzi. To me it seemed a good time to clarify my own feelings as well as to reflect upon and "feel" our own role in the active school. I immediately recalled a young teacher who had been working for five years with children between six and fifteen years of age at a rural school of the one-room variety, situated in a poor and desolate region high in the Andes. He had noticed very quickly that he would be compelled to find new methods of his own, as well as goals, for his pupils, since the regulations and guidelines of the Ministry of Education were more a hindrance than a help. So he worked in his own way, more or less alone and with no understanding forthcoming from his surroundings, and without having sufficient knowledge of inner learning processes and the importance of concrete material. Finally he heard of our Pestalozzi School. The following day he sent his schoolchildren home and traveled down to Tumbaco to get to know our work. He sat one entire morning among the children, watching them in their activity. This was his commentary at the end of said morning: "I'm used to being among children. But this morning I felt completely bowled over by the vitality of these children. Among them, I was a nothing. The children paid attention to me only if they had nothing more important to do. As long as they were busy with their own things, I disappeared from their consciousness completely. I've never felt so unimportant, so insignificant. Now I know that in spite of all my good intentions and reforms, I've stayed the boss of the children at my school."

During a walk along the beach I gained a little more understanding of this feeling that we adults get in our association with children of an active school. Their vitality is like the force of the sea. It is an earthy natural power that seems to us wonderful and—at the same time—awesome or unsettling, even frightening. If we place ourselves, drawn up to our full size and with all our strength, in front of the children, we appear as rocks to them, against which the sea crashes, then roils, and retreats again as quickly as possible. Only a short exchange or communication between these two forces takes place. The ocean wears away stone but leaves little of its own treasure. Yet the more level the beach, the longer and the more intimately water and land come together. The force of the waves gradually adjusts to the form of the beach, and from the depths of the ocean are left the most astonishing treasures after the tide has gone out again. The shore changes shape as well, with every high tide, yet it is a give-and-take with no violence.

If we take this image as a pattern or guide, it gives us a feeling for the basic attitude or position of a teacher in the active school system, who tries to "flatten out" to the inside as well as the outside. Instead of a teacher's feeling "shot" and "burned out" at the end of a school day, this position provides a feeling of peace and enrichment after the work of the day despite our being tired. Every day we should be in a position to gather up the treasures left behind by the children: not just essay notebooks kept in a beautiful hand and pictures painted just as beautifully, but above all a new understanding of their reality. Every day we should perceive in ourselves any or all of the fine changes that have resulted through the effects coming from the children. And when we lay out new work and new materials for the next day, it should feel as though we are placing our treasures on the shore so that the sea can take them readily and without force—in exchange for its own wonderful riches.

In his *Psychologie et Pedagogie*, Piaget makes the assumption that in the inner attitude of the adult—and particularly of the pedagogue—lies the reason that the active school is still not widespread. In his opinion it is the inveterate and ingrained manner of teachers giving "lessons"—their resistance to taking on all the many and varied actions that the open classroom requires—that is sadly responsible for this. Piaget says that the work of an elementary-school teacher should really be at the same level as a scientist's, since a scientist is best able to observe the development of children day by day, to put them in touch with new situations, and to make an analysis of the resulting observations. Unfortunately, reality is far removed from this ideal. Here in Ecuador at least, where the active system is still unknown, we need all our strength to work for its survival on a daily basis. Yet we do hope to find time later on for the evaluation of our experience.

I would present a false picture, however, were I to describe the work of the active teacher only from its positive and worthwhile side, to sing its praises as an ideal. We ourselves often feel pressure from many sides, last but not least from inside. This pressure is not so easy to shake off after stopping work for the day, or on weekends or even on vacation. There is pressure from external insecurities with which we have to deal. Whereas private schools in this country are regarded as "good business" because they work with a large number of children, offering them, however, little more than the necessary classrooms and teachers, a schoolyard, and perhaps a sports field at best, the active school can never be content with already existing materials. In progressive countries children have access to libraries and other institutions that are friendly to them. Financial support is often forthcoming from state or private sources. Here we will have to wait a long time before receiving any such aid from the authorities. The survival of our school stands and falls with the conviction of the parents who decide to "enter into this experiment" with us. Furthermore, it is our wish to make it possible for children of poorer families to attend the school if their parents have become convinced of its value. Some paying parents find this not entirely satisfactory. They fear having to finance the education of other people's children. Aid from abroad normally comes marked "only for poor Indio children." However, we find such differentiations or limitations too restrictive. We would like to try to make a more humane education available to all who feel the need or desire for it, so that human beings can grow up developing a spontaneous social consciousness capable of finding new solutions for the future of the country.

As teachers of the active school system, we enjoy none of the advantages of the traditional school. The future of our school is by no means assured. Our budget still does not provide for fixed salaries for ourselves. We have neither the prospect of social security pensions nor health insurance. All personal interests must take a back seat to the progress of the school.

On the other hand, however, it is a necessity to satisfy the Ministry of Education, to fill out all desired papers and forms, to cultivate important contacts and relationships, and to prove our readiness to cooperate by means of lectures, presentations, and free entry of all sorts of visitors. This aspect of the work is often time-consuming as well as frustrating. Yet it must receive its due attention so that this alternative is not nipped in the bud.

Finally, there are the never-ending insecurities and fears of the parents of our children, which are felt by us as pressure as well. Parents often bring a child to us who shows unmistakable signs of "school damage": asthma, bed-wetting, nightmares, and all the other symptoms that may throw shadows on family life. As a rule, the child sheds the symptoms causing its family such worry after a few weeks or months in the open classroom. Soon, however, the child's parents forget why they brought their child to us in the first place and press us to "take the child in hand" at last, so that it does not stay behind the children of relatives and friends (meaning, in most cases, that it collects less information learned by rote). If we wish to prevent parents from urging a return to the "old" or "tried-and-true" methods, out of fear of themselves or their environment, we must be prepared to devote both time and attention to them.

Yet the main pressure usually comes from the demands we make of ourselves. The various functions of the new teacher, as described in detail in *The Open Classroom Reader* by Charles Silberman, are manifold, and a specialization for the individual teacher is possible only to a limited degree. Whereas a teacher is normally guided for the most part by the instructions or directives of the general curriculum, with the teacher's part in terms of responsibility and decisions to be understood as within this framework, the teacher at an active school must stand on his or her own two feet at every moment. This teacher is responsible for the configuration of the room, the selection, purchase or manufacture, and maintenance of all the numerous materials that are to offer stimulus and opportunity for self-direction for the learning done by the children. This aspect alone is enough to keep our hands full. All attempts to share this responsibility with other volunteers who do not work directly with the children have failed after a short period of time. Only those who see the needs and changing interests of the children day after day can feel motivated enough to be constantly thinking of new things, undaunted by the work connected with this. When parents offer to produce materials, they often need such a long time for it, unfortunately, that the interest of the children has meanwhile jumped over to a completely new area. If I write in my notebook one day, for example, that "Roberto is enthusiastic about volcanoes," I would prefer to have suitable material on hand the very next day.

Every weekend I need a few hours to get the schoolroom in order: preparation of new things, noting down the interests of children on cards, or gathering other material for individual or group work. When touching each material in order to dust or move it to another place, I think of a whole series of new possibilities for use. These must be written down so that they do not remain only fleeting thoughts or ideas but are at hand during the hubbub of a school morning.

Teachers from other schools who come to visit have a hard time understanding how "teaching" can be done when children follow their own interests, perhaps with each one doing something different, or with spontaneous formation of groups that have not been organized by the teacher. To feel comfortable, to be up to this situation in our active school, I must put myself into a state of mind that unites and blends the highest possible level of attentiveness with a great degree of relaxation. As soon as I feel anxious, agitated, or tense, I am unable to give the children real help in their learning without communicating or passing on this tension to them. In the active system it is impossible to hide one's own frame of mind from the children. We do not work with neutral concepts most of the time but with concrete materials through which the children express themselves naturally. While using these objects, the children show themselves as they really are. So it is easy for them to assess me as well in my handling of materials and to read my state of mind or my moods in every movement that I make.

It is not always easy for me to accept the open expression of emotions of the children and not feel affected by them. We have long been accustomed to schoolchildren who keep their real feelings hidden or let them out only after careful observation—"what kind of face will the teacher make"—as a trial balloon. Adults are horrified in most cases at the outbreaks of rage, very expressive language, and aggressivity children exhibit among themselves and toward each other. Disgraceful and shocking behavior of juveniles is rebuked in general. In the United States, it is reported, there are already parents' associations against adolescents with weapons. Only once in a while, and then with great hesitation, does an educator dare to entertain the thought that all this rage and aggression could have been built up over—or indeed by means of—years of forced good behavior. Endless sitting still, constant attention to what the teacher wants, and the effort to "make good" in the many years of personal dependency transform our children, in the course of time, into pressure cookers that will have to explode sooner or later.

In the active school system, it becomes important to avoid a dangerous building up of repressed feelings and suppressed energy. Through their freedom of speech and movement, active children are constantly "running into" or "up against" the environment as well as fellow human beings, sometimes "lightly," sometimes "harder," thus having the opportunity to give vent to the feelings generated by these "collisions." In their games, in their reading and writing, they bear witness to their fears, their anger, their hopes and joys. We adults who share their daily lives cannot help but feel with the children, in the process feeling ourselves as well, and coming into contact with our own fears, our anger, and our wish for personal happiness. The children do not have a "stencil" of a teacher in front of them—they have normal human beings whose feet hurt when someone carelessly steps on them and who say so openly.

Another difficulty, often unexpected in the open classroom and of which I have already made short mention, is the circumstance that children do not always esteem and appreciate our wonderful ideas and tireless work as much as we would hope. Some of the material we make for the children receives hardly any attention. Other material is used for completely different purposes than we had intended or imagined. All in all, we must be prepared for as well as accept the fact that children have a much greater need for play than we would think possible. Our perturbation may be partial in the case of didactic games, the educational value of which can reassure us; it is much more acute, however, when it comes to free play, which seems entirely inexplicable and often "unnecessary" to us, games in which our participation is declared superfluous or even undesired. I have mentioned this type of game or play several times. Here I would simply like to remark upon what a source of conflict the sight of children playing with complete abandon can be for a teacher. Shortly before the end of the school year, for example, the following scene took place. One child had pulled a radish out of another child's lovingly cultivated plot of garden. The gardener began to defend his property by slinging balls of mud. This small incident climaxed unexpectedly in a real battle, in which all the children participated with enthusiasm. It went on for more than an hour. Should we teachers allow the children to "waste" a valuable school morning like this? Would it not be appropriate in this situation to nip this warlike outburst on the part of the children in the bud, so that they learn something "useful"?

Every day we subject ourselves to the discipline of writing down our observations in the classroom, keeping a diary about each child as well as the events of the day. While writing, recalling, and reflecting, we are often able to "feel our way into" individual children and situations, to comprehend connections that remain unconscious in the hurly-burly of the morning. By keeping notes we get new ideas for this or that child, are able to take a close look at our own mishaps or errors, can make decisions for new behavior or a new attitude. Through this practice, little by little and in the course of time, we sharpen our powers of observation and increase our attention, which should be directed at the individual as well as the whole. Instead of remembering that this morning "about ten children" were working in the garden, we begin to see each individual child in our mind's eye—how the child's movements seemed to us, whether it took on a role of leadership or copied others, whether it got involved in arguments, how it solved problems.

Gradually we learn to differentiate what the origin of the many varied actions of the children seems to be. Do they follow from an original need that—following the laws of the child's own growth—incites the child to activity? Or is the child's need a "second-hand" one, so to speak, and the child is showing interest in an activity in order to gain the attention or affection of adults or other children? How can we facilitate and encourage every child to gain more and more experience with actions corresponding to its own self? How can we avoid a process of education in a child that blocks the paths that keep it in contact with its personal inner guidance, in bewildering situations of its life as well? Children who have the habit of making sure "what they should do next" or guessing what is desired of them, because parents and teachers "know what's best for me," will have difficulty finding their own way later on.

The longer we work with the active method, the clearer it becomes to us that it is not a modern yet closed system that avoids the problems of the traditional school and thus, as such, is better than the old system. As Schumacher writes in *A Guide for the Perplexed*, education cannot be a "convergent problem" for which a solution is reached as soon as we have brought all factors into accord by logical means. It is in reality more a "divergent problem," because it has to do with life in all its manifold levels of consciousness, not with material conditions.

John Holt compares the new teacher to a specialist who works in a travel agency. Such agents do not dictate to a client the destination of the journey; they inquire politely about the client's wishes and possibilities, give assistance with their knowledge and connections, help with the planning of trips. They cannot guarantee, however, that the trip will really be a success, and they do not see it as their duty to check whether the traveler follows all advice given. This comparison seems very accurate to me, as it emphasizes the freedom of decision and action accorded to the "customer." Yet there is no pointer in regard to the extent of responsibility that we, as adults, take on: for the children, it is not a question of a vacation—the basis of their whole life is at stake. Educators like Pestalozzi, Rousseau, and others even bring in the principle of love, through which a teacher is put in a position to transcend the antitheses that must be reconciled in divergent problems if life is to remain unhurt.

Experience at an active school teaches us that we are not dealing with only two areas of knowledge, as is commonly assumed: the subject matter to be taught and the teaching methods, which are often considerably behind the most recent findings of psychology, however. According to Schumacher there are four areas: first, my own "interior" or inner self; second, how others see me; third, what it looks like in the inside of another; and fourth, what the other person—or the world—looks like from the outside. Indeed, he speaks of these as worlds one, two, three, and four.

Normally the field of education takes into consideration, above all, the last area: the stuff of knowledge that we spread out before the learner and the typical reactions to these learning situations, which in turn can be modulated by means of various methods. Piaget's works point clearly to the fact—if I have understood them correctly—that teaching methods that take into account only the external reactions of learners to the learning stimuli offered are in the long run obstructive to real development (see Skinner's learning machines and indeed any and all methods coming from behaviorism). If we as teachers wish to serve living growth rather than only a mechanical learning process, we cannot help but take the inner self of the other—the child in this case—seriously. This interior is for Piaget the place in which the structures of comprehension and thought are formed. For Janov it is the origin of all emotions, which unconsciously, yet inexorably, determine our actions, our personality, our self. For others it is the seat of a lower—or higher— consciousness that waits for discovery and out of which can come human actions that leave the laws of "unsatisfied needs" behind.

Only an adult who has made contact with his or her own self can assess the importance of such experiences in others and accord them the place that they deserve. Teachers are to have the same right to growth as their pupils. They, too, are to be open to the world, able to see new and interesting sides of it. This increases the teacher's feeling for life, without a doubt. A teacher who does not know this openness soon experiences the work of teaching as toil and drudgery that only deadens the mind. This view to the outside, even if it constantly renews itself, remains without real value if it doesn't correspond to an expansion of one's own inner space, from which comes direction and meaning.

Finally, let us give some thought to Schumacher's second "world" as well: "how others see me." According to Schumacher, this area contains an important key to true understanding, without which the other three can easily lose their balance. We will assume that with our work, we wish not only to earn a living and provide for our old age but to do something good and valuable as well. In the active school the children give us a multitude of opportunities to examine our ideals and check the genuineness of our intentions. The children give us many hidden and open signs through which we can find out their true opinion and their real feelings about our person and our actions: the way, for instance, we can feel an entire "news agency" at work behind our back at a traditional school. (There are said to be teachers who never write anything on the board with their back to the class, preferring instead to perform the most complicated dislocations in order to keep an eye on the class.) To the extent that we are able to be ourselves with the children, not playing a role that we slip out of after the end of class, the children are themselves, too, and show us openly the effects on them of our good intentions.

In this connection, I think of how I had once arranged a beautiful still life on a table one day at the end of the school year. The older children were invited to try writing a description of it. When I explained the exercise to them, they looked at me, wrinkling their foreheads, and asked what it would be good for. I tried not to show my embarrassment at this—I had really believed that they would share my admiration for this still life—yet faced with the critical standpoint of ten-year-olds, it was difficult to find a sensible explanation for such work. They must have recognized my dilemma, since one of them then said generously, "I think it's stupid to describe something like that, but never mind—I'll do it to please you." The others agreed with their classmate and wrote very good papers, which, however, were not comparable to what they would have written had they been able to write about something that interested *them*.

Whenever I feel dissatisfied, out of sorts, or too easily tired in my work with the children, I try to think about how the balance among these four worlds of Schumacher's could have been disturbed. Taking stock like this in such a situation, however, is only possible for me if I am prepared to "go into" or "give myself to" the moment and put considerations of expediency on the back burner. This is not an easy exercise. My feeling of life is more deeply influenced by my school years than I would ever have suspected. Unconscious yet very much present in me: the forty-five-minute rhythm and the vague feeling that real life begins when I have accomplished this or that. It is astounding that even the many adult years of my life spent in South America, with its less pronounced sense of time measured by the clock, have not been able to diminish or eliminate the habits formed in childhood.

Life in the present is something we adults must make ourselves conscious of, building up a sense of it once again, becoming aware, before we can feel how natural it is for children. In our daily practice in the active school, we can gradually learn to live with the children in this sense. Yet the difficulty of including the parents of the children in this "magic circle" still remains. Parents send their children to school so that they learn everything they will need for secondary school, for university study, and, finally, for life—life seems always to begin "later" for most people—"so that they get on, so that something becomes of them, so that they can be happy later on in life."

The hidden meaning of this "so that": we know what we are learning and teaching, and what it is good for. If, however, we take into account all four "sectors" of knowledge for our "program," this program changes into a plan for a journey into the unknown, for which we equip ourselves, children and adults alike.

CHAPTER SIXTEEN

Pedagogy or Therapy?

S ome years ago I worked as a music teacher at a traditional
school and often wondered about the fact that the other subject
teachers were able to discuss grade averages, performance curves,
and behavior problems during our meetings before report cards
were due to be given out without any mention whatsoever of the
personalities of the children in question. I myself had only two
weekly class hours in each class and would have liked to hear more
about the pupils. Yet most of my colleagues could only report
on children who were especially bad or particularly good in their
subject or who drew attention to themselves as a result of the disturbances they caused. The vast majority of children were characterized at these meetings only through a numerical grade with two
digits behind the point, which then had to be rounded up or down
according to consensus. One day a homeroom teacher presented the
record of marks for the current trimester of a twelve-year-old boy.
They had gone down considerably in comparison with those of his
previous report card. The vice principal of the school was just about
to draft a recommendation to the effect that the boy would have to
take care in the future not to be expelled. (The good schools permit
themselves the luxury of sorting through their pupils and eliminat-
ing those who cannot keep up or do not conform to norms of school

267

behavior.) Then the homeroom teacher spoke up again, requesting that the particular situation of this pupil at the moment be taken into consideration. His father had had an automobile accident a few months before, which had left him a paraplegic in a wheelchair. It could therefore be assumed that this had something to do with the boy's difficulties in his school subjects. Would it not be better to wait with the warning and give the pupil some time first to regain his balance? The answer was short and wise: "We are a pedagogical institution, not a place of therapy." The warning remark was entered on the report card and at the end of the school year the child transferred to another school.

At another elite school in Quito, a little girl threw a stone at the head of another child. Blood flowed, tears as well. The respective mothers were phoned, and they came immediately. "How could you allow this bad girl to hurt my poor child?" was the accusation flung at the allegedly inattentive teacher. The mother of the guilty four-year-old snapped at her daughter, "Why are you so bad?" Things calmed down only after it was announced that the bad girl would be expelled from the school on the spot. Are there only faultless and good children at the good schools? Where do all the bad ones go?

A young teacher who took part in our summer course provided the following data from the elite school at which she teaches: of fifty-six children between six and seven years of age (two first-grade classes), thirty-one are under neurological and/or psychological treatment. Of these, seventeen take sedatives regularly, on the advice of the school psychologist.

In Ecuador, teaching reading and writing to the rural population is one of the priorities high on the list of government policy. But compulsory school attendance can be achieved only to a limited extent and with difficulty, and there is hardly any development in teaching methods. Both in urban and in rural schools the results are dubious at best, and the specialists at the Ministry of Education are continuously concerned about equipping the existing schools with special "learning centers," which have long since become common in the developed countries. These are by no means centers for the handicapped but are for clinically normal children who have either behavioral abnormalities or other apparently inexplicable blocks in some area of learning. As teachers already have their hands full with the keeping of discipline in their classes as well as getting through the curriculum, they are in urgent need of help for children with difficulties in adapting. The demand for psychologists, neurologists, or specialists who, in particular circumstances or under special conditions, can get the necessary subject matter into the heads of blocked children as well is constantly on the increase. From the experience of other countries, we know that such children who are taken out of the mainstream feel themselves labeled or singled out. And not only that: this "stamp" follows them, in the form of written references to their difficulties on report cards or in files, for the rest of their school careers.

The effects of this selection principle seem to me, however, to be problematic not only for those who are "branded" and become accustomed to a life with tranquilizers, perhaps upon the advice of a school psychologist, from a very early age; it seems tragic as well for the "normal" ones, the "good" and "well-behaved" ones, all of whom systematically learn always to do the "right thing" and to beware of "mistakes." Young people in all countries have indeed been revolting against this self-image fostered over many years, but many of them have learned only that they are "against" something, not what they are really "for." Indeed, how should they find the way back to themselves, after so many years, and to their own inner guiding force? From the time they were small children, they have been used to receiving direction and instruction from outside; they lack the security and self-confidence of knowing when and if their own compass can be relied on. So, as young adults, they run here and there, supporting or resisting one thing or another, railing at or battling this or that, yet seldom do they find their way in their own lives.

Who decides, at the end of the day, which children are "normal" and which need some form of therapy? And where does the urgent desire to isolate the "others" or the "difficult ones," sending them off to specialists, come from? In the villages of Ecuador, the handicapped are still part of normal everyday life, whatever their handicap may be. In their families they take over certain tasks that they are up to and participate in public life as well. But in the cities, in this and other countries, they are already hidden for the most part and are the recipients of "special" treatment.

In between the group of children with differing types of handicaps and the group of normal children who conform to prevalent school conditions, there is a growing number of "slightly damaged" children. For their problems the experts in their specialized fields create more and more new specialist terms. In the confidential files of schools, to which, in many places, not even parents have access, code words appear from preschool age up to the end of a child's school years: "specific learning disability," "behavioral disturbance," "minimal brain disorder," "hyperactivity," and many more. Peter Schrag and Diane Divoky, in *The Myth of the Hyperactive Child*, have exposed hyperactivity as a myth; they report that the multitude of children unable to adapt to the general norm, thus becoming suspected of a certain abnormality, is continually increasing. Estimates vary widely, lying between 10 and 40 percent of the entire school population for the United States.

The study clearly establishes that in most cases there is no proof of organic or psychological disorders. A child's nonconformity to the demanded learning rhythm, its maintenance of strong personal convictions or dislike of sitting still in school, is sufficient to result in the child's being turned over to a psychologist or learning specialist. The number of children being given tranquilizers for the duration of their school careers is also growing—not only in the United States but in Ecuador as well, where everything is done to assure the happy future of children through an education at a "good school." Are these school diseases a creation of the growing number of specialists, or do the specialists make their appearance on the scene as a result of the number of "diseased" children? One thing is sure: children bearing labels like "hyperactivity" or "learning disability" who transfer from a traditional to an active school lose the typical symptoms of their disorder, sometimes after only a single week.

Equally disquieting is the number of children in Ecuador who, despite their having been declared normal, are still not normal enough to endure the demands of an elementary school—or even a kindergarten—without suffering any damage. At the elite schools in Quito, eighty children are chosen from approximately four hundred applicants for nursery school by means of tests. Of these eighty, the fifty "best" go on to preschool, and thirty of those continue on to first grade. These are all children from families of good standing, without nutritional or other problems of growth. Already at preschool age, they feel "rejected" or "chosen"—both of which are questionable bases for a young life. The rejected children can still find a place at a school of somewhat less esteem. Those of the middle and lower classes—if they get to start school at all—often have serious problems of undernourishment or a lack of the simplest forms of a culture of daily life. If these children fail, they do not get a second chance. They join the multitudes who have no hope of taking part in, let alone being a part of, the country's progress.

Paul Goodman emphasizes in *Compulsory Mis-Education* that this would have been no overly great misfortune for the affected children in earlier times. In all fields of life, it was often the "dropouts" who were able to attain the highest and most remarkable feats of achievement. For people who did not take every step of the ladder in the course of what was by no means a universal school system at that time, there were still various paths open to them. Today things are different: for all practical purposes, there is no other path to happiness, success and fulfillment of all wishes than via "the one and only alma mater."

Yet it is this obligatory institution itself that sets the stage very early on, much too early, for an entire life. With children who were forced to suffer deficiencies in the initial years of their lives, the problems come to light all the more quickly. In some cases, there may have been prenatal problems, in others the effects of an unnatural birth, unloving or careless treatment as a small child, or one of the manifold insecurities with which small children are obliged to come to terms by themselves, because we adults live in our own world and do not understand their real needs.

Even children who enter school with the highest expectations, full of energy and curiosity, frequently exhibit all sorts of alarming symptoms after only a few years: from a general weariness of school, sinking concentration, and/or decreasing curiosity, to headaches, bed-wetting, stomach problems, frequent colds, and even suicide attempts. Between these two extreme poles are to be found all degrees of irritation, lack of self-confidence and zest for life, aggressivity, cynicism, and everything else that makes life unpleasant for families and the rest of the general population. Admittedly, all of these represent pathological symptoms of our civilized world, yet school seems to be the place where they are cultivated. We could, for instance, take the widespread and growing malady of legasthenia, a deficit in sensory-motor coordination believed by specialists to cause difficulties in reading and writing. In his little booklet about the school printing press, Hans Jörg remarks that in schools that use this as a method of work and activity for the children, no cases of legasthenia were observed! With this work technique, children—in addition to having the possibility of intensive verbal communication—often get up off their chairs, move back and forth, touch the letters with their fingertips, set and take apart blocks of type, and do a whole series of practical work steps that appeal to all five senses as well as give the child pleasure in its own activity and the concrete result of its efforts.

Here we come a little closer to the nucleus or heart of the problem. Our experience with the active school system gives us sufficient proof that it is possible to educate in harmony handicapped and normal children, among them children of differing temperaments and levels of intelligence, without using the principle of selection. More than this, our experience shows that children who exhibit all sorts of "minor damage"—and thus would have been quickly removed from a traditional school or placed in the hands of specialists—can find surroundings here that allow them not only to calm down but to recover as well, where their positive sides can come to the fore. At an active school, children are not obliged to behave in a way that runs contrary to their nature as children. Sitting still and speaking only when spoken to—this is possible for schoolchildren only with suppression of their natural predisposition. For those who are already under pressure on the inside, it is the worst thing that can be asked or expected of them. According to Piaget, freedom of movement and speech is basic to the formation of healthy structures of comprehension. A positive grasp of reality comes about only to the degree that the natural needs of the child are respected. Egocentric behavior will continue for as long a time as the pressure of unsatisfied needs necessitates it. At this age, freedom of movement alone and in itself is indispensable in order to start therapy of repressed emotions and create a long-term connection between the structures of feeling and thinking. At this age it is impossible to separate the "hygiene of personality" connected to feelings from intellectual ideals. The school should give children legitimate and unceasing opportunity to free themselves of inner tensions, whatever the origin of these tensions may be. For the same reason, the school should at all costs avoid producing such tensions itself. For us at Pestalozzi there is no doubt about it: if we give children not only permission but new stimulus and incentive on a day-to-day basis to move spontaneously and in a way that corresponds to their nature as such, school unites the principles of therapy and pedagogy in one current.

In this practice of a free association with things and people, there is one wholesome factor already implicit, included automatically, so to speak: whereas the traditional school sets teacher and pupil against each other in a way that allows no escape (the child has a teacher it does not like for the entire school year, and a teacher is faced with difficult pupils for the duration as well), the active school transforms this face-to-face confrontation into a triangle. Children and teachers work with each other, among one another, and with the material within the dynamic framework of the prepared environment. According to their mental state at the moment, children and teachers have the opportunity to be together with or to avoid the others, while concrete materials that are of interest to both adults and children give them a common ground on which to meet. Let us imagine that we are in a completely empty room with a child, either our own or an unknown child. There may be nothing more difficult for an adult than to have to approach a child directly, without a medium. However, if we have something at hand that arouses the interest of the child, it does not take long until the child admits us to his or her own personal magic circle.

Every day we experience how children "forget all their sufferings" and "heal themselves," when they lose themselves in a self-chosen activity with things that hold their interest to such an extent, when they reach such a high level of concentration, that they feel at one with the world, even if only temporarily. This feeling of oneness—long since forgotten and buried in the case of most of us adults—is the "magic potion" that can heal all the ills of childhood. But its secret formula must be found by each child on its own and applied in the dose it alone can prescribe for itself. We adults cannot invent the therapy for children from outside and "administer" it to them.

What, then, is the role of the adult in this therapeutic process? It is derived from a change of stance, a transformed attitude, which makes it possible to find any behavior of children "normal" in the sense that it is the intelligent answer of the child's organism to the conditions of its life. If we wish to change the behavior of the child, because it is hard for others to tolerate, we must change the conditions of the child's environment and leave it to the child to find new and more satisfactory responses—for all concerned—to these new conditions. We approach each child with complete and entire respect, letting the child feel accepted, even if the child itself feels full of conflict. If we must correct a child, for the protection of other children and the objects that are to be of service to all, we draw the child over close to us and try to hug him or her, if the child permits this. Thus the child can feel the acceptance of its person, and it will be easier for him or her to accept the correction of unsuitable behavior without feeling attacked on the level of its person.

In the case of an overly shy or fearful child who mistrusts adults, we offer opportunities for interesting activities either alone or with others, if that is possible, and leave it at that for the present. We try to come into contact with the child, without posing a danger to its integrity, by means of looks, fleeting touches, or a friendly word. Every now and again we remind the child, "If you need me, you can call me." One seven-year-old boy needed a full year before he called me for the first time and showed me his work! Our readiness to play "dumb" games with the children is an important aid in gaining their confidence and thus being able to make contact, even with the most shy of them. Maybe they stand there with their mouths open when another child knocks us over in the course of play. A child's eyes tell us whether it secretly wishes to play similar games one day. Later we invite the child to come closer or to join in the game, with small gestures, but without touching the child. Thus trust is built up bit by bit. It may take weeks or months, but someday even a child like this will open up to the world and its fellow human beings with a great feeling of happiness.

Freedom of movement and an outlet for physical energies are of great importance for the aggressive and "hyperactive" children in particular. Sometimes it is not enough for them to hoe the ground or kick a ball to let out anger. A seven-year-old boy to whom we supplied a carpet beater and an old mattress during an attack of rage screamed at one point, "I don't want to hit any mattress! I want to hit *somebody!*" He needed a strong man who could take a real fistfight with the boy and who did not end the fight leaving him with more bewilderment and new feelings of guilt but with a bigger and bigger hug instead. At the close of this improvised therapy session, the child sat and cried on the lap of his new friend for a long time, gasping out between sobs, "All grown-ups are liars, liars, liars!"

In every school year it comes to light that a few of our children—most of them from families not suffering want—are little thieves. They steal the food of their schoolmates, school materials, and office supplies. When this comes to our attention, usually through the complaints of other children, we not only try to show these small criminals more affection, we also have a basket within reach of the teacher that is filled with fruits, cookies, small whatnots. Once in a while one of us calls the wrongdoer over and gives him or her, under the seal of secrecy, a little present, together with a small hug. It can be a shell, a few marbles, something to eat—it depends on what seems to be the primary need of this child. This remedy results in great success in most cases. The child gradually begins to feel loved and accepted, receiving something when it is least expected. A connection is made between the authentic need for love and acceptance and the substitute, namely the attempt to satisfy this need by the theft of something. As a result of our acceptance, rather than punishment, the child finds the strength to change its behavior and make real friends.

The presence of the adult takes on new significance in this context: it is not the role of the doctor who makes a diagnosis and prescribes suitable medicine but rather that of a good guardian spirit that creates new and more helpful conditions for children so that they can find as well as restructure themselves. During this process the adult is available should the child need help. The adult, however, does not determine the course or direction of the process from outside. Each new level of consciousness requires a leaving behind of something, a separation from former habits. This brings with it feelings of pain. Another person who has been through such transitions can offer security here in this situation, without stealing the child's wonderful feeling of personal accomplishment or triumph.

The common schoolroom for all can and ought to benefit the growth of all children, the normal ones as well as those suffering from certain ills. In very special cases, which I will report on a bit later, an additional individual therapy may be necessary for a certain length of time. Here I would like to cite a few examples of children who came to us with difficulties and were helped considerably by the environment of the active school system.

Santiago came to us as a six-year-old. He had been described as hyperactive and dangerously aggressive by three previous kindergartens. On his first day at our school, before we could blink an eye, he had scattered a considerable amount of the didactic material all over the grounds, opened all the doors of the rabbit hutches, gone after the llamas, and given kicks to dogs, cats, and most of his classmates; he finally landed, exhausted and crying, in the arms of a teacher. And that is where he landed again and again when the world threatened to collapse around him. Other than that, he had experiences of a positive nature in a huge sandpile, realized a number of incredible projects using water, bridges, mud, and stones, chased insects every day, climbed up trees, and played soccer to the point of exhaustion. Later he laid out a small garden and was devoted to it.

When Santiago began to show interest in different materials, he started a rock collection, and he built boats of balsawood for a duration of three weeks, which he then sailed on the pond. Little by little his movements became less hectic, less hurried, calmer. He was able to work at the school printing press for periods of fifteen minutes at a time and learned to read fluently in one month with this. The Montessori material for arithmetic fascinated him even though it frustrated him, because the many beads and chains kept flying off the table. Gradually, however, his movements became more orderly, though he soon developed the inclination to switch over to mental arithmetic as quickly as possible, so as to shorten the period of time spent with the difficult handling of these materials. It need hardly be said that his social behavior improved noticeably, and he was soon a popular companion and buddy for all the adventurous small boys. When one of the children hurts itself during a walk or gets stung by a bee, Santiago is the first one there to offer comfort and help. It is no wonder, either, because he knows what pain is from his own experience.

Soon after he entered our school, we were able to have our first talks with Santiago's mother. It turned out that she herself had been treated with tranquilizers since the age of fourteen in order that she might take life more calmly. She had always seen herself as an intellectual, marrying one as well, a sociologist. When she was expecting Santiago, she was horrified at this, resisting the idea of being a mother. For two years she was unable to get rid of a feeling of aversion toward her own child. She can vividly recall scenes in which she hit her small child mercilessly for minor offenses. A psychologist tried to make clear to her what damage she was doing to the child by her behavior. Since then she has been making an effort, together with her husband, to give the boy "positive attention." Yet she is still considerably inhibited in her direct expression of feelings, certainly in part because of the effect of the medications. Thus she addresses herself to the child in an intellectual manner, encouraging all impulses that prove his intelligence. Santiago has been fighting for the right to be himself since the day he was born.

Another child who would have been sent to a specialist long since were she still going to a traditional school is Alba. When she came to us at the age of four, her role of enfant terrible in the family was very familiar to her. She never wearied of fighting everything and everybody. She was an eternal troublemaker, broke everything, and never played happily by herself like other children of her age. Through lots of opportunity for practical activity, her behavior gradually became more tolerable, but she still showed much less harmony and was more of a "changeling" than all the other children of her age group. Her older sister, who had gone to nursery school here and then been sent to another school, came back to attend our primary school when Alba was six years old. Alba's behavior worsened immediately. Compared with Alba, her sister seemed quiet and beautifully well behaved, a model pupil. At the age when other children have long since begun to learn to read and write, it was still impossible for Alba to sit still for more than five minutes. But she exhibited great care, concentration, and perseverance in all practical work.

In the course of the years, we had close contact with the parents of these two girls. It turned out that Alba had been born with a hip defect. According to the doctor's instructions, she had to live with a pillow between her legs, day and night, in her first two years of life. At the same time, her parents were overworked and under considerable strain in their new hardware store. The child often showed impatience in her uncomfortable position—which hindered her from crawling or learning to walk—which the parents in turn usually regarded as unacceptable behavior. So Alba grew up with the feeling of being an undesired intruder, in addition to coping with her motor limitations. She was continually compared with her nice sister. When, following our recommendations, the parents started to observe Alba more closely in her spontaneous activity at home, they were astounded to find that she most loved to lie in bed and move her arms and legs back and forth like an infant. She was making up for what she had not been able to do in those first two years. She gradually perceived the security of being respected at home as well, not forced into attaining school achievements. It did not take long for her to show interest in all that can be learned at school. But as soon as her parents took note of this, they wanted to spur her on to faster progress. Alba immediately took flight back to her old behavior and her rebellious personality. We convinced the parents anew that the most important thing for Alba was complete love and acceptance with no strings attached. Only with that would she feel secure enough to be able to learn like other children. She has since learned to read and takes home a new book from the library every week.

Freedom of movement, free play, and the experience that the child's decisions are respected in the prepared environment have therapeutic as well as educational effects. Free symbolic play takes on the most important role in this process. All teachers consciously encourage this play, as it constitutes, both for normal and abnormal children, a spontaneous and natural play therapy. Children who have forgotten how to play like this may need a lot of time before they dare to make up, in front of their teachers, for what they have missed. The older the child, the greater the hesitation before deciding to jump in, but no child under the age of twelve can resist for long. If we adults are near the playing children, our respectful observation, listening, and occasional verbal reflecting of their play provide additional security that enables them to play out their personal problems and free themselves from them. We do, of course, have myriad other things to do in the active school system and thus cannot always give this aspect the amount of attention it merits. For particular cases, therefore, we have made the decision to offer help in the form of individual therapy in our playroom, when parents are in agreement. This nondirective type of play therapy is described in detail by Virginia Axline. Although we have information about the problem of the child in question, coming from reports of the parents and our own observations, we do not make any diagnoses in this therapy. Often the adult only repeats the actions and words of the playing child, without any explanatory comments, allowing the child to go as far in its expression and its own diagnosis as its own integrity allows.

David, who came to us at nine years of age because of his hyperactivity, showed only minor improvement after a number of weeks. He could never stay at one activity for longer than ten minutes and constantly tried to torment or disturb the other children. So we decided on an individual play therapy, in agreement with his parents, to be supplemented by regular talks with them. In the course of this work, the story of the child's history came out in bits and pieces, a story his parents had tried to keep as secret as possible. Up to the age of five, David had been a quiet and happy child, so normal in every respect that his parents felt completely safe in leaving him in the care of their housemaid while they went about their own lives. When he was five, the maid committed suicide in front of him. She expired just upon arrival at the hospital to which his parents had driven her after arriving home. Soon after this experience, David lost his power of speech and turned into a child completely dominated by fear. A psychologist recommended a school for disturbed children. By means of the therapy that was administered there, David gradually regained his speech, but his behavior became more and more intolerable. He could never be left alone after this and repeatedly attempted to throw himself in front of a car. The general impression he gave was one of greater and greater derangement.

After five sessions of play therapy, David was already daring to express with dolls what had been going on inside him for the last four years. Like every five-year-old child who often believes that it is the cause of everything going on around it, he had had to live with the overpowering and unbearable conviction that he was responsible for the death of the housemaid. His feelings of guilt were exacerbated by a state of bewilderment caused by the continually new and different stories that his parents invented in regard to the disappearance of the maid. With these attempts to cover up what had happened, they effectively prevented the child from talking to them about his terrible feelings. In further sessions of play therapy,

David was able to act out his guilt in a variety of versions. Almost unnoticeably, his hyperactive behavior began to disappear, and he invented new possibilities of dissolving his tensions within the free atmosphere of the school.

We often find ourselves discussing the question of whether the active school and all the possibilities connected with it for the child to structure its behavior anew are meaningful and/or make sense only if conditions at home begin to adapt to the child's needs. In spite of all our efforts, not all parents can or wish to make changes in favor of their children. However, it seems to us that even in cases in which a child has to return to a disadvantageous or even destructive situation day after day, thus being compelled to turn the active school into a place of therapy rather than one of learning, this positive experience gives the child strength to be able to deal with his or her home situation. At the very least, the child does not grow up with the conviction that life is a dead end with no escape but comes to believe that there must be ways out. So we cherish our hope that the child's experience in an active school will provide the courage necessary to continue the search for alternatives, all through its life.

CHAPTER SEVENTEEN

A Look Back and a Look Ahead

S ince the first publication of this report on our experience at Pestalozzi, more than fifteen years have passed. It is nothing less than a miracle that more than twenty years have gone by since the foundation of our Pesta, as the school is affectionately called, and we have survived many a storm, been through both expected and unexpected experiences, gained a number of new insights, and earned a few gray hairs in the process.

External developments go hand in hand with those of the internal kind. The original concept of an alternative school has become more radical, undergoing its transformation into a deeper understanding of processes of growing and maturity.

We started our first kindergarten for Leonardo in Colombia. His negative experiences in primary school gave us the courage to take the plunge and create a new kind of primary school for our second son, Rafael, which developed into what is now the Pestalozzi school. Both of our sons have grown up in the meantime. Leonardo is thirty-three years old now, and—most recently—a father himself. Our first grandchild, a baby girl who is named Miranda, was born just a few months ago. And we find ourselves in a new process: being—and becoming—grandparents.

When we permitted Leonardo, at the age of twelve, to leave

secondary school, he stayed home for more than a year. During this period of time, he was apparently able to "reproduce" contact to his own self. After a few months of "doing nothing," he began baking bread in order to earn the money for a new bicycle and explored on horseback the area surrounding the inactive volcano called Ilalo, the impressive contours of which rise to one side of Pesta. Then he began to read with a passion. At the age of fourteen he again made an attempt to attend a traditional secondary school, but his capacity for self-study had grown so much that the classes soon started to bore him. In his free time, often until late at night, he began writing his own short stories, until he raised blisters on his hand. At sixteen he gave up secondary school once again, earned the money—at a job he had chosen himself—for a flight to Europe, and spent a year there, working at various jobs, taking courses, and traveling. When Leonardo was seventeen he showed up in Ecuador again, with the manuscripts of two new books. As he was still wavering as to whether he should attempt to earn his school-leaving certificate of secondary education, an unexpected opportunity arose for him to go to sea as a sailor on a private sailing boat taking course for the South Pacific. Following these six months of adventure, he returned home full of desire and energy for getting back to his studies. In four months of private study, he prepared himself for the external examinations leading to the awarding of an American high-school diploma, which he then passed in Washington, D. C. Six weeks after his arrival in the United States, he was able to matriculate at a university to begin study. In the two years that followed he earned his own living, at the same time taking so many class hours that he went through college with a double subject load; but after two years with a scholarship and a place on the Dean's list, he decided to concentrate on his writing and on sailing the South Pacific. Since then Leonardo has brought together much travel experience, as well as experience in myriad jobs, both at sea and on land (on various continents), with the writing of short stories, novels, and poetry. He has constructed a house of wood near Pesta and is trying to build up an existence that allows him to find a balance between an active, practical life and the life of a writer. After publication of regular articles in a national newspaper and various magazines here in Ecuador, several of his novels started to come out in 1996, in this country and in Germany.

I tell this story of a "dropout" here for the benefit of parents who see no alternative between the horrors of a life as a good-for-nothing and the constricting necessity of compelling a young person to sit in school year after year or go through a regulated period of job training.

Our second son, Rafael, the then two-year-old "founder" of Pesta, is now twenty-four years old. He remained at Pesta until he was eighteen, attending our secondary school, of which I will give a short description a bit further on in this chapter. In earlier editions of this book, I described how Rafael, at the age of eight, summed up the event of his learning to read using the following words: "Up to now I only saw the letters with my eyes and wrote them with my hand. But now I've learned to make them resound in my heart." After that it took a few more years for Rafael to find enough pleasure in books of some length that he was ready to sacrifice his other important activities for reading. But in all those years, he loved to listen to stories of all kinds. And when he did begin to read intensively and continually, he devoted evenings, above all, to this activity, often reading until late at night, while his days were filled primarily with experimentation, adventures, play, and concrete types of work. Even as an adolescent, he combined a childlike openness with an astonishing ability to grasp complex situations. As a young adult, he feels as much at home with practical work as with reflection and analysis in regard to his experiences. In his relationships with peers, older persons, and children, he shows the same sureness, including the difficult art of setting limits or drawing the line, something that normally causes adults great difficulties. It seems to be one of the particular characteristics of active children that they show dignity in their being children, rather than perceiving it as a sort of disease from which one must be cured as fast as possible. They play representative games up to and into the years of puberty, often sharing them with younger children, and still enjoy games involving movement, without the necessity of competition or matches of physical strength. Above all, they always find something interesting to do; are much less dependent on outside entertainments; have fun with practical work, excursions of exploration, and trips; and make friends easily with children and adults alike.

When we compare children who have spent years of their growth in the active system with others who spend the greater part of their time sitting on chairs and at desks, the first thing we notice is their greater sureness and harmony of physical movement. Even without pressure, they help to keep common rooms in order. They can solve conflicts, in most cases, in a way that we adults would never come upon. They can often tolerate stress situations better than we can. One father told the following story about his ten-year-old daughter, Isabel: "My mother came to stay with us for a few days. She's one of these elderly people that you can't please, no matter what you do. She found fault with meals, with the haircut of our four-year-old, with our furniture and the disorder in the kitchen. She caused so much tension in the house that we all started to bite our fingernails and fight with each other, because we couldn't stand any more. Naturally, her grandmother also started in on Isabel, who was trying out recipes from her children's cookbook in the kitchen, as usual. To our complete astonishment, Isabel grasped the situation far better than any or all of us were able to—my only idea was to put my mother on the next plane to Guayaquil—and found the right solution by intuition: she asked her grandma to cook the most famous traditional Ecuadorean recipes with her during her visit, so that she could learn them. My mother was charmed by this interest. The two of them went off together happily to get all the ingredients from the market, and then spent every free hour in the kitchen. My mother really came alive—I haven't heard her laughing like that since she was young. Every meal became a culinary feast. But the best of all was that this grandmother of ours had finally found a worthy place in this incomprehensible modern household she never had been able to understand."

Another story was recounted to us by the parents of Christian when he was around nine. Christian had been one of our "impossible" boys who for years spent the majority of the morning with games of movement and maybe half an hour per day at the most with structured material—yet showing an ability to organize that proved his good concrete operational capabilities. On a trip to the coast, the family had a car accident. The injuries were minor; Christian, with one bloody head wound, had got the worst of it. But his parents found themselves in a state of shock and suddenly had no idea in their heads of how to deal with the situation of their damaged car and the aggressive other driver who had crashed into them. To their surprise their son, whom they usually regarded as more or less a "failure," began to give them the necessary guidance, step-by-step. Since this experience, Christian has been in a position to circumvent the decision of his parents to transfer him to a "decent" school, year after year. He has now been at Pesta for seven years. Recently, in the course of a parents' evening at school, his father exclaimed, "Well, finally! Now you've explained all of this here so that I can understand it!"

In my other books, *Sein zum Erziehen* ("To Be in Order to Educate"), *Kinder im Pesta* ("Children in Pesta"), and *Freiheit und Grenzen* ("Freedom and Limits"), I have described a number of experiences and processes of both children and adults that have impressed us over the years. Therefore, I would like to go into some external aspects of our work here at this point.

OUR RELATIONS WITH
THE MINISTRY OF EDUCATION

Although the Ministry of Education was soon recommending our preschool kindergarten as a model, resulting in our receiving numerous visits from groups of educators from all provinces of the country, at its start the primary school worked for three years without official recognition.

On the dissolution of a military junta of many years in Ecuador and its replacement by a democratically elected government, the inflexible education law experienced a reform. In its new form, parents were accorded the final decision in regard to the type of school for their children, thus opening a door for alternative forms of education. Pesta received its official approval and the license for operating on the basis of the method "education through the spontaneous activity of the child," yet in all those years there was no official primary-school certificate for this "school category." Children who transferred to the traditional system had to take a test worked out by the ministry in order to be graded in terms of the normal system of marks. This changed in 1998. Under the current administration, experimental schools are given the task of "breaking out of the framework set up by the law and gaining entirely new experience in educational practice." A number of seminars, in which authorities together with the heads of all experimental schools in the country attempted to set down new regulations and guidelines, brought to light that up to then, only Pesta had fulfilled this above condition of such "illegality." In June 1989 we organized, in cooperation with the Ministry of Education in Ecuador, a one-week seminar during which theory and practice of the "educational method of spontaneous activity of the child" were presented and discussed. Delegations from the Saraguro tribe of Indians in the far south of Ecuador and from the active school of one of the poorest areas in Quito participated in this seminar as well, thus making clear that alternative education is not the privilege of intellectual or wealthy elites. On the contrary, it signifies a real chance for the "underdeveloped" to arrive at a solution for many problems that have remained unsolved to date. Since August 1989, children who have worked in the active system up to the equivalent of the third secondary grade (approximately equal to the sophomore year of high school in the United States, about fifteen to sixteen years of age) receive an official certificate from the Ministry of Education in Ecuador that attests to emotional, social, and intellectual maturity rather than subject matter or knowledge learned by rote.

ORGANIZATION OF THE SCHOOL

Soon after official recognition of the school in 1982, we followed the initiative of parents and gave the school, up to that point our private undertaking, the legal status of a foundation, with the name Fundacion Educativa Pestalozzi. The general meeting of its members elects the representatives for the board of directors, who have since been responsible for administration of the school. Since 1990 all responsibility for decisions relating to pedagogy and administration lies with a team of (now) seven adults, all of whom work directly at the school and are parents at the same time. They are assisted by other interested parents. The aim of the foundation is, in addition to the operation of the kindergarten and primary schools, the sharing of our experience with interested persons at home and abroad upon demand.

Despite the earlier insecurity of a school-leaving certificate, more and more parents have decided in the last few years not to send their children from Pesta's nursery school to a school of the traditional system, leaving them with us instead. Parents of primary-school children sign a contract with us for each new school year, stating their agreement with our method and accepting the obligation to take part in a course for parents once a month.

At the preschool kindergarten as well as the primary school, a small percentage of differently handicapped children are accepted every school year and integrated into our normal operations day. The prerequisite for acceptance of these children has meanwhile become this: they must not be undergoing any special therapies outside school, unless it is in clear agreement with our staff. This condition, which may seem very hard at first glance, follows from the experience we have had over the years. In the course of time it became very clear that children whose handicaps are "treated" by therapies coming from outside do not utilize the possibilities of a nondirective and relaxed environment in a positive way but try to get rid of their tensions—which arise again and again through constant directive handling—in it, whereas children who open up to this environment in their own way go through unexpected developments, coming from their own inner healing force of nature, that are incomprehensible even to specialists.

The necessity to integrate very different social classes increased more and more as well. Since 1992 the Pestalozzi II kindergarten has no longer been working separately, owing to the fact that social structures in the Tumbaco valley, as an area just outside Quito, have changed greatly. Pestalozzi I has taken some of the children from the parallel kindergarten, after it had been utilized years ago as a last resort by Indio families from various provinces and of different "nationalities." Such families, having settled in Quito for reasons of jobs, found themselves in a dilemma: at public schools their children had to stop wearing their traditional costumes, cut their long hair, often worn in braids, and put on school uniforms. At Pestalozzi they sought respect for their individual and cultural differences. Inhabitants of poorer areas of Quito and Tumbaco, Indians of various tribes and cultures, and children of the middle and upper classes now mix more and provide us with the proof that our respect for the "inner plan of development of children" that we try to put into practice in turn leads to an amazing ability in the children to respect each other in regard to their individual, social, and cultural differences.

Out of this practice of social integration grew the problem of financing scholarships, or free places, that has accounted for approximately 30 percent of our budget in all these years. As the government grants us no support, we have attempted to make up for this inevitable deficit in a variety of ways, all of which represent activity that costs us a great deal of time and energy.

WORK WITH ADULTS

Something that gained more and more significance in regard to the functioning of this way of dealing with children was the work with teachers and parents. Experience showed us beyond the shadow of a doubt that we adults represented the greatest problem in the relaxed environment. For this reason we devote two afternoons a week for work with the teachers. Three afternoons are reserved for private talks with parents and practice with concrete materials. Two evenings a week are for group work with parents of the various age groups or meetings of our board of directors for the solution of problems. On Saturdays we give introductory courses on the problems of upbringing and education in the situation of our modern society for interested teachers from other schools, representatives of projects beginning to work with the active method, or especially interested and/or involved parents. Since 1990 part of our work with adults has been our regular introductory and advanced seminars for parents, teachers, and educators of all kinds in Europe who have set their feet on a new path in the search for new forms and methods.

The model of a "completely different" school, in which human beings of many different social classes and nationalities are treated with the same respect, has always drawn attention from groups looking for alternatives themselves. Many have come to visit us, in the course of their search for ideas and exchange. From some of these many visitors have come initiatives like the popular day nurseries supported by Terre des Hommes, which have been working for the initiative of the child for more than ten years now. In the slums of Quito and the Indio communities, there were various initiatives to put into practice active methods that respect children's own cultures. This is a sector in which the pressure of politicians and programs of development aid in favor of uniform schooling is very great. The tempting offer that is made, namely to incorporate underprivileged or disadvantaged children into the miracle of progress by means of a school education, often convinces many parents here, as in other countries, to bow to compulsory schooling, even if it goes against their culture and the harmonious development of their children. This pressure from outside makes it hard for such projects to yield to the growing desire for change in education, yet small initial efforts have been made; "new beginnings" are to be seen in various places, despite the difficulties.

Owing to all these developments, there was polarization on the part of "old" Pesta parents, who had consciously or unconsciously hoped that Pesta would be an elite alternative school, guaranteeing their children higher intellectual and social standards. When the first five Indio teachers began to work and children with braids and ponchos had the same rights as those with curly blond hair, we saw waves of departing children from "better" families. Seldom, however, was anyone prepared to admit the motive openly. Most of those who fled to the safety of recognized and socially accepted school conditions did it as secretly as possible. "Active schools" were suddenly founded, and they promised parents observance of all ministerial regulations and the valid curriculum, thus the possibility of recognized school certificates, and active methods at the same time. In one year we lost 30 percent of our paying pupils at one blow. Yet Pesta survived this storm as well and was able to expand through the new parents who found their way to us, coming because they were searching for this alternative out of the need for a truly new beginning in life.

THE PROJECTS OF SECONDARY SCHOOL AND AUTODIDACTIC UNIVERSITY

In the course of time, we were confronted with the problem of whether our alternative should really end for children following their completion of an active primary school. We had seen again and again that children who had lived many years in the free system had no difficulty making the transfer to the usual school system, becoming the best in their class in most cases and able to skip a grade in some cases. We assumed that the concrete operational phase of development, lasting until about the twelfth year of life, demands a prepared environment in which children can solve problems in concrete situations and thus develop the cognitive structures for the laws and regularities of the physical world—meaning, therefore, that this phase has been completed for the most part by the end of the Ecuadorean primary-school period.

In addition, Pesta had been accommodated since its foundation on premises that were terminable every year, according to our contract. The owner of the property lived in the United States. Prices for property went up and up; in spite of ever increasing rent, the owner received fewer and fewer dollars for our sucres because of the inflation of our local currency. A sale of the property became more and more likely. Our project for an alternative secondary school was turned down by Pesta's board of directors, with no hope of approval as long as no permanent construction on land of our own could be realized. Yet the financial situation of the foundation allowed no dreams of land purchase.

One day, however, Maria, an Indio girl who had suffered greatly during her earlier sojourn at a normal school, flatly refused to leave Pesta to attend secondary school. Her father wrote an inflammatory letter to the board of directors in which he officially entrusted the further education of his daughter to us, because he had found the results so entirely satisfactory up to that point in time. He appealed to our feelings of humanity, which would certainly not allow us to "deliver up" his daughter to a traditional secondary school with all the dire consequences that would entail. His letter ended with the remark that "only the most courageous may dare to operate outside the law."

At this meeting a member of the board offered to become the girl's tutor. Maria remained at our school. Amid the hubbub of one hundred primary-school pupils, she had to create her own space, together with her tutor. As soon as two other girls who had just transferred to a traditional secondary school got wind of this new constellation, they came back—and an "illegal secondary level" was founded against all odds.

An earlier concept of ours for an alternative secondary school, albeit in vague form as yet, was then taken up again. Step-by-step it went through a process of gradual further development, and it is being put into practice at present, step-by-step, with approximately thirty-five young adolescents between thirteen and seventeen years of age. Following naturally from our experience with the older primary-school pupils (aged from ten to thirteen), who spend three days a month "sniffing the air" at a great variety of places of work in the adult world, and who regard this opportunity as a very important part of their program, the model for the older children gradually ripened to maturity. The basic idea is that youngsters of this age group find themselves in a period of transition from the concrete operational stage of development just coming to an end (which can still be very strong, especially in boys of this age) to the stage of formal thinking. The question of what the authentic needs of this new developmental stage are brought us to the conclusion that this age attaches more and more significance to dealing with the world of new and open social experience—exactly the opposite of the otherwise usual isolation in preacademic schooling or the specialization for particular occupations already determined. The result of this reflection led to a model of secondary school in which the young people get practical work experience or exposure to a different culture from their own each year at different points in time during the school year and spend the rest of the time in a prepared environment corresponding to their intellectual, emotional, social, and "playful" needs. The processes adolescents go through in the course of these changing experiences clearly show that this new practice satisfies their authentic needs more than an abstract study program that forces them to sit still for hours on end. It has become obvious to us that through such interaction between growing organisms and a more and more complex environment, new structures of comprehension are formed that correspond to the biological plan of maturing for this age group. Each adolescent chooses a tutor among the adults with more experience at Pesta who helps him or her with orientation in this very open life situation. The tutor gives the pupil the security of being available, also after school hours if need be, offers an open ear in times or situations of difficulty, and can also build a bridge to parents when necessary. If a boy or girl does not get along with the respective tutor any longer, he or she has the option to choose someone else.

From these years of experience, as a logical consequence, a new project has developed since 1995, to which we have given the name Autodidactic University. The basic structure consists of an organization with so-called offerers from all sorts of areas of work and knowledge who open up their practice and their theoretical knowledge. Persons of any age (from eighteen on, because this coincides with legal coming of age in Ecuador) have the opportunity, upon mutual agreement and arrangement, to make use of the experience, the concrete work opportunities, and the knowledge of the offerer. We have three different levels: (a) a first taste of it, then (b) practice, and finally (c) deeper involvement.

The considerations leading to this structure have been manifold—for example, the fact that Pestalozzi "graduates," after many years of experience in making decisions and working on their own projects, must begin a course of study and share the same fate as many other young people, all of whom are forced to follow a pre-scribed curriculum plan for years before they have the possibility of seeing in everyday practice whether they would like to work in this field at all. "Lost time" and prestige do not permit many to change to something else after years of study. The two opportunities for a "first taste" and "practicing" open up to young people a variety of different experiences, thanks to which they can broaden their hori-zons, switch from one area over to another without losing face, and finally come to a decision in regard to the sector into which they want to go deeper, that is to say, study. Moreover, during the period of practice they can even earn money. There is an agreement be-tween university and employer that this employer is not under any legal obligation to offer steady or permanent employment.

Other grounds for this structure are provided by our conviction that theory without practice is nonsense but that all reflection based on concrete experience is a true human need. Furthermore, it is to be seen on the normal labor market to an increasing extent that certificates and degrees of education without practical experience are less and less attractive. Yet up to now there have been only very few opportunities for students to gain concrete experience in addi-tion to their studies.

During the short time that this autodidactic university has been in operating existence, it has shown not only that young people in search of a profession find new possibilities here but that adults who already have occupations in which they are working also gain new experience by the hour or day, thus enriching their lives. In some cases, offerers are registered as autodidactics as well, which replaces the accustomed hierarchy of teacher and learner by a constellation of cooperation and exchange. Moreover, there are offerers who have not even completed a school education but can offer experience and knowledge worthy of attention and interest in their field or from their culture (for example, representatives of Indio communities).

We are involved in the creation of a prepared environment for all these offerers and autodidactics, together with their tutors, who act as go-betweens for both of them, in which they can meet as desired for their mutual exchanges. The central coordination office of this "university" awards no public diplomas. Instead it provides certificates that describe each experience in terms of type and level. We believe that certificates such as these will be useful for finding starting positions or niches in our rapidly changing economic system. Pestalozzi pupils with certificates from their nine years of basic education with us can make use of the offers of this "university"—which we are calling the Autodidactic Network—before they are eighteen, as so-called tadpoles. We are still looking for a way to certify their activities and accomplishments, but this allows them to continue to enjoy the prepared environment of the school and thus move back and forth between the two worlds of adolescence and adulthood.

FINANCIAL ORGANIZATION

In our society of today, there seems to exist only a dim awareness of the fact that an environment corresponding to the needs of young people growing up ought to be one of our highest priorities. In the "progressive" countries it is especially obvious what efforts are put into prepared environments for cars, for instance. Let us compare this with the fainthearted and irresolute attempts to do the same for children and with the widespread myth that the best place to keep children is in the classroom, where they spend the greater part of the day sitting still. On the other hand, more and more of those in positions of responsibility express their worry over the various problems connected with today's youth, a source of concern for all. Discussions about the budget for education are conducted around points such as square meters per child, salaries of teachers and school psychologists, costs of laboratories and school equipment, by which is meant schoolbooks and visual material, above all. But when do we hear anything about creating environments in which children can really *live*—at home, at school, in urban surroundings?

Within this general framework, Pesta, like probably every alternative that addresses itself to the real needs of children, is constantly attempting to solve its financial problems. The accusation is often hurled at us that we have no right to create such an environment unless we can guarantee that all the children in the world will then have the same chance. As this unfortunately cannot be achieved by individuals, we have found ourselves in the same dilemma for many years: trying to find a balance between paying and nonpaying children, since social integration has been a part of our principle of respect for children since the very beginning of our school. An active school requires the constant repair and replacement as well as expansion of available materials, which—together with scholarships—make up a very large portion of the budget. Although we have had state recognition for some years now, we have never received any subsidies from the state. Anyway, an annual inflation rate of 80 percent makes any financial planning a cliffhanger. So it does seem a miracle that Pesta has made it through all these years. The most important factor has probably been the readiness of parents to pay the school tuition for their children, despite their own financial difficulties (we have very few parents for whom tuition fees for Pesta do not constitute a high percentage of their entire family income). Only a few are in a position to pay more than the amount set by the Ministry of Education (52 percent of pupils cannot pay tuition or can pay only part of it). The second important factor is the willingness of teachers to work for a minimal salary. That is their contribution to make it possible for the school to survive, for themselves and for the children. In many cases this can also mean a possible long-term dependency on one's extended family. Many a young man who wanted to have a family had to choose between working with us and taking another job that offered better pay. A further contribution to the maintenance of the school has been the readiness of some staff members to sacrifice their own vacations in favor of giving summer courses for interested people. With these, some salaries can be covered during the summer, and course fees go back into the school budget as donations.

About 10 percent of the annual budget was made up by donations from abroad in earlier years. We have always tried to make donors conscious of the fact that the establishment of environments suitable and beneficial for children should be a social aim in and of itself. For some donors the idea of social integration was in the foreground of their reflection; others wanted to make sure that their money would be spent only on the poorest. The widespread notion also prevails that projects should get aid only at the start, then help themselves as they go on—quite an illusion in the situation of a country in which the majority of the population gets poorer every year.

In order to set something creative against this tendency of inevitable impoverishment, an exchange ring was founded within our Fundacion Educativa Pestalozzi in October 1994, based on the LETS (local exchange and trading systems) concept practiced in Canada and England. Since then there has been an exchange market taking place here every Saturday, which not only serves as an exchange for goods and services of all kinds but has become a new social center of activity. The offered selection of simple meals permits more than a hundred people (adults and children) to eat together every week, make all sorts of contacts, and get to know one another in a relaxed atmosphere much better than would be possible at the regular parents' evenings. At the Saturday market, goods of all kinds are offered (there is even a truck bringing in "biologically correct" vegetables that always attract particular attention). This assortment of products is augmented by a regular handbill with announcements of "supply and demand." Parents in especially difficult financial circumstances can make application to make partial payment of school tuition fees in "*recursos*," our local unit of "exchange" currency.

For many this alternative economy has proved itself to be a real help. A savings and loan cooperative, which functions without interest, has opened up new possibilities for staff as well as some parents to make purchases and to bridge difficult situations that would otherwise have remained without any hope of a rapid solution. This "cash and loan office" has been in existence since December 1993; it has regularly been able to grant loans amounting to three times the deposits, following the principle of circulation of money.

All these years Pesta has lived from hand to mouth, as they say. We were often unable to say how we would cover our fixed operating costs from one month to the next. In the twelve years that we worked on our leased premises, we always tried to pay at least the rent on time, in order not to give the owner any grounds to serve notice on us. Under such conditions it was impossible to think of buying property ourselves, let alone buildings of our own.

Then, however, in 1987 a number of unforeseen events came together that, when we look back upon them today, seem like pure fiction to us. Contrary to any form of planning or imagining, constellations occurred that finally led to the purchase of land at the foot of the old volcano Ilalo. And then, through a new and fortunate shuffling and congealing of unforeseen factors, the funds donated to us for the purchase of this land were also sufficient for the construction of the most needed infrastructures.

The building for the primary school was constructed in the traditional half-timbered style by twenty Saraguro Indians in cooperative work. Another building for various purposes was built by architects and a local construction company out of wood and brick. The two makeshift pavilions that had accommodated preschool kindergarten and primary school on our rented premises were taken along to the new site. Today they see service as our school office and a center for the exchange market, while a generous donation from Dutch friends enabled us to construct a new kindergarten building, round and entirely of wood.

And so here we are, in beautiful surroundings and without fear of termination of contract since 1989, with a view of the eastern and western mountain ranges of the Andes, at the edge of a deep canyon, continuing to work on the prepared environment for children and adolescents.

HOW CAN ONE KEEP ON IN SPITE OF THE MANY DIFFICULTIES?

This book tells the story of how we, with conviction and enthusiasm, have worked on an alternative in order to make a different experience of school possible for our own son and later for many other children. After more than twenty years we notice that, other than external resistance and obstacles, perhaps one of the greatest hindrances to successful continuation of this work lies in the danger than the enthusiasm at the start gives way to, and is replaced by, routine—the motivation at the beginning receives no further nourishment. This natural tendency toward inertia, however, is countered by our urgent need and wish to gain a deeper and more varied understanding of our work, and to share this with interested people who so desire. This has led us into experiencing a natural opportunity for our own inner growth in our work with children, a process that we consciously undertook, as I have tried to describe in *Sein zum Erziehen*. By looking at our situation anew, over and over again, from new and different angles and viewpoints, our reasons for keeping on with this work, in which concrete and obvious results are only to be seen once in a while, like an unexpected surprise gift, became more radical and even stronger.

It never fails that people who have their first contact with our alternative way of dealing with human relationships ask us the following: "Don't you think that children who grow up in such a way will have a hard time adjusting to 'real' life later? How can children learn what they are going to need later on if they don't grasp how serious and hard life really is and don't learn to do what they don't like? Can they learn at all if they follow their own interests, being happy doing it, wasting most of the day in play? Isn't it our duty to lead them to abstract thinking as quickly as possible, so they can be successful in later life?"

I have just been hearing from one mother—who, after a lot of back and forth, finally took her children out of Pesta—about how happy she is now that her three children are finally learning discipline, in part by practicing military marches on three different brass instruments.

It remains to be seen where such discipline will lead. At Pesta this woman's oldest daughter had found it especially hard, without the usual force administered in other schools, to do something on her own, to solve concrete problems, and to concentrate. Her son, because of his tendency to get into a rage, was constantly in conflict with his classmates during free play and looked for support from adults a number of times every day because he was not able to solve his own problems. Their little sister longed to go back to a traditional school because one could "go to sleep so wonderfully during classes"! It is obvious that such symptoms are closely tied to the parents' lack of understanding or putting their insights into practice, and it is parents like these who find it especially hard to stick it out in an alternative system that actually calls upon them to check their own attitudes and try out new things as well.

But experience has shown us not to give up too easily—it is worth the effort, despite the many setbacks. In the appendix to Herbert Kohl's book *On Teaching,* we can read through considerable research data on the later life and fate of pupils coming from alternative schools. This data confirms not only that "alternative pupils" achieve an acceptable standard in their occupations but that their personal and family life is happier on the average in comparison with the control groups. In addition, they show a remarkable difference in that they exhibit stronger interest in new areas of study and a greater social sense of responsibility.

In the older children who have remained with us despite the earlier "illegality," we can observe an increasing ability for critique. Most of our primary-school pupils, who from the age of ten on gain experience of various kinds in the world of work on three days of every month, in both city and country surroundings, are simply pleased to have the opportunity of getting to know the world—though as they still depend emotionally on the attention of adults they might fall victim to manipulation if the respective employer offers affection or an especially delicious pizza in return. Pupils on the secondary level look at the world of adults with very critical eyes and quickly notice when someone's occupation is not a real vocation, or if a person pretends to have more knowledge than is really the case or makes distinctions of social class with customers or staff. They already ask themselves very basic questions, such as whether it is really worthwhile to conform to many of the values that most adults accept so readily. And they criticize not only easily visible violations of human respect that they have observed, for instance, at a five-star hotel, but also, for example, the subtle arrogance of scientists toward fellow citizens with a lower level of education at an experimental biology laboratory of world renown.

Parents of our young people must also reckon with such critical attitudes and opinions. If desired, the older children take part in their parents' conversations with us. Tania's mother used the occasion of such a talk to complain about her daughter's lack of a sense of order. "Why do you have to throw your dirty socks all over your room before you put them in the laundry basket?" was her accusing question. Tania countered with, "It seems to me that your constant fighting with my father stinks up the house more than my socks!"

In a world that understands very well how to establish prepared environments for cars, factories, commerce, and offices yet does not bother about what children need in order to grow up into full and complete human beings, the work exemplified by Pesta means a constant swimming upstream, against the current. In this daily work, which is also subject to doubt on the part of many people, one thing crystallizes for us more and more: we do not wish simply to adapt the children to the existing world in a nicer way than a regular school would do. The longer we devote ourselves to this task, the clearer it becomes to us that the issue is a completely new way of looking at education, a view or standpoint that could well be called a change of paradigms.

In his introductory remarks addressed to the participants in a seminar on experimental schools in Ecuador in June 1989, Mauricio robbed them of their feeling of well-being that comes from taking part in a successful ritual by saying, "All of us sitting here suffer from a disease that is far more dangerous than AIDS. We suffer from a disease that is beginning to endanger all of civilization—even the survival of our planet is at stake. This disease is AEDS, or acquired educational deficiency syndrome. What makes this disease so dangerous is that we have not yet recognized its devastating effects, or are in fact proud of them."

The mistake made in the usual method of educating human beings up to now is that it goes against the most important biological given factors and principles of life, thus preventing a healthy and harmonious unfolding of development.

Especially in the second chapter of his book *Leitmotiv vernetztes Denken* ("Main Topic: Interconnected Thinking"), Frederic Vester explains the connections between our present educational practices that are regarded as normal, with their tendency to force early abstraction, and the more and more dangerous unsolved problems of our civilization. He emphatically warns us that teaching methods that do not pay serious heed to biological processes of development and the reality of the whole human being, that is to say, that disregard human ecology, lie at the root of the problem and lead to not recognizing living connections and thus to the inability to live in harmony with ourselves and our world. David Elkind mentions in his books many of the devastating effects of conditions of life that do not respect authentic human needs. His data could be supplemented by new statistics from developing countries as well as, to an increasing extent, the industrialized nations.

Instead of conforming to the "normality" of our endangered world—making the luxurious attempt to go new ways, perhaps, but still heading for the same goal of material success—an *Erziehung zum Sein* or "education for being," as the literal translation of the original German title of my book would read, places itself on the side of life. Dealing with life, learning to know and respect its basic principles—this is the alternative to the "nonbeing" that threatens us human beings as well as our environment, our space of life, if we disregard and/or mistreat the realities and laws of life. All life is one, and any and all effort to bring human beings to respect and consideration toward nature is useless and nonsensical, even if we make it a required subject in elementary school, unless we make it possible for our children to have direct interaction with the world, instead of separating them from it by high school walls and subjecting them to lectures by adults who teach knowledge they themselves have gained only from books or taken over from people who "know." When an adult speaks of his or her own experience, hopes, errors, or problems, this alone leads to a threefold increase of attention. How much higher, then, is the concentration of children when they have direct experience in concrete situations of life through their own initiative.

There is prevailing general agreement that we bear great responsibility for the condition of the world we pass on to our children, and we must devote our full attention to it. Yet that alone is not enough if we change nothing in the quality of our relationships. The first step takes place as soon as we cease to impose ourselves, with our manipulations, our interpretations, and our constant giving of directions, between children and young people and the living world, and instead try to stand by them in their own natural activity that fosters growth. Such a change of attitude and stance makes us almost of necessity free for more respectful and loving relationships.

Connected "network" thinking, regarded by Vester as absolutely necessary for the solution of our survival problems, cannot be taught, on principle. It develops spontaneously through the invigoration, inner networking, and flowing connection of all inner structures of feeling, of intuition, up to and including formal thinking. But that is possible only by means of concrete and direct interaction with an environment that does not merely permit the need and desire for autonomy and spontaneous action but consciously enriches the possibilities for this as well. Why is all the research that proves the inner "network connections" of body and mind taken seriously by our general educational sector only when it comes to fitting individuals who have fallen out of norm categories back into the prevailing norms, thus exerting better control over the incorporation of each and every individual into the prevailing system of values? Who is afraid of whom when it comes to daring to take decisive steps in the general school system: teachers, of educational authorities; parents, of teachers; or teachers, of parents? Or are all of them afraid of themselves, because they would have to deal with something new, for which they themselves received no education, that would call into question the entire path of education that they themselves took, that is to say, were obliged to take?

The law of education in Ecuador gives parents the last right of decision concerning the type of education they prefer for their children. Other countries, democratic in other respects such as form of government, apparently do not grant this right to parents. Despite this, I am convinced that, were enough parents to gain awareness of the internal and external connections in issues of education, these parents could influence public opinion in such a way that changes in the school system would no longer be limited to "subversive" individual teachers or the even fewer educational authorities "working underground," so to speak. Even in countries that accord greater freedom in the choice of educational methods, there is apparently a lack of people who can do something with this freedom and share concrete experience with others.

In the higher animal world it is normal than a mother defends her young with incredible courage and rage, if need be. A mother hen will even do battle against snakes in order to protect her chicks. Only we human beings, out of mistaken social consciousness and without entertaining any doubts, would think of delivering our children into the hands of a system, year after year, that has an environment that systematically goes against the basic conditions for living interaction with the world, thus also precluding the development of emotional and intellectual security in later life.

The task we have been given is certainly not easy. But the central question is not whether it is easy or not but, rather, how great the necessity is. And it appears to us that the necessity is as great in the developed as in the underdeveloped countries. Despite all differences, we find ourselves in a similar situation. Our task is to save the quality of our human life and—at the same time—save our world, hurting as it is. I would like to close these pages about the experiences of an active school in Ecuador with the final words of Schumacher's *Guide for the Perplexed*:

> The art of living is always to make a good thing out of a bad thing. Only if we *know* that we have actually descended into *infernal regions* where nothing awaits us but "the cold death of society and the extinguishing of all civilized relations," can we summon the courage and imagination needed for a "turning around." . . . This then leads to seeing the world in a new light, namely, as a place where the things

modern man continuously talks about and always fails to accomplish *can actually be done.* . . . Can we rely on it that a "turning around" will be accomplished by enough people quickly enough to save the modern world? This question is often asked, but no matter what the answer, it will mislead. The answer "Yes" would lead to complacency, the answer "No" to despair. It is desirable to leave these perplexities behind us and get down to work.[1]

---

1. Schumacher, *A Guide for the Perplexed,* 139–40.

Bibliography

Axline, Virginia. *Dibs: In Search of Self*. Boston: Houghton Mifflin, 1964.

———. *Play Theory: The Inner Dynamics of Childhood*. Boston: Houghton Mifflin, 1947.

de Bono, Edward. *The Mechanism of Mind*. New York: Penguin Books, 1977.

———. *Po: Beyond Yes and No*. New York: Penguin Books, 1973.

Dauber, Heinrich, and Etienne Verne. *Freiheit zum Lernen: Alternativen zum lebenslänglichen Verschulung. Die Einheit von Leben, Lernen, Arbeiten*. Reinbek, Germany: Rowohlt, 1976.

Deakin, Michael. *The Children on the Hill*. London: Quartet Books, 1973.

Dewey, John. *Progressive Education*. Vol. 5. 1928. Reprint, in *Dewey on Education,* edited by Martin S. Dworkin. New York: Teachers College Press, 1965.

von Ditfurth, Hoimar. *Der Geist fiel nicht vom Himmel*. 9th ed. Munich: Deutscher Taschenbuch Verlag, 1988.

Elkind, David. *Child Development and Education*. New York: Oxford University Press, 1976.

Freinet, Celestin. *L'enseignement du calcul*. Cannes: Edition de l'Ecole Moderne, 1962.

———. *Methode naturelle de lecture*. Cannes: Edition de l'Ecole Moderne, 1961.

Furth, Hans G., and Harry Wachs. *Thinking Goes to School: Piaget's Theory in Practice*. New York: Oxford University Press, 1982.

Goodman, Paul. *Compulsory Mis-Education*. New York: Penguin Education, 1964.

Holt, John. *What Do I Do Monday?* New York: Pitman Publishing, 1970.

Illich, Ivan. *Celebration of Awareness*. Garden City, NY: Doubleday, 1970.

Janov, Arthur. *The Feeling Child*. London: Abacus, 1979.

———. *The Primal Revolution*. London: Sphere, 1975.

Janov, Arthur, and E. Michael Holden. *Primal Man: The New Consciousness*. London: Abacus, 1977.

Jegge, Jürg. *Angst macht krumm*. Reinbek, Germany: Rowohlt, 1983.

———. *Dummheit ist lernbar*. Reinbek, Germany: Rowohlt, 1982.

Jörg, Hans. *Von der Eigenfibel zur Arbeitslehre: Einführung in die Schuldruckerei*. Wuppertal-Ratingen-Kastellaun, Germany: Henn, 1970.

Jung, C. G. *Memories, Dreams, Reflections*. Translated by Aniela Jaffe. 3rd ed. New York: Vintage Books, 1963.

———. *The Undiscovered Self*. New York: Mentor Books, 1957.

Koestler, Arthur. *Janus: A Summing Up*. New York: Random House, Vintage Books, 1979.

Kohl, Herbert. *On Teaching*. New York: New American Library, 1967.

———. *Reading, How To*. Harmondsworth, England: Penguin, 1974.

———. *Thirty-Six Children*. New York: Bantam Books, 1976.

Leonard, George B. *Education and Ecstasy*. New York: Delacorte, 1968.

Mander, Jerry. *Four Arguments for the Elimination of Television*. New York: Morrow Quill, 1978.

Marshall, Sybil. "Art." In *Primary Education in Britain Today*. Edited by Geoffrey Howson. New York: Teachers College Press, 1969.

Montessori, Maria. *The Absorbent Mind*. New York: Dell, 1979.

———. *The Child in the Family*. London: Pan, 1970.

———. *Discovery of the Child*. New York: Ballantine, 1986.

———. *Dr. Montessori's Own Handbook*. New York: Schocken, 1988.

———. *From Childhood to Adolescence*. New York: Schocken, 1976.

———. *The Montessori Elementary Material*. New York: Schocken, 1973.

———. *The Montessori Method*. New York: Schocken, 1988.

———. *The Secret of Childhood*. New York: Ballantine, 1977.

————. *Spontaneous Activity in Education: The Advanced Montessori Method.* New York: Schocken, 1965.

Ortega y Gasset, José. "La psicología del cascabel," in *El Espectador*, vol. III. Madrid: Biblioteca Nueva, 1961.

Parkinson, C. N. *Parkinson's Law and Other Studies in Administration.* New York: Ballantine, 1957.

Pearce, Joseph Chilton. *Evolution's End.* San Francisco: HarperCollins, 1992.

————. *Magical Child: Rediscovering Nature's Plan for Our Children.* London: Paladin, 1979.

————. *Magical Child Matures.* New York: Bantam, 1983.

Piaget, Jean, *Judgement and Reasoning in the Child*, trans. M. Warden. New York: Harcourt Brace & World, 1926.

————. *The Moral Judgement of the Child.* New York: Harcourt Brace Jovanovich, 1932.

————. *Play, Dreams, and Imitation in Early Childhood.* 3rd impression. London: Routledge and Kegan Paul, 1972.

————. *Psychologie et Pedagogie.* Paris: Bibliotheque Mediations, Editions Denoel, 1969.

————. *To Understand Is to Invent: The Future of Education.* New York: Penguin Books, 1976.

Rosenthal, Robert, and Lenore Jacobsen. *Pygmalion in the Classroom.* New York: Holt, Rinehart, and Winston, 1968.

Sagan, Carl. *The Dragons of Eden.* New York: Random House, 1977.

Samuels, Mike. *Seeing with the Mind's Eye.* New York: Random House, 1975.

Schrag, Peter, and Diane Divoky. *The Myth of the Hyperactive Child.* New York: Dell, 1975.

Schumacher, Ernst F. *Good Work.* New York: Harper and Row, 1979.

————. *A Guide for the Perplexed.* New York: Harper and Row, 1977.

————. *Small is Beautiful,* London: Harper and Row, 1973.

Silberman, Charles. *The Open Classroom Reader.* New York: Vintage Books, 1973.

Taylor, Gordon Rattray. *The Natural History of the Mind.* London: Secker and Warburg, 1979.

Toffler, Alvin. *Future Shock.* New York: Bantam Books, 1971.

————. *The Third Wave*. New York: William Morrow, 1980.

Vester, Frederic. *Leitmotiv vernetztes Denken*, 2nd ed. Munich: Wilhelm Heyne Verlag, 1988

Wild, Rebeca. *Freiheit und Grenzen: Liebe und Respekt*, 2nd edition. Freiamt, Germany: Mit Kindern wachsen Verlag, 1998.

————. *Kinder im Pesta*. Freiamt, Germany: Arbor Verlag, 1993.

————. *Sein zum Erziehen*, 6th edition. Freiamt, Germany: Arbor Verlag, 1998.